מצוקה

ArtScroll Judaica Classics®

kol dodi
on the torah

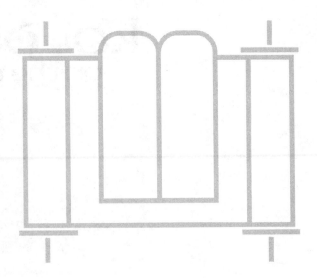

kol dodi

Published by

Mesorah Publications, ltd

in conjunction with

MESIVTHA TIFERETH JERUSALEM

קוֹל דּוֹדִי עַל הַתּוֹרָה

on the torah

COMMENTS, INSIGHTS AND IDEAS
ON THE WEEKLY SIDRAH,
ADAPTED FROM THE SHIURIM OF
RABBI DAVID FEINSTEIN

by
Pinchos Osher Rohr

FIRST EDITION
First Impression . . . February 1992

Published and Distributed by
MESORAH PUBLICATIONS, Ltd.
Brooklyn, New York 11232

Distributed in Israel by
MESORAH MAFITZIM / J. GROSSMAN
Rechov Harav Uziel 117
Jerusalem, Israel

Distributed in Europe by
J. LEHMANN HEBREW BOOKSELLERS
20 Cambridge Terrace
Gateshead, Tyne and Wear
England NE8 1RP

Distributed in Australia & New Zealand by
GOLD'S BOOK & GIFT CO.
36 William Street
Balaclava 3183, Vic., Australia

Distributed in South Africa by
KOLLEL BOOKSHOP
22 Muller Street
Yeoville 2198
Johannesburg, South Africa

THE ARTSCROLL JUDAICA CLASSICS ®
KOL DODI ON THE TORAH
© Copyright 1992, by MESORAH PUBLICATIONS, Ltd.
4401 Second Avenue / Brooklyn, N.Y. 11232 / (718) 921-9000

ISBN:
0-89906-071-4 (hard cover)
0-89906-072-2 (paperback)

Typography by CompuScribe at ArtScroll Studios, Ltd.
4401 Second Avenue / Brooklyn, N.Y. 11232 / (718) 921-9000

Printed in the United States of America by Noble Book Press Corp.
Bound by Sefercraft Inc., Quality Bookbinders, Brooklyn, N.Y.

Dedicated to the memory
of our beloved father

ר׳ שלום יעקב ב״ר צבי ז״ל

נפטר א׳ טבת, תשי״ט

תנצב״ה

He came to these shores as a young man
in the early part of this century and fought
the battle for Torah and *Yiddishkeit*
against the overwhelming assimilationist
trends of his day. His *tzedakah,* kindness
and *chesed* towards family and community
were his hallmark. May the *tzedakah* given
to enable publication and distribution
of this important volume be
an uplifting for his *neshamah.*

יחיאל מיכל ועטרה דזשייקאב ומשפחתם
Marvin and Atara Jacob and Family

In memory of

Leibish Ben Dovid ע״ה

and

Endel Bas Mordechai ע״ה

They personified the richness of Eastern European Jewry,

its warmth, generosity, and love of Torah.

The fruits of their accomplishments — their children —

brought seeds to the New World, planted and nurtured them,

and raised new generations that are the living tribute

to their blessed memory.

Dedicated by

Mr. and Mrs. Nathan Berger

תשורת שי לזכות זכרון לנפש

רפאל יצחק בן אפרים ליפר ז״ל

Raphael I. Laifer

נפטר כ״ז טבת תש״נ

אנחנו משתתפים להפיץ ספר זה

לשם הרבצת התורה

מאת

אשתו מרת מלכה תחי׳

בנו אפרים ורעיתו חיה פעשא שיחיו

ונכדיו אריה ורעיתו חנה אסתר שיחיו

ובתם תמר עטרה שתחי׳

אברהם חיים ורעיתו יעל דפנה שיחיו

וטובה תחי׳

מצבת זכרון

ר' אליהו ב"ר אליעזר ז"ל
נפטר כ"ח שבט

וזוגתו יעטע בת ר' משה הכהן ע"ה
נפטרה יו"ד כסלו

❧❧

ר' יוסף ב"ר שמעון ז"ל
נפטר י"ג מנחם אב

וזוגתו בילא בת ר' גדליה ע"ה
נפטרה ח' אדר

❧❧

הילד אליהו צבי ב"ר יוסף שמעון ע"ה
נפטר י"ב מנחם אב

תנצב"ה

„זה ספר תולדות אדם",
This is the book of generations of man
(*Genesis* 5:1)

This is dedicated to the memories of

זלמן בן אברהם משה ע״ה

Solomon Zerring

ו׳ שבט תשמ״ח / January 25, 1988

שלימה בת מרדכי ע״ה

Sylvia Zerring

August 20, 1986 / ט״ו אב תשמ״ו

Their life was a book of kindness and devotion, of *nachas*
and joy, of generations binding the future with the past.
— As the parents of Elliot, Jacqueline, and Marvin
— as the grandparents of Erin and Julie
they remain etched in our memories as rare people
whose sensitivity and commitment were lavished
not only on their immediate loved ones,
but on their extended family — the entire Jewish people.
May we always be inspired by their kindness and concern,
and may we follow in their path of *tzedakah* and *chessed*.

Elliot, Marvin, Jacqueline, Erin
Julie and Family

יהי רצון

שיהיה חוט של חסד

משוך על משפחת

רפאל אריה

לאריכת ימים

ושנות חיים

This is dedicated
to the memory of our parents

Louis and Fanny Miller

ר׳ אליעזר בן ר׳ מרדכי ע״ה

מרת פייגא בת ר׳ אריה לייב ע״ה

who nurtured seeds of Jewish growth
during their exemplary lifetimes;

and to our brother and his wife and son

Emanuel, Lillian, and Philip Miller

ר׳ עמנואל בן אליעזר ע״ה

וזוגתו מרת לאה אסתר בת ר׳ פייוועל ע״ה

ובנם פייוועל ע״ה

whose lives ended in a tragic accident
with their futures still ahead of them;

and to our brother-in-law

Myron Silver

משה בן ניסן זכריה ע״ה

Mr. and Mrs. Milton Miller

In loving memory of
our dear parents and grandparents

Lisa & Manfred Schuster, ע״ה

חסד ואמת נפגשו, צדק ושלום נשקו

(תהלים פה:יא)

Bobbie and Leon Gerstle,

Dena, Dodi, Aliza,

Avi, Moshe and Yechiel

In memory of

my beloved parents

דוד אלטער בן ישראל הלוי, ע״ה

נפטר כ׳ אדר תש״ט

פייגא ליבא בת משה, ע״ה

נפטרה י״ג אדר תש״ן

dedicated by their beloved son

Louis Green

In memory of

my beloved parents

אריה דוב בן ר׳ יצחק יהודה, ע״ה

כ״א כסלו, תשל״ה

סאשא מינא בת ר׳ נתן, ע״ה

ג׳ שבט, תשמ״ב

dedicated by

their beloved daughter

Selma Lipner

In loving memory

of my dearest parents

אברהם יצחק בן ר' זעליג ע"ה

בלומה בת ר' אברהם ע"ה

dedicated by their daughter

Mrs. Bessie Swerdin

לזכר נשמת

ר׳ אברהם ראובן ב״ר דוד יהודה ז״ל

נפטר י״ב תשרי תשי״ט

ואשתו

חיה פייגא בת ר׳ יחיאל מיכל הלוי ע״ה

נפטרה י״ז ניסן תשל״ה

חיה רחל בת איידל מינקא

לרפואה שלמה

לזכר נשמת אמי מורתי

זלאטא בת ר׳ קלמן, ע״ה
נפטר ער״ח טבת תשנ״ב

ולזכר נשמת חמי

ר׳ שלמה ב״ר אריה ליב, ע״ה
נפטר יו״ד אייר תשנ״א

וזוגתו

מרת מרים בת ר׳ יחזקאל, ע״ה
נפטר ט״ו מרחשון תש״ם

תנצב״ה

In loving memory of
my Mother

Lois Simon Rohr, ע״ה

who was taken from us
while the work on this sefer was in progress
Erev Rosh Chodesh Teves 5752 (December 6, 1991)

and my Parents-in-Law

Solomon Crugman, ע״ה

departed 10 Iyar 5751 (April 24, 1991)

Miriam (Myra) Crugman, ע״ה

departed 15 Cheshvan 5740 (November 5, 1979)

May they find peace and repose in Gan Eden.

๕ Table of Contents

Foreword   13

ספר בראשית / Sefer Bereishis

בראשית / Bereishis   19

נח / Noach   25

לך לך / Lech Lecha   31

וירא / Vayeira   39

חיי שרה / Chayei Sarah   45

תולדות / Toldos   49

ויצא / Vayeitzei   55

וישלח / Vayishlach   60

וישב / Vayeishev   67

מקץ / Mikeitz   72

ויגש / Vayigash   79

ויחי / Vayechi   85

ספר שמות / Sefer Shemos

שמות / Shemos   95

וארא / Vaeira   101

בא / Bo   107

בשלח / Beshalach   111

יתרו / Yisro   116

משפטים / Mishpatim   122

תרומה / Terumah   128

תצוה / Tetzaveh   134

כי תשא / Ki Sisa   141

ויקהל / Vayakhel 148

פקודי / Pekudei 154

ספר ויקרא / Sefer Vayikra

ויקרא / Vayikra 161

צו / Tzav 166

שמיני / Shemini 170

תזריע / Tazria 175

מצורע / Metzora 179

אחרי מות / Acharei Mos 183

קדשים / Kedoshim 187

אמר / Emor 191

בהר / Behar 197

בחקתי / Bechukosai 202

ספר במדבר / Sefer Bamidbar

במדבר / Bamidbar 209

נשא / Naso 213

בהעלתך / Beha'alosecha 217

שלח / Shelach 222

קרח / Korach 226

חקת / Chukas 230

בלק / Balak 235

פינחס / Pinchas 239

מטות / Matos 244

מסעי / Masei 248

ספר דברים / Sefer Devarim

דברים / Devarim 255

ואתחנן / Vaeschanan 261

עקב / Eikev 266

ראה / Re'eh   270

שופטים / Shoftim   274

כי תצא / Ki Seitzei   278

כי תבוא / Ki Savo   282

נצבים / Nitzavim   286

וילך / Vayeilech   291

האזינו / Ha'azinu   296

וזאת הברכה / Vezos HaBerachah   300

Foreword

ר' נְחוּנְיָה בֶּן הַקָּנָה הָיָה מִתְפַּלֵּל בִּכְנִיסָתוֹ לְבֵית הַמִּדְרָשׁ וּבִיצִיאָתוֹ תְּפִלָּה קְצָרָה. בִּכְנִיסָתוֹ מַהוּ אוֹמֵר? יְהִי רָצוֹן מִלְּפָנֶיךָ שֶׁלֹּא יֶאֱרַע דְּבַר תַּקָלָה עַל יָדִי . . . וְיִשְׂמְחוּ בִי חֲבֵרַי.

R' Nechuniah ben Hakanah would recite a brief prayer when he entered the study hall and when he left it. When he entered it he said, "May it be Your will that no mishap occur through me . . . and that my fellows rejoice through me" (Berachos 28b).

A s I began to supply the material on which this work is based, I prayed that the ideas expressed here be correct, and that they bring the joy of Torah study to those who use it. The riches inherent in the Torah are infinite and it has been my privilege to have spent my life mining them, I hope to the best of my ability. By sharing them with the public through this *sefer*, it is my wish that the readers will share my own joy and will find in its pages ideas and interpretations that will please them and, most of all, that will motivate them to broaden and deepen their own study.

When R' Nechuniah left the study hall, he would thank Hashem שֶׁשַּׂמְתָּ חֶלְקִי מִיּוֹשְׁבֵי בֵית הַמִּדְרָשׁ, *that You have placed my lot with those who dwell in the study hall.* I echo his prayer of gratitude, and I add a prayer that, through this *sefer,* I may bring many readers into the "study hall" of those who listened to these words of Torah when they were first expounded. Until now, the contents of this *sefer* were shared only with the people who were in our study hall on Friday mornings; now they can reach an audience unbounded by schedules and geography. To be able to "expand" one's *bais midrash* by bringing Torah to multitudes is a privilege that brings with it the responsibility to do so clearly, accurately, and in a manner that will be of the greatest benefit to as many people as possible. I am grateful for the privilege and I pray that it has been fulfilled properly.

The world was created for the sake of Torah study, and it is the Torah of the Jewish people that preserves the universe. Consequently, those who study the Torah are the true citizens of the world; others are tantamount to aliens in a land to which they do not contribute. Moreover, the Sages (*Yevamos* 96b) expound that those whose Torah teachings survive them continue to live in both worlds, even when their physical lives are over. This is based on the words of King David: אָגוּרָה בְאָהָלְךָ עוֹלָמִים, *I shall sojourn in Your tent forever (Tehillim* 61:5). The Sages render the word עוֹלָמִים in its other meaning, *worlds,* i.e., this world and the World to Come. The Torah is eternal and as long as one's Torah is studied here, he is alive in the most meaningful sense. Therefore, I am further grateful that those who have made this *sefer* a reality have given eternity to the author of its contents.

I would like to dedicate this *sefer* to the memory of דוד ליב בן מנחם מענדל ז"ל who was taken from us on כ"א טבת, תשנ"ב. I knew him for less than two years, but during that time we became good friends. He listened to the *shiurim* on which this *sefer* is based, and told me that they changed his outlook and influenced him to become much more involved in giving to worthy causes. It is most appropriate, therefore, to dedicate these words to his memory. תנצב"ה.

I am deeply grateful to those who brought this work to fruition. PINCHOS OSHER ROHR wrote it based on notes and cassettes. He succeeded in capturing the ideas and presenting them lucidly and accurately. RABBIS NOSSON SCHERMAN and AVIE GOLD reviewed and edited the text, thereby improving it significantly. RABBIS YESOCHER GINZBERG and CHAIM FINKELSTEIN contributed their notes on most of *Bereishis*. RABBI STANLEY BRONFELD, the English Studies principal of our Yeshivah and a lifetime friend, has attended the *shiurim* and encouraged this undertaking; he also read many of the pages and offered helpful opinions. I would also like to thank my many *talmidim* throughout the years; were it not for my obligation to teach them, the *divrei Torah* would never have come to fruition. וּמִתַּלְמִידַי יוֹתֵר מִכֻּלָּם. Finally, my deep thanks go to RABBI MEIR ZLOTOWITZ, a very close friend of my family and of the Mesivtha, and to members of the MESORAH HERITAGE FOUNDATION staff. May they be blessed with continued success in enriching the Jewish people with more and more works of Torah and books that bring them closer to our Father in Heaven.

Rabbi David Feinstein
I Adar, 5752

kol dodi
on the torah

סֵפֶר בְּרֵאשִׁית

Sefer Bereishis

פרשת בראשית
Parashas Bereishis

בְּרֵאשִׁית בָּרָא אֱלֹהִים אֵת הַשָּׁמַיִם וְאֵת הָאָרֶץ: — *In the beginning of God's creating the heavens and the earth* (1:1).

According to *Rashi,* the word בְּרֵאשִׁית, *bereishis,* is grammatically a construct noun, *in the beginning OF* something. Immediately we are faced with the question, "in the beginning of what?" *Rashi* explains that it means in the beginning of Hashem's creating the heavens and the earth. We have translated this verse in accordance with *Rashi's* understanding, in contrast to the familiar rendering, *In the beginning, HASHEM created . . .*

To answer this question, we will suggest a different object of the preposition "of," one that seems self-evident to us. As *Rashi* points out, the *Chumash* is not a history book, but rather a lesson in Torah, the laws and statutes we need to know in order to live according to Hashem's will and to fulfill His purpose in creating us. Thus the unstated subject of this, the Torah's first verse, is the Torah itself, which existed from the outset. Thus we can read our verse as follows: *In the beginning of the Torah, HASHEM created the heavens and the earth.* What does this mean?

The Sages tell us that before Hashem created the world, He first made the Torah, which He then used as a blueprint and guideline for designing the world. In other words, He created a world to fit the Torah, to provide situations in which the Torah can function. For example, the Torah contains a commandment to honor one's father and mother. Therefore Hashem designed the world to include the institution of parenthood, which would allow fulfillment of this commandment.

Thus the Torah not only preceded the creation of the world, but was also the entire reason for the creation. *Rashi* comments on the verse (ibid. 1:31), *and there was evening and there was morning, the sixth day,* that the whole world was kept in suspense as to whether it would continue, until the "sixth day" of Sivan, when the Jews accepted the Torah at Mount Sinai.

Nonetheless, the converse is also true. Just as the Torah is the justification for the world, the Torah has no meaning unless it is practiced; this is why the Torah was given to human beings. The Sages say (*Shabbos* 88b) that when Moshe went up to heaven to receive the Torah, he had to argue with the angels, who claimed to be more worthy recipients than the Jewish people.

"Were you ever slaves," Moshe asked, "that you need to be commanded to remember that you were freed from Egypt? Do you have parents to honor? Do you eat, that you need to be given laws of *kashrus?*" Finally they had to concede that the Torah was intended for humans, and not for them.

This, then, is the meaning of our verse: *In the beginning of the Torah, HASHEM created the heavens and the earth* —the Torah did not begin until it had a physical world in which it could be practiced.

❧ ❧ ❧

וַיְהִי־עֶרֶב וַיְהִי־בֹקֶר יוֹם שֵׁנִי: — *And there was evening and there was morning, a second day* (1:8).

The phrase וַיַּרְא אֱלֹהִים כִּי־טוֹב, *And HASHEM saw that it was good,* appears in the account of each of the six days of creation, except for that of the second day. *Rashi* says that the word *good* does not appear in the account of the second day because the work of creating the waters above the firmament and those below the firmament was not completed until the third day when the lower waters were sent down to form the oceans. The goodness of a creation is not realized until it is finished. Thus the Torah says twice on the third day, *And HASHEM saw that it was good,* once for the the work of the waters, which was finished then, and once for the creation of vegetation.

There remains a question, however. Why did Hashem put off completing the work of the waters until the third day? We cannot say that He did not have enough time for it; each creation was accomplished by an utterance (see *Avos* 5:1), which could have taken only an instant, and certainly did not need a whole day.

The Sages said (*Shabbos* 156a) that the work of the second day was not called "good," because on that day *machlokes* (strife) came into being. When Hashem created the firmament to separate the waters beneath it from the waters above, all the water wanted to be in the lofty heavens above the firmament, and there was strife among the particles of water. Finally Hashem ordered half of them to go below the firmament, and the "unlucky" ones were resentful of their more fortunate fellows. This is why the word "good" is not used in describing the work of the second day.

From the way Hashem handled this conflict, we can learn an important lesson in how to deal with our fellow humans. Once He saw that bad feelings had been aroused, He stopped what He was doing and gave everyone time to cool off, as the Sages said (*Avos* 4:23), *Do not placate your fellow when he is angry.* This is why the work of the water was not completed until the third day, when the water below the firmament had come to accept, and even be thankful for, its lot.

So too, we must learn to be sensitive to someone else's feelings, especially if he is not happy with his lot in life. When we have no choice but to impose an unpleasant decision on someone, we should think of his feelings and give him time to reflect on what we are doing. Hopefully by the next day, or the next week, when he has had time to become used to the idea (and we have found ways of presenting it to him in a favorable light), he will agree that it is *good.*

❧ ❧ ❧

וַיֹּאמֶר אֱלֹהִים יְהִי מְאֹרֹת בִּרְקִיעַ הַשָּׁמַיִם — *God said, "Let there be luminaries in the firmament of the heaven"* (1:14).

The word מְאֹרֹת, *luminaries*, in this verse is written without the *vav* that normally indicates the plural form. *Rashi* points out that as it is spelled here, this word could mean מְאֵרָה, *curse*, because the day on which the luminaries were created is more susceptible to certain sicknesses (may Hashem protect us from them).

We would like, however, to suggest another way of understanding this "curse." Often in Torah literature the concept of *light* is used to symbolize wisdom (*Shabbos* 156a). Left uncontrolled and unchanneled, wisdom can be the greatest curse; but if it is nurtured and directed in the right way it becomes a powerful *light*, revealing infinite treasures which would otherwise be hidden from us, and showing us the way to attain them. Without wisdom, we are like the blind men who sit starving at a banquet because they cannot see the food directly in front of them waiting to be eaten; with it we can be, spiritually, the best-nourished people in the world.

Thus someone who reads the written Torah in his own way, ignoring the traditional interpretations handed down through the generations, would read the word מְאֹרֹת as it is spelled, and for him it would be a *curse*. However, someone who accepts this rich tradition and reads the word as it was meant to be read would know that it really is a *light* which can guide him to the greatest blessings the world has to offer.

❧ ❧ ❧

וַיֹּאמֶר אֱלֹהִים נַעֲשֶׂה אָדָם בְּצַלְמֵנוּ כִּדְמוּתֵנוּ — *And God said, "Let us make man in Our image, after Our likeness"* (1:26).

The commentators ask, to whom was Hashem speaking when He made this statement? *Rashi* comments that this verse teaches us about Hashem's humility: Since man was to be created in a form similar to the angels, they might well be hurt, and therefore He consulted with them before He created man. It was only His humility that made Him do this; He was certainly not beholden to them and was not required to ask their advice.

The Sages say (*Sanhedrin* 38b) that when Hashem first put this question to the angels they answered, *What is man that You should remember him and the son of man that You should favor him?* (*Tehillim* 8:5). Upon hearing this, Hashem, so to speak, pointed His finger and destroyed this whole group of angels.

Then He created more angels, who gave the same answer and were also destroyed. Finally the third group answered differently, "Master of the World, You ask us if You should create man. What do You want of us? We see that You want human beings, so create them."

Why did Hashem destroy the two dissenting groups of angels, instead of simply creating man over their protests?

As we said above, the purpose of creation was to give man the opportunity to learn and observe the Torah. Man is the culmination of creation; everything else, including the angels, was made to serve him and aid him in accomplishing his purpose. The Sages taught that a righteous person is on a much higher level than any angel and that the angels are jealous of this potential, which they lack.

Thus, when Hashem asked the angels if man should be created, He was really testing them, to see if they would fulfill the role for which they were made. By answering that man had no place in creation, they failed the test. Because they would not accept the task Hashem had assigned them, to serve man and help him observe the Torah, they were superfluous in His plan and He therefore destroyed them.

Though it may seem paradoxical to us, this demonstrates Hashem's humility. Hashem certainly had a right to force the angels to serve man against their will, since He had created them. However, out of humility He chose not to impose His will on them and instead replaced them with other angels who would, hopefully, accept His plan of their own free will.

☙ ☙ ☙

וַיְבָרֶךְ אֱלֹהִים אֶת־יוֹם הַשְּׁבִיעִי — **God blessed the seventh day** (2:3).

Rashi comments that this verse refers to a blessing which would come only in the future, when Hashem caused manna to come down from heaven in the wilderness. The day before the Sabbath, the Jews gathered a double portion (see *Shemos* 16:22) and on the Sabbath itself no manna came down at all. In this way, everyone could see the blessing of the Sabbath.

How does this apply today, when we no longer have the manna? There is nothing physical that sets the Sabbath apart from the rest of the week, so how do we appreciate its blessing?

Later in this *parashah,* man was given the curse of hard work: *By the sweat of your brow shall you get bread to eat* (3:19). However, this curse does not apply to the Sabbath. The Sages said (*Beitzah* 16a) that all of man's provisions are rationed for him, except for the expenses of the Sabbath. For one day a week, Hashem provides for all of our needs, absolutely free of charge, as if we were guests at His table. No matter how much we spend in honor of the Sabbath, it will not be subtracted from the amount we were allotted on *Rosh Hashanah.*

In the Wildernesss this was made manifest through the manna; every Friday everyone gathered a normal portion, but when he took it home and measured it, he found that it had miraculously become twice the normal amount. Also, as *Rashi* says in *Shemos* (16:22), the manna which they ate on the Sabbath tasted much better than the weekday manna. Thus their needs for the Sabbath required no extra work at all.

This blessing remains with us today. It may seem that we work for six days to earn seven days worth of food. In truth, however, this is not so. The work we do in six days gives us only six days worth of livelihood. What we need for Sabbath comes directly from heaven, in fulfillment of the blessing Hashem gave to the seventh day.

❧ ❧ ❧

פרשת נח
Parashas Noach

נֹחַ אִישׁ צַדִּיק תָּמִים הָיָה בְּדֹרֹתָיו — *Noah was a righteous man, perfect in his generations* (6:9).

In his well-known commentary on this verse, *Rashi* cites two seemingly conflicting opinions of the Sages. According to one of them, if Noah was righteous even in his corrupt generation, how much more righteous would he have been had he lived in a truly righteous generation. And according to the other, Noah stood out as righteous only by comparison to his exceptionally wicked contemporaries; had he lived in the time of Abraham he would have been insignificant.

We believe that these two opinions are not really in conflict. Both agree that to say that Noah was perfect in *his* generation means that he was not the best person of all the generations. In a society in which no one else had any appreciation of Hashem's role in the world, his level of faith in Hashem made him exceptional. Even so, his level was not the highest attainable; he was merely a one-eyed man in the kingdom of the blind. Also according to both opinions, he did not reach as lofty a level as Abraham did.

Clearly, when the Torah described Noah as *perfect in his generations,* it meant that he reached a high plateau. And if he was able to attain spiritual achievements which the Holy Torah described as *perfect,* in spite of the corrupt environment of his generation, we believe that all opinions would agree that had he come from a background like Abraham's, he would have raised himself up to be the equal of Abraham. It is only Noah, *as he was,* who was inferior to Abraham, but that is only because his generation prevented him from achieving his full potential.

There is a powerful lesson for everyone in this: No one has any excuse for shirking his struggle for self-perfection. If Noah was able to win the Torah's praise as a perfect man in his generation, surely all of us can aspire to the same relative level, whatever obstacles and handicaps we may have to overcome.

❧ ❧ ❧

נֹחַ אִישׁ צַדִּיק תָּמִים הָיָה בְּדֹרֹתָיו אֶת־הָאֱלֹהִים הִתְהַלֶּךְ־נֹחַ: — *Noah was a righteous man, perfect in his generations; Noah walked with God* (6:9).

In this verse the Torah describes three traits that Noah possessed in his lifetime: he was *righteous,* he was *perfect,* and he *walked with Hashem.* Let us examine what each of these means.

Noah was born with the trait of righteousness. The Sages tell us that he emerged from the womb already circumcised, which is a sign of a righteous person (*Avos d'Rabbi Nosson* 2:5). Even as a child he was always kind and well behaved, not like other children who have to struggle to overcome their natures and mold themselves to be good.

Similarly, the description *perfect* means that someone has faith that Hashem knows what is best for him, and therefore accepts happily whatever Hashem gives him. This was another stage of Noah's life.

Finally, the Torah says that Noah *walked with God.* This verse uses the Divine Name *Elokim,* which generally refers to Hashem's attribute of justice. Noah walked with God because he saw that He was just and always kept His word. When Hashem said He would reward someone, He did so immediately; similarly when He said He would give punishment, it was swift in coming. Even when Hashem delayed bringing the Flood by one hundred and twenty years, Noah realized that it was so that his construction of the ark would be a warning to his contemporaries to repent, as Hashem had commanded. This is what is meant by the phrase *he walked with* God.

Abraham, however, was different. His faith did not waver even when he did not see immediate justice. Moreover, he was willing to put off his reward for generations. This is why Hashem told Abraham (17:1), *"Walk before Me and be perfect,"* meaning, "walk before Me and have faith, even though it will be generations before your reward will actually come."

❦ ❦ ❦

וַיּוֹלֶד נֹחַ שְׁלֹשָׁה בָנִים אֶת־שֵׁם אֶת־חָם וְאֶת־יָפֶת: —
Noah had begotten three sons: Shem, Ham, and Japheth (6:10).

Why does the Torah tell us that Noah had *three* sons? It could have simply listed their names and let us count them for ourselves. Indeed, at the end of the previous *parashah* (5:32), the Torah does just that. What can we learn from the number *three*?

The *Talmud* (*Yoma* 62b) asks a similar question regarding the two he-goats mentioned in the service of *Yom Kippur* (see *Vayikra* 16:5). There is a general rule that when a plural noun appears without a specific number, it indicates exactly two, the smallest plural number. Nevertheless, the Torah specifies *two* he-goats, and the *Talmud* derives from this superfluous number the requirement that the two must be a pair, like twins, similar in appearance and value.

Here also we can say that the superfluous number *three* teaches us that Shem, Ham, and Japheth were like triplets in some sense. Even though they were born in three different years, they all inherited equally their father's ability to perfect themselves in all of the three ways in which Noah perfected himself, as described above. Each could have nurtured in himself righteousness, perfection and the quality of walking with Hashem. That they developed strikingly different personalities, with only Shem emulating his father, was not because Hashem decreed that it be so, but rather resulted from the way each one chose to react to the trials of the wicked generation in which he grew up.

❦ ❦ ❦

וַתִּשָּׁחֵת הָאָרֶץ לִפְנֵי הָאֱלֹהִים וַתִּמָּלֵא הָאָרֶץ חָמָס: —
*Now the earth had become corrupt before
God; and the earth became filled with violence*
(6:11).

The wording of this verse, *corrupt before Hashem,* implies
that only in Hashem's eyes was the world corrupt; in the
eyes of men, seemingly, everything was proper.

The Sages taught (*Sanhedrin* 57a) that the root שָׁחֵת, *corrupt,*
always refers to immorality and idolatry. In human terms, it is easy to
imagine that these are not crimes at all. Who is hurt when someone
worships an idol? Who is affected by the "private" lives of consenting
adults, even if they are relatives who are forbidden to each other by
the Torah? Surely the people thought of these as "individual"
matters which would never lead to real crime.

Hashem knows otherwise. Thus the verse continues, *and the
earth became filled with violence.* In the end violence erupted into
the public's attention in a way no one could deny. Finally, it became
clear that what seemed like harmless and private acts had led to a
situation out of human control. The signs were present all along, but
only Hashem knew what was happening.

If the sins of that generation had remained purely "private" ones,
sins between man and Hashem, the world would have remained a
viable place and would not have deserved the almost total
destruction visited upon it. However, Hashem in His supreme
wisdom knows that such transgressions of His law will always
produce the bitter fruits of injustice and violence.

The Sages (*Nedarim* 91a) told a story about a man who spent an
afternoon once in the company of a married woman. When the
woman's husband came home suddenly, the surreptitious visitor hid
himself, and remained in hiding until he saw the husband raise a
glass to drink from it. "Stop!" he cried, "I saw a poisonous snake
drink from that glass."

From this act of mercy, the Sages concluded that the visitor could
not have committed a sinful act with the woman. They knew that the
sin itself would have dulled his human compassion to the point
where it would not have troubled him to watch while someone else
unknowingly poisoned himself.

Thus sins which appear to be purely "private" do not remain that way forever. Eventually the attitude they create breaks out into the open and leads to a climate of anarchy, about which the Sages warned (*Avos* 3:2), *Were it not for fear [of the government], a person would swallow his fellow alive.*

❧ ❧ ❧

וַיַּעַשׂ נֹחַ כְּכֹל אֲשֶׁר צִוָּה אֹתוֹ אֱלֹהִים כֵּן עָשָׂה: —
Noah did so; just as God commanded him, so he did (6:22).

Seemingly the last two words of this verse, כֵּן עָשָׂה, *so he did,* are redundant; we have already been told that Noah did as Hashem commanded him. Why then does the Torah include these words? Throughout the Torah, we find that this phrase is usually used to praise someone for obeying Hashem's command even though he would not benefit from doing so and might even lose. How does this praise apply to Noah?

If someone had asked Noah why he was building an ark, a natural answer would have been that he wanted to save himself and his family from the coming flood. However, his motivation was higher than that. The word כֵּן literally means *correct* or *upright,* as we find in Joseph's brothers' answer to his charge that they were spies, כֵּנִים אֲנַחְנוּ, *We are upright men* (*Bereishis* 42:11).

In these seemingly extra words, the Torah testifies that Noah acted correctly, and uprightly, in keeping with the spirit of Hashem's command. *Rashi* (ibid. 6:14) says that Noah spent one hundred and twenty years building the ark so that the people of his generation would ask him what he was doing, and he could warn them to repent for their sins before Hashem brought a flood to destroy the world. He knew that if they repented, even at the last moment, the flood would be averted and all of his work would be in vain. In that case he would be left looking like a complete fool, the man who spent one hundred and twenty years building an ark for a flood that never came.

And yet, Noah continued his work for one hundred and twenty years, all the time with the *correct* frame of mind. He understood that the process of building was desirable in itself, and that even if the ark was never used, he would still have done Hashem's will by performing the commandment he had personally been given.

This attitude of Noah's can teach us a valuable lesson in many areas. For example, on Succos we have the *mitzvah* of taking the four species, an act that does not accomplish the slightest physical change in the world. Yet, like Noah, we rejoice in the *mitzvah* for its own sake, because we know that we are doing Hashem's will with the *correct* attitude.

It is noteworthy that Noah did not enter the ark with the same lofty attitude. The commentators say that Noah delayed his entry until the rising waters left him no choice, as the Torah says, . . . וַיָּבֹא נֹחַ . . . אֶל־הַתֵּבָה מִפְּנֵי מֵי הַמַּבּוּל, *Noah went . . . into the ark because of the waters of the flood* (ibid. 7:7). Thus we do not find the same praise in connection with his entry into the ark. There the Torah says simply, וַיַּעַשׂ נֹחַ כְּכֹל אֲשֶׁר־צִוָּהוּ ה', *And Noah did according to all that Hashem had commanded him* (ibid. 7:5), but does not say כֵּן עָשָׂה, *so he did.* This is because his motive then was only to save himself and his family, and not total obedience to the command of Hashem.

❀　❀　❀

פרשת לך לך
Parashas Lech Lecha

וַאֲבָרְכָה מְבָרֲכֶיךָ וּמְקַלֶּלְךָ אָאֹר וְנִבְרְכוּ בְךָ כֹּל מִשְׁפְּחֹת הָאֲדָמָה: — *I will bless those who bless you, and he who curses you I will curse; and all the families of the earth shall bless themselves by you* (12:3).

T his verse is difficult to understand in light of a teaching of our Sages: הֲלָכָה הִיא בְּיָדוּעַ עֵשָׂו שׂוֹנֵא אֶת יַעֲקֹב, "It is a *halachah* (law): it is known that Esau hates Jacob" (see *Rashi* to *Bereishis* 33:4). If the nations always hate the Jews, to whom was Hashem referring when He told Abraham, *I will bless those who bless you*? When does anyone ever bless his enemy?

In order to answer this question, let us look at the history of the Jewish people and their relations with the other nations. Generally when the nations prosper and things go well for them, the Jews under their rule enjoy good treatment at their hands. Conversely, when the nations undergo misfortunes, such as war and famine, they always hold the Jews accountable, even though there is no rational reason for doing so.

The most recent example of this is the current wave of problems in Russia. The Jews are among the first to bear the blame for the political and economic instability there. Even though Jews have had almost no role in Russian politics for the last several generations, the Russians somehow find excuses to accuse them.

In our verse, the Torah explains why this occurs. Hashem says that when He wants to reward Abraham's descendants, He will cause the nations around them to prosper. Since prosperous people do not begrudge the well-being of others, even those they consider enemies, they will then bless the Jews. Thus, Hashem blesses the nations in order to give the Jews a share in their neighbors' peace and prosperity, so that the tolerance and benign feelings of the nations will enable the Jews to learn more Torah and do more *mitzvos*.

However when Jews go astray and Hashem, in His kindness, finds it necessary to remind them to return to the path He has set for them, He afflicts the nations with various hardships, which in turn awaken deep-seated hatreds. Then they curse the Jews and hold them responsible for their problems, even though they cannot explain rationally how the Jews are involved. Though *they* do not realize it, they are right — because Hashem is cursing their people only because the Jews have neglected the Torah.

Thus the Torah tells the Jews that when Hashem wants to bless (or, Heaven forbid, curse) them, He does so by giving a blessing (or curse) to the nations. Thus it follows that whenever Jews have problems with their neighbors, they should ask themselves how they can strengthen themselves in the service of Hashem. Similarly, when the nations around them prosper and the Jews enjoy good times, they should look for ways to use their blessings to do more *mitzvos* and grow further in Torah.

❦ ❦ ❦

וַיְהִי כַּאֲשֶׁר הִקְרִיב לָבוֹא מִצְרָיְמָה —And it oc-*curred, as he came close to enter Egypt* (12:11).

The word הִקְרִיב literally means "to bring something close." It is most commonly used to describe the offering of a sacrifice, during which the owner and the *Kohen* "bring" it to the Altar.

This word is also used in *Parashas Beshalach* to describe how Pharaoh approached the Jews at the Sea of Reeds. In explaining what Pharaoh *brought close*, *Rashi* comments that this unusual form indicates that Pharaoh "pushed himself" to be at the forefront of the Egyptians' attack on the Jews — even though he was afraid.

This suggests that, in our narrative also, Abraham had to push himself to overcome something. In the preceding verse, *Rashi* points out that Hashem brought famine only on the land of Canaan and nowhere else in order to test Abraham. The commentators say that this was one of the ten trials Abraham withstood, as described in *Pirkei Avos* (5:4). What was his trial and how did he withstand it?

Hashem had told Abraham to leave his home and go to a foreign land, promising to give him the land of Canaan and make him wealthy in it. But soon after he arrived, there was a famine and he was forced to go to Egypt just to stay alive.

This was Abraham's trial: Would he jump at the opportunity to leave a country which did not live up to his expectations, in spite of Hashem's promises, or would he be reluctant to foresake the land that Hashem had told him would be his, and whose spiritual superiority he had surely already recognized? Would he think that Hashem had treated him unfairly, or that Hashem was not capable of keeping His promises (Heaven forbid)?

The Torah answers these questions with the word הִקְרִיב. Far from doubting Hashem and running away from the land he had been promised, Abraham resisted going to Egypt *every step of the way*. Hashem had told him that his place was in Canaan, and he put off leaving as long as it was possible to survive there. When he finally reached the point where there was no choice, he still had to push himself to leave, as Pharaoh would later have to push himself to overcome his fears of attacking the Jews. From this we can see how great was Abraham's love of the land Hashem had promised him, and how strong was his desire to do Hashem's wishes.

❧ ❧ ❧

וַיִּרְאוּ אֹתָהּ שָׂרֵי פַרְעֹה וַיְהַלְלוּ אֹתָהּ אֶל־פַּרְעֹה וַתֻּקַּח
הָאִשָּׁה בֵּית פַּרְעֹה: — *When Pharaoh's officials saw her [Sarai], they praised her for Pharaoh, and the woman was taken into Pharaoh's house* (12:15).

Immediately upon entering Egypt, Sarah's great beauty was noticed and she was taken to Pharaoh as a "gift." Even though no harm was done to her, the Sages taught that this was a trial of the faith of Abraham and Sarah (*Midrash Tanchuma*).

We can imagine that the trial must have been greater for Sarah than for Abraham, since her honor and her person were at stake. If so, we may ask why did Hashem, Whose ways are totally just and righteous, see fit to subject her to such a terrifying experience?

Many generations later, there was a similar episode when Esther was taken to be a wife of King Achashveirosh. Her uncle Mordechai, the leader of the Sanhedrin at the time, realized that Hashem would subject a righteous woman like Esther to such an experience only if it was required by an overall plan, out of which would come some enormous benefit to the people (see *Rashi* on *Esther* 2:11). Thus Mordechai went daily to the gate of the king's palace to inquire about Esther, waiting expectantly for Hashem's plan to unfold. And, of course, in time it became clear to everyone that Hashem had positioned Esther exactly where she would need to be in order to thwart the machinations of the wicked Haman.

Here also, we may assume that the incident of Sarah's abduction must have been part of Hashem's master plan to accomplish a good purpose. We may further speculate that the benefit realized from the experience was very great, commensurate with the very distressing nature of the experience for Sarah and Abraham. But what was it?

In the short term, we know the outcome. Pharaoh was stricken with severe plagues, which protected Sarah's honor, and was only too eager to give her back to Abraham. He also gave Abraham a sizable gift to assuage Sarah's offended feelings, making Abraham very wealthy as a result.

More importantly, however, this incident set a great example to all of Egypt. Everyone heard about the harsh punishment Pharaoh received for his unsuccessful attempt to impose himself on an unwilling Hebrew woman. This was a lesson that the Egyptian people would not soon forget.

Rashi comments in *Parashas Pinchas* (*Bamidbar* 26:5), that the other nations scoffed at the Jews' scrupulousness in recording their lineage. "While they were in servitude, the Egyptians had control over their bodies. Surely they would also have exercised control over their wives." Therefore, says *Rashi,* the Torah adds the letters *yud* and *hei* to the names of all of the families listed in *Parashas Pinchas,* a reference to one of Hashem's names, as a sign that He Himself testified to the purity of their lineage.

This is truly remarkable. Why would the notoriously licentious Egyptians restrain themselves from taking advantage of their power over the Jewish women? It must be that the lesson of Pharaoh's punishment for his attempt to abuse the honor of a Hebrew woman had left such an indelible impression on the Egyptian character that even hundreds of years later, no Egyptian would allow such an idea even to enter his mind.

We may assume that this was the fruit of Hashem's "master plan" that made Sarah's distress worthwhile: In spite of the abject slavery in which the Egyptians held the Jews for two hundred and ten years, the memory of Pharaoh's punishment afforded Jewish women complete and absolute protection from any harm.

This story contains a powerful lesson for all of us. Whenever we undergo any kind of difficult experience, we must strengthen our faith in Hashem's goodness and believe that His master plan required us to endure that difficulty in order to accomplish something worthwhile. We should remember that, even though the benefits of Sarah's trial were not realized until several hundred years later, the result was nonetheless of incalculable importance. It is only because of the lesson Pharaoh learned from his encounter with Sarah that we can say that we are directly descended from our fathers Abraham, Isaac and Jacob.

❧ ❧ ❧

וַיִּשָּׂא־לוֹט אֶת־עֵינָיו וַיַּרְא אֶת־כָּל־כִּכַּר הַיַּרְדֵּן כִּי כֻלָּהּ
מַשְׁקֶה לִפְנֵי שַׁחֵת ה' אֶת־סְדֹם וְאֶת־עֲמֹרָה כְּגַן־ה'
בְּאֶרֶץ מִצְרַיִם בֹּאֲכָה צֹעַר: — *So Lot raised his eyes and saw the entire plain of the Jordan, that it was well watered everywhere — before* HASHEM *destroyed Sodom and Amorah — like the garden of* HASHEM, *like the land of Egypt, going toward Zoar* (13:10).

When Abraham and Lot agreed to part ways, Lot was attracted by the beauty and fertility of the Jordan valley and decided to go in that direction. In describing the lushness of the valley, the Torah interjects a comment, *before Hashem destoyed Sodom and Amorah.* Seemingly these are not the words of Lot but rather a comment provided by the Torah, that Lot chose to live in that region while it was still in its beauty, before Hashem punished it.

We would like to suggest, however, a different interpretation from this obvious one. The Torah does not state facts without reason; if a fact is given, it is only in order to teach us something we need to know in order to conduct ourselves properly. What lesson is the Torah hinting at in these words?

Lot was an orphan who had grown up in the household of his uncle Abraham. As such he knew that the world was governed by a Creator Who rewards those who do His will and punishes those who sin. The wickedness of Sodom and Amorah was notorious, and we cannot doubt that Lot knew that some day their measure would be full and Hashem would repay them for all their iniquities. Thus, the Torah tells us that Lot knew that these cities were destined for destruction and chose to live there in spite of that knowledge. Why would Lot make such a choice?

Lot was not so stupid as to think that he could sin indefinitely and never be punished for it. Like all wicked people, he knew that Hashem always punishes His enemies, but he thought that he still had time. Intellectually, he knew that he was doing wrong, but his intellect was not strong enough to contain the powerful flames of desire that burned within him.

Lot looked at the lush valley and thought, "Some day this will be laid waste, but that's a long way off. In the meantime, I want to go enjoy myself." The Sages said (*Eruvin* 19a), *Even when the fires of Gehinnom are open before them, the wicked do not repent.* They are like an anesthetized patient undergoing surgery—intellectually they are aware of being cut open but they feel no pain and cannot imagine ever feeling pain.

Had Hashem punished Sodom and Amorah little by little, they might have absorbed the lesson and improved their ways as did the people of Nineveh. But Hashem allowed them to enjoy the lush pleasures of the valley without interference, until it was too late for them to save themselves.

We must learn from Lot's mistake never to be misled when Hashem's retribution is slow in coming — even though, as the Psalmist says, Hashem *frequently withdraws His anger* (*Tehillim* 78:38), the Evil Inclination tries hard to trick us into thinking that we can always postpone repaying our debts to Hashem — lest we wake up one day, like Sodom and Amorah, and discover that the end was a lot closer than we thought.

❧ ❧ ❧

וַיֹּאמַר אֲדֹנָי אֱלֹהִים בַּמָּה אֵדַע כִּי אִירָשֶׁנָּה — *And he said, "My Lord, HASHEM/ELOHIM: Whereby shall I know that I am to inherit it?"* (15:8).

Rashi comments that Abraham was not asking for a sign to prove that Hashem would keep His promise; his faith in Hashem's was complete and flawless. Instead, he was asking through what merit the promise would be fulfilled.

To understand this, we must know that usually when Hashem offers someone a gift, His offer is subject to the condition that the recipient will be worthy of it. If one does not *earn* the object offered, then he will not receive it.

Thus Abraham was asking by what merit he and his grandchildren would be worthy of remaining in *Eretz Yisrael*. That his concern was justified is clear from the fact that his descendants were exiled from their land, first for two hundred fifty years (Jacob went down to Egypt in the year 2238; Joshua led the nation into *Eretz*

Yisrael in 2488), then later for seventy years, and now for nearly two thousand years.

This interpretation explains why there have been so many frustrated predictions by the Torah giants throughout the centuries that the redemption would come at one specific time or another. The times they predicted were indeed suitable for the redemption, but the people weren't worthy of it. The Talmud (*Sanhedrin* 98a) relates that someone once asked the Messiah when he would come.

"Today," was the answer, but the Messiah did not come that day.

The next day the questioner asked Elijah, "Why did he lie to me yesterday? He said he would come today, and he didn't come."

The prophet Elijah answered, "He didn't lie. He said, 'today,' in the sense of the Psalmist, *Even today, if we but heed his call"* (*Tehillim* 95:7). The time was right but the people were not worthy. Let us hope that next time they will be.

Returning to our verse, Abraham asked how he could know that his descendants would not sin and thereby forfeit their rights under Hashem's promise. According to *Rashi,* Hashem answered Abraham that he need not worry. The merit of the offerings that he and his descendants would bring guarantees that the Jews would keep *Eretz Yisrael.* As long as they continue to bring offerings, Hashem will not allow them to stray so far from the path that their promise would be completely canceled.

To this Abraham said, "That is very good as long as the *Beis HaMikdash* stands and they are able to bring offerings. What will happen after it is destroyed? What merit will they have then?"

Answered Hashem, "As long as they recite the order of the offerings, I will consider it as if they had brought them." For this reason, it is important for us to make an effort to say at least some part of the service of the offerings in the daily prayers, so that the merit of the recitation will protect the Jewish people and bring about their speedy redemption.

❧ ❧ ❧

פרשת וירא
Parashas Vayeira

וַיִּשָּׂא עֵינָיו וַיַּרְא וְהִנֵּה שְׁלֹשָׁה אֲנָשִׁים נִצָּבִים עָלָיו
וַיַּרְא וַיָּרָץ לִקְרָאתָם — *He lifted his eyes and saw:
And behold! three men were standing over
him. He perceived, so he ran toward them
from the entrance of the tent* (18:2).

W hen Abraham saw the three men coming across the
desert, he had just had the unimaginable privilege of
having Hashem appear to him. Even so, as soon as the
opportunity to have guests in his home presented itself, he asked
Hashem to excuse him and ran off to invite them. From this incident
our Sages derived, גְּדוֹלָה הַכְנָסַת אוֹרְחִים מֵהַקְבָּלַת פְּנֵי שְׁכִינָה, *Hosting
guests is greater than receiving the Shechinah [the Divine Presence]*
(*Shabbos* 127a).

On the face of it, it is difficult to understand this teaching and the
story on which it is based. Is it not disrespectful to the Creator to say
that His flesh and blood creations have precedence over Him? How
could Abraham, who was known for his unsurpassed dedication to
upholding Hashem's honor in the world, interrupt a conversation
with Hashem in order to invite strangers, mere flesh and blood, into
his home?

The answer to these questions is to be found in the *halachah* (law)
that a hired laborer may not interrupt his work without his
employer's permission. Imagine, for the purpose of discussion, that

Hashem came to visit someone at his job during working hours. If the worker allowed himself to be distracted from his duties, even for such a Visitor, the Torah would say that the worker has *stolen* the wages his employer gives him for the time that he did not work. (How much more is someone guilty of theft if he spends his work time in personal conversations, or otherwise engaged in personal activities. For this reason, one should always clarify with his employers exactly what he is permitted to do on the employer's time.)

When Abraham saw the men approaching, he said to himself, "My job is to take care of strangers here in the desert. These men have been out in the hot sun for hours. They need food, drink and shelter. No one else will give it to them if I don't. Hashem doesn't need me, but they do, so therefore they come first."

In spite of his vast wealth and many servants, Abraham considered himself as no more than a simple workingman, whose job was performing *mitzvos*. The time he spent talking with Hashem was just a lull in his normal workday. The moment that needy guests arrived, his break was over and he had to excuse himself to his Visitor and return to his job. Seen in this light, it was not in the slightest disrespectful to Hashem that Abraham left in the middle of a conversation.

Lest we think that Hashem felt snubbed when Abraham left him, the Talmud (*Megillah* 29a) tells a story that shows that Hashem sees the matter differently.

Rav Sheishes [who was blind] was sitting in the synagogue that had been destroyed and rebuilt in Nehardea. The *Shechinah* came, but Rav Sheishes did not leave.

The ministering angels came and threatened him. Rav Sheishes said, "Master of the Universe! [In an encounter between] an unfortunate one and a fortunate one, who must defer to whom?"

Said Hashem to them, "Leave him alone!"

From this we see that the unfortunate and needy have priority even over Hashem.

❀ ❀ ❀

כִּי־עַל־כֵּן עֲבַרְתֶּם עַל־עַבְדְּכֶם — *Inasmuch as you have passed your servant's way* (18:5).

After he turned away from Hashem, Abraham ran to greet the strangers and, in terms of utmost politeness and servility, offered to serve them food and drink, and begged them not to leave without accepting his hospitality.

The expression which he used is unusual. כִּי־עַל־כֵּן עֲבַרְתֶּם עַל־עַבְדְּכֶם literally means, *because for this you have passed your servant's way*. Why did Abraham say *for this*? If he wanted to give the guests a reason to stay with him, "*because* you have passed your servant's way" would have been adequate. To what was he referring when he said, *for this*?

Abraham believed that the men had been sent by Hashem specifically to give him an opportunity to perform a *mitzvah*. Thus, when he said *because for this you have passed your servant's way,* he meant, "you have come here *for this*, for the purpose of allowing me to perform the *mitzvah* of giving you food and drink."

This gives us a picture of the greatness of our father Abraham. It never entered his mind to complain that the men were causing him trouble and expense at a time when he was not feeling well. To the contrary, he believed that the only reason they were there at all was for his benefit, to give him the opportunity to perform a *mitzvah*. Far from arrogance, his attitude toward them was one of total subservience.

One important lesson emerges clearly from this understanding of our verse: Never pass up an opportunity to perform a *mitzvah*.

The Talmud (*Shabbos* 121b) states, *If someone encounters snakes and scorpions and kills them, it is plain that they were sent to him in order for him to kill them. If he does not kill them, it is known that they were sent to kill him and a miracle was done for him to enable him to survive.* By killing these dangerous creatures, he receives credit for the *mitzvah* of protecting people from danger. Conversely, if he fails to kill them, he has committed a crime punishable by death, and was kept alive only by Divine mercy.

A vital lesson emerges from this: We must never pretend that we do not see an opportunity to perform a *mitzvah*. People sometimes ask why Hashem does not feed the poor Himself, if He loves them as much as we are told. The answer is simple: Hashem also loves the *rest* of His people, and wants them to have the merit of feeding the poor (*Bava Basra* 10a). Someone who closes his eyes to the poor not only forgoes that merit, but also incurs Hashem's displeasure, Heaven forbid.

May our lot always be with those who learn from our father Abraham and grasp eagerly at every opportunity to help those in need.

❦ ❦ ❦

— וַיֹּאמְרוּ אֵלָיו אַיֵּה שָׂרָה אִשְׁתֶּךָ וַיֹּאמֶר הִנֵּה בָאֹהֶל:
They said to him, "Where is Sarah your wife?"
And he said, "Behold! In the tent" (18:9).

When the angels, who came to announce that Sarah was about to conceive, asked Abraham where she was, he answered, "הִנֵּה בָאֹהֶל, *Behold! In the tent.*" Later in the *parashah* (22:1), *Rashi* comments that the similar word הִנֵּנִי is an expression denoting both humility and readiness. Here also, we may assume that when Abraham referred to his wife with this word, he wanted to praise her modesty to his guests, telling them that she was in her place at home, where she was expected to be. Of such a woman the Psalmist says (45:14), *All the honor of the King's daughter is within.*

After Abraham's answer, one of the angels gave Abraham and Sarah the happy tidings: שׁוֹב אָשׁוּב אֵלֶיךָ כָּעֵת חַיָּה וְהִנֵּה־בֵן לְשָׂרָה אִשְׁתֶּךָ, *I will surely return to you at this time next year, and behold Sarah your wife will have a son* (v. 10). He also used the word הִנֵּה, *behold*—the same word Abraham used to describe his wife—to indicate that it was because of Sarah's modesty that she merited to have a child, because children are the sign of a modest woman.

For this reason, when a *sotah* (a woman whose husband has suspected her of infidelity—see *Bamidbar* 5:11-31) is cleared of her husband's suspicion, she can be assured that she will soon conceive. Hashem grants her fertility as a sign of her recognition that the purpose of the act of which she was suspected is solely to bring children into the world. As such, she would never profane that act with a man other than the one to whom she is sanctified.

❦ ❦ ❦

וַתַּשְׁקֶיןָ אֶת־אֲבִיהֶן יַיִן בַּלַּיְלָה הוּא — *So they plied their father with wine on that night* (19:33).

The term בַּלַּיְלָה הוּא, *that night,* is peculiar. Normally the Torah would express *that night* as בַּלַּיְלָה הַהוּא, with an extra *hei.* This unusual form occurs elsewhere in the Torah (see our commentary on *Parashas Vayishlach* 32:23), and the Sages (*Niddah* 31a) taught that the use of the word הוּא, literally *he,* in place of הַהוּא, *that,* refers to Hashem, the *He* par excellence. Whenever this form occurs, it indicates that Hashem intervened specially in the events under discussion. In our verse, it means that Hashem supplied the daughters with wine specifically for this purpose.

Rashi comments on our verse that Lot's family had not had time to bring wine along with them in their hurried departure from Sodom; the wine they used was specially provided for them in the cave, so that they might bring forth two nations. (It is worth remembering that the royal Davidic dynasty came out of these two unions, through the Moabite Ruth and the Ammonite Na'amah.)

Seeing that the wine had been Divinely provided, Lot's daughters concluded that Hashem favored their plan, which was motivated by a sincere sense of duty, since they were under the impression that the whole world had been destroyed. Nonetheless, we may assume that Hashem intended to cause Lot to undergo this indignity to punish him for the life style he had embraced in the wicked environment of Sodom.

❧ ❧ ❧

כִּי אָמְרָה אַל־אֶרְאֶה בְּמוֹת הַיָּלֶד וַתֵּשֶׁב מִנֶּגֶד וַתִּשָּׂא אֶת־קֹלָהּ וַתֵּבְךְּ . . . אַל־תִּירְאִי כִּי־שָׁמַע אֱלֹהִים אֶל־קוֹל הַנַּעַר בַּאֲשֶׁר הוּא־שָׁם: — *For she said, "Let me not see the death of the child." And she sat at a distance, lifted her voice, and wept . . . "Fear not, for God has heeded the cry of the youth because he was there"* (21:16-17).

The angel told Hagar not to be afraid, Hashem has heard the voice of *Ishmael* and will keep him alive. The Torah does not say, however, that Hagar was answered, even though she wept loudly. Why were her cries ignored?

We may say, however, that the Torah answers this question in these very words: Hashem answered Ishmael *because he was there,* because he was asking Hashem for relief from *his* problem, not someone else's. *Rashi* (v. 17) reminds us that Hashem listens to the prayer of someone who is sick more than to the prayers of those who pray on his behalf. Thus, Ishmael's prayers for himself carried more weight than his mother's.

Without question, the cry of a mother for her suffering son is deep and heartfelt. Nonetheless, there is a basic difference between one's prayers for oneself, where the only concern is the problem at hand, and the prayers of someone else, into which the personal feelings of the petitioner always enter, however slightly. Thus Hagar asked, *"Let me not see the death of the child."* She was concerned for the pain *she* would feel if her son were to die, more than for his pain. Therefore, her tears are the tears of an outsider. There is a sincereity in someone's prayer for his own life that no one else can possibly duplicate.

This explains another saying of the Sages (*Berachos* 13a), *Whoever prays for someone else, and he himself needs the same thing, he will be answered first.* Only one who needs the very same help that he is requesting for someone else can put himself in the position of the other one and cry genuine tears. Therefore, the supplicant will be answered first, before the other person.

This is why the Torah testifies that, even though Hagar cried, Hashem listened to Ishmael's tears.

❧ ❧ ❧

פרשת חיי שרה
Parashas Chayei Sarah

וַיָּבֹא אַבְרָהָם לִסְפֹּד לְשָׂרָה וְלִבְכֹּתָהּ: — *And Abraham came to eulogize Sarah and to cry for her* (23:2).

Baal HaTurim points out that the word וְלִבְכֹּתָהּ, *and to weep for her,* is written in the Torah with a small *chaf,* to indicate that Abraham did not weep excessively, because Sarah was already old and had led a full and holy life. Why, however, did the Torah choose to reduce the size of the letter *chaf,* and not one of the other letters? A small *beis* would seem more appropriate, since the root word for crying, בכה, begins with this letter.

Whenever a righteous person is taken from us, however old he is, we still cry. There are two reasons for this: For one thing, we cry because the departed has lost the ability to perform *mitzvos* and add further to the abundant register of merits he accumulated in his lifetime. We also cry for *our* loss, because the righteous person is no longer available to suffuse the world with his holy influence. Thus Abraham cried because Sarah could no longer grow to higher levels of holiness.

How does this explain why the *chaf* was reduced in size? *Rashi* comments (ibid. 23:1) that just as Sarah was without sin at the age of twenty, so even in her old age she remained sinless. Perhaps the small *chaf,* whose numerical value is twenty, is an allusion to the fact that until her death, Sarah remained as sinless as she had been at the age of twenty. Thus, the letter *chaf* alludes to Sarah's full lifetime of one hundred and twenty-seven righteous years. But since this "twenty-year" stage of her life lasted for more than one hundred years, the *chaf* is written small.

☙ ☙ ☙

— וַיְדַבֵּר אֶל־בְּנֵי־חֵת לֵאמֹר: גֵּר־וְתוֹשָׁב אָנֹכִי עִמָּכֶם
And he spoke to the children of Heth, saying: I am an alien and a resident among you (23:3-4).

It is incongruous to find the terms *an alien* and *a resident* used together; they seem to contradict each other, and all of the commentators have addressed themselves to this problem. We may suggest, however, that Abraham may have meant the following: "You Hittites consider me to be an alien because I moved here from Haran, and you probably think my family roots are there. Therefore you will argue that I should take Sarah there for burial, since that is her native land.

"Let me say, therefore, that Hashem has promised to give this land to my offspring after four hundred years of exile and servitude. After that time, then, we will be residents here. Thus, I claim my right to bury her here now, in the land that my descendants will inherit, so she will be among her children."

It is not uncommon today for people to send their relatives to be buried in *Eretz Yisrael*. Even though it may be inconvenient to visit them for the present time, in the (hopefully near) future, we will have unlimited perpetual visiting rights.

Abraham did not insist that the Hittites honor his ownership rights as a citizen. He admitted that he had acted like a sojourner and therefore they were justified in giving him only the rights of an alien and making him pay for the land. But he wanted to clarify for them the situation as it was, that he would not be talked out of it, so that they could give him a prompt decision.

☙ ☙ ☙

אֶרֶץ אַרְבַּע מֵאֹת שֶׁקֶל־כֶּסֶף בֵּינִי וּבֵינְךָ מַה־הִוא —
Land worth four hundred silver shekels —
between me and you—what is it? (23:15).

Ephron the Hittite finally names his price, four hundred silver shekels. How did he arrive at this figure?

As we said above, Abraham had agreed to conduct the transaction as an "alien" with no legal claim to the land. Ephron must have realized that, for some reason, Abraham was willing to pay any amount of money for that particular parcel of land. He also knew (possibly because Abraham had said so in explaining why he considered himself a "resident") that in approximately four hundred years Abraham's descendants would take possession of the land for free.

Thus, we may surmise that Ephron thought of the money he was getting from Abraham not as an outright purchase, but rather as a rental fee, at one shekel a year, until such time as the land would anyway pass out of his ownership. This was not a purely arbitrary figure — for in connection with the redemption of a field which someone has sanctified, the Torah fixes the rental value at the same amount, one shekel a year. For example, if one redeems his sanctified field ten years before *Yoveil*, he must give ten *shekalim* for the redemption (see *Vayikra* 27:16-18).

❊ ❊ ❊

וְאַבְרָהָם זָקֵן בָּא בַּיָּמִים וַה' בֵּרַךְ אֶת־אַבְרָהָם בַּכֹּל: —
Now Abraham was old, well on in years, and
HASHEM had blessed Abraham with every-
thing (24:1).

Abraham became concerned about his son's future, and so he started to look for a suitable mate for him. Why does the Torah pick this juncture to inform us that Hashem blessed Abraham with everything?

The Sages (*Bava Basra* 17a) said that each of the Patriarchs tasted of the World to Come already in this world, basing this teaching on the fact that the blessing of *everything* is mentioned in connection with each of them.

Perhaps it was only now, after he had withstood the last of his ten trials, that Abraham finally ascended to the level of living in the World to Come. If so, he would have no further need for wealth, and was therefore willing to give what he had to help secure his son's future. Thus, the blessing of *everything,* that is the taste of the World to Come, played an important role when Abraham looked for his son's mate, for it was because of that taste that he gave Isaac all his material goods.

❧ ❧ ❧

וַיֹּסֶף אַבְרָהָם וַיִּקַּח אִשָּׁה וּשְׁמָהּ קְטוּרָה: — *Abraham proceeded, and took a wife whose name was Keturah* (25:1).

The word וַיֹּסֶף, which in this context is best translated *he proceeded* or *he continued,* literally means *he added.* If we take the word in this sense, we are faced with the question: To what did Abraham add?

We may also ask why Abraham married again, when he was about one hundred and forty years old. We are told that he was already privileged to experience the taste of the World to Come (*Bava Basra* 17a), so the pleasures of this world would not have held any appeal for him, as the Sages taught (*Avos* 4:22), *Better one hour of spiritual bliss in the World to Come than the entire life of this world.* What, then, motivated him to take another wife?

Even though he had tasted the World to Come, he also understood the purpose of *this* world, as the Sages said (loc. cit.), *Better one hour of repentance and good deeds in this world than the entire life of the World to Come.* While the pleasures of this world no longer attracted him, he still valued the opportunity to do *mitzvos,* which is the entire purpose of our stay in this world. Therefore, he wanted to *add* to the *mitzvos* he had already done and to *continue* to occupy himself with the *mitzvah* of *be fruitful and multiply,* for which purpose he needed to take a wife.

❧ ❧ ❧

פרשת תולדות
Parashas Toldos

וַיִּתְרֹצֲצוּ הַבָּנִים בְּקִרְבָּהּ וַתֹּאמֶר אִם־כֵּן לָמָּה זֶּה אָנֹכִי
וַתֵּלֶךְ לִדְרֹשׁ אֶת־ה': וַיֹּאמֶר ה' לָהּ שְׁנֵי גוֹיִם בְּבִטְנֵךְ
וּשְׁנֵי לְאֻמִּים מִמֵּעַיִךְ יִפָּרֵדוּ — *The children
agitated within her, and she said, "If so, why
am I thus?" and she went to inquire of
HASHEM. And HASHEM said to her: "Two
nations are in your womb; two regimes from
your insides shall be separated"* (25:22-23).

The Torah relates Rebecca's anxiety and confusion about the
children she was carrying. As *Rashi* relates, when she went
by the Torah schools of Shem and Eiver, Jacob struggled to
get out, and when she went by temples of idol worship, Esau tried to
get out.

Let us consider carefully the question Rebecca asks, "לָמָּה זֶּה אָנֹכִי,
If so, why am I thus?" which means, "Why has *this* happened to
me?" Normally, the word *this* is used to refer to a tangible object,
something at which we can point (thus at the Passover *Seder*, we lift
up the *matzah* and say, "this *matzah*" or the *marror* and say, "this
marror"). To what was Rebecca referring when she said, "Why has
this happened to me"?

The Sages often interpreted the word זֶה, *this*, as referring to the
number twelve, its numerical value. In our verse, then, we may
suggest that זֶה refers to the twelve tribes of Israel.

At this point, Rebecca thought that she was carrying only one child, who she knew through prophesy would be the father of the Jewish people. She was confused because this child seemed to be drawn to both Torah and idol worship, and this prospect troubled her greatly. Idol worship is a terrible thing in itself, as she knew from her childhood as Laban's sister. However, she also knew that someone who applied Torah knowledge to idolatry was far worse. Therefore she went to Shem, the leading Torah scholar of the time, to ask what Hashem was doing.

Now, finally, we can understand the question Rebecca asked Hashem, לָמָּה זֶּה אָנֹכִי. Let us examine it word by word: לָמָּה, *Why will,* זֶּה, *the twelve tribes,* who will emerge from the child I'm carrying ever be privileged to stand at Mount Sinai and receive אָנֹכִי, the Ten Commandments, which start with the words אָנֹכִי ה׳ אֱלֹהֶיךָ, *I am HASHEM, your God,* if they keep wanting to run after idols?

To this, Shem answered that she was really carrying two children, who would father two nations, one of which would devote itself to Torah and the other to idolatry.

❧ ❧ ❧

וַיֹּאמֶר עֵשָׂו אֶל־יַעֲקֹב הַלְעִיטֵנִי נָא מִן־הָאָדֹם הָאָדֹם הַזֶּה כִּי עָיֵף אָנֹכִי עַל־כֵּן קָרָא־שְׁמוֹ אֱדוֹם: — *Esau said to Jacob, "Pour into me, now, some of that red, red stuff for I am exhausted." He was therefore called Edom [red]* (25:30).

I t is surprising that only now, after this incident, does the Torah first call Esau by the name Edom (Red). From the moment he came into the world, he had been distinguished by his redness, as the Torah says (ibid. 25:25), וַיֵּצֵא הָרִאשׁוֹן אַדְמוֹנִי, *the first one emerged red.* The commentators say that not only did he have copious red hair, he also had an exceptionally ruddy complexion. Yet for some reason he was never given the name *Red* until he asked for some of Jacob's red stew. What was there about this request that finally earned for him a name that would have been natural all his life?

In all generations and cultures, ruddy people have been considered more likely to have violent, and in extreme cases even murderous, temperaments. King David had a red complexion, which would have led the prophet Samuel to suspect murderous tendencies in him (see *Malbim* to *Shmuel I* 16:12). David, however, was able to channel this aspect of his character so that it was manifested only in desirable ways. In fact, he was known for his kind and charitable nature. As a shepherd, he ran to save his sheep and directed his "red" nature to killing the beasts of prey that attacked his charges (see *Shmuel I* 17:34-36).

To return to our *parashah*, until this incident there had been doubt as to which direction Esau's potentially explosive personality would take. Only now, when he returned from the field after a day of violence and blasphemy (see commentaries to this verse), was it apparent that he had turned to wickedness. He himself emphasized this shift in his nature when he asked for *some of that red, red stuff*. From now on, just as he had turned to violence as a way of life, he would look for the redness in everything, even the food he ate. Therefore he now deserved to be called by the name *Red*, which would not have been fitting if he had channeled his nature to the good, as did King David.

❦ ❦ ❦

וַיֹּאמֶר יַעֲקֹב הִשָּׁבְעָה לִּי כַּיּוֹם וַיִּשָּׁבַע לוֹ וַיִּמְכֹּר אֶת־בְּכֹרָתוֹ לְיַעֲקֹב: — *Jacob said, "Swear to me as this day." He swore to him and sold his birthright to Jacob* (25:33).

I n exchange for the stew Esau wanted, Jacob demanded that Esau sell him his birthright and Esau agreed. Jacob then insisted that Esau take an oath, which he did. The purpose of this oath was not to establish that he would not deny the sale; Hashem knows the truth in any case, and Esau, murderer and thief that he was, could certainly not be relied upon to honor his oath, but would deny the sale.

Therefore, we must say that Jacob's intention in demanding the oath was something else. He was afraid that Esau would acknowledge that the sale took place, but claim that it was void because he had been charged an unreasonable amount. To prevent that, Jacob asked him to swear that the food he received was worth as much to him as his birthright. By saying that Esau despised the birthright, the Torah confirms that it had so little value to him that even a pot of lentils was worth more.

The passage concludes, *Jacob gave Esau bread and lentil stew, and he ate and drank, got up and left. Thus Esau spurned the birthright* (25:34).

In this week's *Haftarah,* Hashem speaks through the prophet Malachi to chastise the Jewish people for the contempt with which they treated the Temple service. The *Haftarah* begins by stressing the difference between Jacob and Esau, saying that the Jews have behaved like Esau: "You have made My table disgusting by bringing rotten and wormy bread. You have insulted Me by offering blind and lame animals. You act as if the whole service is an enormous burden."

This is in contrast to the attitude Jacob displays toward the service of Hashem in our *parashah.* He so much valued the opportunity to serve Hashem that came with the birthright that he actually *paid* for it, and risked his life to receive his father's blessings. His commitment and love for the service should be an example to all of his descendants. No aspect of serving Hashem should ever be a burden to us, but rather an act of love, which we desire with every fiber of our beings.

❧ ❧ ❧

צֵא הַשָּׂדֶה וְצוּדָה לִּי צָיְדָה: — *Go out to the field and trap game for me* (27:3).

The Torah spells the word צָיִד with an extra *hei* at the end. As it is written, צֵידָה, it means literally *food* or *provisions;* but as it is pronounced, צָיִד, *trapping* or *trapped game.* What can we learn from this difference between the written and spoken forms?

On the surface, Isaac was simply telling Esau to go hunt an animal for him. Implicitly, however, Isaac instructed his son to bring an animal which would be *food* for *him,* food which was not only *kosher* but also permitted in every sense. Thus, *Rashi* explains that

Isaac meant food from ownerless animals, not animals which Esau had stolen. *Gur Aryeh* explains that Isaac wanted Esau to hunt far away from private lands, so as to be extra-scrupulous not to capture someone else's animal, even by accident.

This shows us Isaac's great insight into his son's character. Isaac knew that, however much or little Esau may have been submissive to the will of Hashem, he could still be relied on at least to respect his parents. If Isaac made it clear to Esau that he wanted not just any trapped animal, but an animal which would be *food* for *him*, food which satisfied all of his special strictures, Esau would honor his father's wishes. This is why the Torah writes צֵידָה, *food*, even though the word is to be pronounced in keeping with its surface meaning, צָיִד, *trapping*.

※　※　※

וַתֹּאמֶר לוֹ אִמּוֹ עָלַי קִלְלָתְךָ בְּנִי אַךְ שְׁמַע בְּקֹלִי וְלֵךְ קַח־לִי: — *But his mother said to him, "Your curse be on me, my son. Only heed my voice and go fetch them for me"* (27:13).

Rebecca told Jacob to go to Isaac pretending to be Esau and thereby receive the blessings which Isaac intended to give Esau. Jacob objected that his father might well recognize him from the feel of his skin, and would then curse him for his duplicity. In other words, Jacob wanted to reject Rebecca's advice because it was he, rather than his mother, who would run the risk of his father's curse. Since he had so much at stake, while Rebecca was not personally involved, he felt he should trust his own judgment rather than hers. Rebecca responded by trying to reassure him: "Your curse be on me, my son."

This reply is difficult to understand. As a promise, her words were meaningless—if Isaac were to curse Jacob, Rebecca would have no power to deflect that curse onto herself. Her offer should not have resolved Jacob's fears, and yet, without further objection, he obeyed her instructions. How did Rebecca's answer reassure him?

Her reply was not a literal offer to accept on herself the brunt of Isaac's curse, which she could not have done. Rather, she wanted him to know that, because she was his mother, any harm which came to him would hurt her as much as it would him. He should not feel that she was telling him to take the blessings only because she was not personally at risk, for she did feel the risk as much as he did. Once Jacob realized that, he saw that he could trust her advice and immediately went to do as she had told him.

❈ ❈ ❈

פרשת ויצא
Parshas Vayeitzei

וַיַּחֲלֹם וְהִנֵּה סֻלָּם מֻצָּב אַרְצָה וְרֹאשׁוֹ מַגִּיעַ הַשָּׁמָיְמָה
— *And he dreamt, and behold! A ladder was
set earthward and its top reached heavenward*
(28:12).

Baal HaTurim points out that the *gematria* (numerical value)
of the word סֻלָּם, *ladder,* is equal to that of the word
קֹל, *voice,* one hundred thirty.

From this we may adduce an interesting symbolism: Just as the
ladder in Jacob's dream connected the earth to heaven, allowing the
angels to ascend and descend on it, so our voice is the vehicle which
connects us to heaven, for our prayers ascend and are heard in
heaven.

This same symbolism is strikingly expressed in the liturgy of the
High Holy days. One of the best-known affirmations of Hashem's
mercy is a boldly simple statement consisting of seven words: וּתְשׁוּבָה
וּתְפִלָּה וּצְדָקָה מַעֲבִירִין אֶת רֹעַ הַגְּזֵרָה, *Repentance, prayer and charity
mitigate the evil decree.* In most prayerbooks, each of the first three
words has a word of explanation printed over it in small print. Over
וּתְשׁוּבָה, *repentance,* is the word צוֹם, *fasting;* over וּתְפִלָּה, *prayer,* is
קוֹל, *voice;* and over וּצְדָקָה, *charity,* is מָמוֹן, *money.* The numerical
value of each of these "explanatory" words (without the *vav,* which
may be omitted without changing the meaning) is the same: one
hundred thirty! If we would appreciate the power that these means
of expression have to convey our needs directly to Hashem, and to

arouse His compassion for us, we would certainly approach them far more seriously.

It should be noted that in order for the above equation to come out, the words must all be written without a *vav*, since the Torah spells סֻלָּם, *ladder*, without a *vav*. We may speculate that the Torah gives this variant spelling so that the value of סֻלָּם will equal the word סִינַי, *Sinai*. This, we may suggest, is an allusion to that glorious moment in our history when every Jew stood united and received the Torah directly from Hashem Himself. Just as Jacob's ladder connected him directly to Hashem, the Revelation at Mount Sinai was also a ladder between Heaven and earth.

❊ ❊ ❊

וְעֵינֵי לֵאָה רַכּוֹת — *Leah's eyes were tender* (29:17).

In those days, it was common for women to cover themselves completely, leaving only the eyes exposed. A woman's beauty, therefore, could be judged only through her eyes, as the Sages said: *If a bride's eyes are beautiful, no further description is necessary* (*Taanis* 24a).

Rashi cites Rava's interpretation (*Bava Basra* 123a) of this verse that Leah's eyes were unattractive because she cried so much. Everyone said that since she was Laban's elder daughter, she would have to marry Esau, the elder son of Rebecca; the prospect of being the wife of such a wicked person so distressed her that she spent most of her time crying.

The Sage Rabbi Elazar (ibid.) seemingly found such an explanation hard to accept. It was inconceivable to him that the Torah would needlessly mention such a blemish in a woman as righteous as Leah. Therefore he interpreted the Torah's description רַכּוֹת to mean not *tender*, but *regal* or *aristocratic*. *Onkelos* gives a similar interpretation, יָאֲיָן, which suggests that her eyes were seemly and beautiful.

We may explain, then, how *Rashi* who cited Rava's opinion may be reconciled with the opinion of Rabbi Elazar: Though Leah's eyes were different from those of the other maidens of her time, being red and puffy from excessive crying, we need not consider this in any way a blemish. To the contrary, the Torah focuses on this aspect of her appearance in order to *praise* her, for only a noble and sensitive soul such as hers would have felt such overwhelming revulsion at the thought of marriage to the wicked Esau that she could not control her tears. Thus, both Rava and Rabbi Elazar would agree that the Torah mentions Leah's puffy eyes for they are where her majestic inner beauty was manifest.

Because of this sincere, unaffected devotion to goodness, she received the greatest blessings a mother could hope for: Among her children were Reuben, Jacob's firstborn; Levi, ancestor of all the *Kohanim* and Levites; and Judah, forefather of the Royal House of David, including the Righteous Redeemer, may he come soon and free us from the wickedness of the world. Thus, Leah was regal in an additional sense, that the leaders of Israel, its Kings and *Kohanim*, were all descended from her.

❧　❧　❧

מַלֵּא שְׁבֻעַ זֹאת וְנִתְּנָה לְךָ גַּם־אֶת־זֹאת בַּעֲבֹדָה אֲשֶׁר
תַּעֲבֹד עִמָּדִי עוֹד שֶׁבַע־שָׁנִים אֲחֵרוֹת: וַיַּעַשׂ יַעֲקֹב כֵּן
— *Complete this week and this one also will be given to you for the work which you will do for me for another seven years. And Jacob did so . . .* (29:27-28).

Why did Jacob agree to Laban's proposal without protest? Under any legal system, he could certainly have claimed that the seven years he had already worked were for Rachel, not for Leah; therefore he now had a right to marry Rachel without any further payment. If Laban had tricked him into marrying Leah, that was Laban's error, but Jacob owed him nothing for her, especially since Jacob had taken pains to make it clear that he wanted only Rachel (*see Rashi* on 29:18).

Laban's claim that it was not proper for a younger daughter to marry before her older sister was no defense. Even if it were true, he should have said so before the seven years started. Why, then, did Jacob ignore his rights and acquiesce to Laban's trickery without protest?

Jacob's behavior was motivated by his strong respect for the feelings of another human being. He knew that if he insisted on his right to marry Rachel without further payment, Leah's self-esteem would have been shattered. Imagine—Leah would see that her new husband was willing to work seven years for her sister but did not consider her worth even one day of his time. What a blow to her dignity!

From this story, we see the lengths to which the Torah expects us to go to avoid hurting someone's feelings. Rather than cause any slight to Leah's self-respect, Jacob gave up another seven years of his life to work for his conniving father-in-law, in an atmosphere diametrically opposed to the pure Torah environment he had known in the house of his father Isaac. How much more so must we be careful in our everyday speech and actions to avoid giving even the slightest offense to another person's feelings.

❧ ❧ ❧

וַתַּהַר לֵאָה וַתֵּלֶד בֵּן וַתִּקְרָא שְׁמוֹ רְאוּבֵן כִּי אָמְרָה כִּי־רָאָה ה' בְּעָנְיִי כִּי עַתָּה יֶאֱהָבַנִי אִישִׁי: — *Leah conceived and bore a son, and she named him Reuben, as she had declared, "Because HASHEM has discerned my humiliation, for now my husband will love me"* (29:32).

Leah's explanation of her son's name reveals an important character trait that she instilled in him—a concern for the troubles of other people. Thus, twenty-three years later when the brothers were plotting to kill Joseph, it was Reuben who persuaded them to spare his life and throw him into a pit instead. Later, when Reuben came back and found Joseph missing from the pit, he was so devastated that he tore his garments and said to his brothers (ibid. 37:30), *"The boy is gone! And I—where can I go?"* As *Rashi* paraphrases his words, "Where can I flee from my father's grief?" Such was the nature he had acquired from the name his mother gave him that he could not bear to see the sorrow of another person.

The Sages (*Berachos* 7b, see also *Rashi*) explained the name Reuben as a contraction of two words, רְאוּ, *see,* and בֵּן, *son.* Leah said prophetically, "See the difference between my son and my father-in-law's son (Esau): Esau hated his brother and wanted to kill him for taking his birthright, even though he had sold it of his own free will. My son will acquiese graciously when his birthright passes to Joseph, and even endanger his life to save Joseph's."

Perhaps we can add another level of meaning to this interpretation of Reuben's name. רְאוּ בֵּן, *"See! A son!* Esau hated his brother so much that he was willing to kill him in spite of the anguish this would cause his father. That is not the behavior of a devoted son! Reuben is a true son, who is so concerned about his father's feelings that he will save the brother who had taken his birthright."

❧ ❧ ❧

> וַתַּהַר וַתֵּלֶד בֵּן וַתֹּאמֶר אָסַף אֱלֹהִים אֶת־חֶרְפָּתִי:
> וַתִּקְרָא אֶת־שְׁמוֹ יוֹסֵף לֵאמֹר יֹסֵף ה' לִי בֵּן אַחֵר: —
> She [Rachel] conceived and bore a son, and
> said, "God has taken away my disgrace." So
> she named him Joseph saying, "May HASHEM
> add on for me another son" (30:23-24).

These verses reveal a double meaning to Joseph's name. One is from the word אָסַף, *to gather up and remove,* because Hashem *removed* Rachel's disgrace over her barrenness. The other is יֹסֵף, *to add onto* or *increase,* a prayer that Rachel should be granted another son.

We find that Joseph fulfilled both of these meanings, although in different senses than the ones Rachel intended. During the years of famine, Joseph *gathered all the* grain in Egypt, and thus was able to *remove* the shame of hunger from his brothers. Later when the Jews settled in *Eretz Yisrael,* the portion of Joseph's descendants was the fertile breadbasket of the whole country. We see this in Moshe's final blessings to the tribes in *Parashas Berachah: His land is blessed by* HASHEM . . . *with the bounty of eternally fertile hills, with the bounty of the land and its fullness (Deut.* 33:14-16).

In the other meaning of the word, to *increase,* the census of the Jews taken just before their entry into *Eretz Yisrael* reveals that Joseph's descendants were the most numerous of all the tribes (see *Bamidbar* ch. 26).

❧ ❧ ❧

קול דודי על התורה   בראשית / ויצא   □   59

פרשת וישלח
Parashas Vayishlach

וַיִּשְׁלַח יַעֲקֹב מַלְאָכִים לְפָנָיו אֶל־עֵשָׂו אָחִיו אַרְצָה שֵׂעִיר שְׂדֵה אֱדוֹם: — *Then Jacob sent angels ahead of him to Esau his brother to the land of Seir, the field of Edom* (32:3).

L et us consider how each of the brothers approached this meeting, their first in twenty years. Esau stood firm in his hatred for Jacob, who had "tricked" him out of his birthright and then "deceived" their father into giving him Esau's blessings. Certainly he was wary of Jacob's message to him, "I, your servant Jacob, lived with Laban until now," which *Rashi* interprets to mean, "Even though I lived with Laban, I kept the six hundred and thirteen *mitzvos* and did not learn from his wicked ways."

Let us imagine how Esau might have reacted to this message. "He wants me to think that he's the sincere and honest brother I knew as a child, not the conniver he became later. He must be hoping that I'll wait for him to come to me here, full of gifts and brotherly affection. Meanwhile, he'll slip around me and run to our father, and then I won't be able to do anything to him. I'll outsmart him and go out to attack him with my four hundred soldiers!" Such was Esau's thinking.

Jacob's strategy is harder to fathom. He must have known that Esau might very well react with suspicion, and that he was taking a great risk by announcing his presence. Would it not have been better for him to keep quiet and hope that Esau would not notice him?

True, Hashem had told him to return home, and had promised Jacob that He would be with him (cf. 31:3). But if Jacob was so confident of Hashem's protection, why did he react with such fear to the news that Esau was coming to meet him with four hundred men? He even took the defensive measure of dividing his entourage into two camps so that at least one would survive.

Although Jacob was confident that Hashem's promise of safe conduct gave him total security, he knew that Hashem did not want man to rely exclusively on a miracle, which would detract from his merit. Therefore he took whatever steps he could to protect his family and thereby minimize the miracle that would be required to save them. This explains also why he sent messengers with gifts to Esau—even though he knew that Hashem would surely arouse his brother's compassion towards him, he had to make an effort on his part to placate him.

When he heard that Esau was marching against him, his fear was not of Esau but rather of Hashem. The fact that Hashem even allowed Esau to threaten him showed that Hashem wanted him to be afraid, and it was Hashem's displeasure that caused him concern. He was confident that with prayer and repentance, Hashem would save him and arouse Esau's compassion for him. When that happened, Jacob would surely be pleased to see him. In the meantime, however, he knew that the real meaning of Esau's anger was that Hashem was displeased with him.

❧ ❧ ❧

וַיָּקָם בַּלַּיְלָה הוּא וַיִּקַּח אֶת־שְׁתֵּי נָשָׁיו וְאֶת־שְׁתֵּי שִׁפְחֹתָיו וְאֶת־אַחַד עָשָׂר יְלָדָיו וַיַּעֲבֹר אֵת מַעֲבַר יַבֹּק: — *But he got up that night and took his two wives, his two handmaids and his eleven sons and crossed the ford of the Jabbok (32:22).*

The term בַּלַּיְלָה הוּא, *that night,* is peculiar. Normally the Torah would express *that night* as בַּלַּיְלָה הַהוּא, nearly the same but containing an extra *hei.*

We find the same expression once in the previous *parashah* (30:16), וַיִּשְׁכַּב עִמָּהּ בַּלַּיְלָה הוּא, *so he was with her that night. Rashi* comments there that the word הוּא (literally *he*) refers to Hashem, and that this unusual usage tells us that Hashem intervened on that night to arrange for Leah to conceive Issachar.

Here, also, we may assume that this unusual usage tells us that Hashem intervened on that night, when Jacob crossed the river Jabbok. What did Hashem's intervention consist of?

Previously, we find that Jacob had been exceedingly anxious about his upcoming meeting with Esau, as we have explained earlier. When his messengers returned from their mission to Esau, the Torah relates (32:8), *Jacob became very frightened, and it distressed him.* In his prayer to Hashem, Jacob says, *"I have been diminished by all the kindness and all the truth that You have done to Your servant."* As *Rashi* restates this, "My merits have been diminished in consequence of all the kindnesses which You have already shown me. Therefore I am afraid; perhaps since the promises were made, I have become soiled by sin, and this may cause me to be delivered in Esau's hands."

Yet, after this night, we do not find that Jacob was afraid any more. Obviously Hashem gave him a sign that night which completely dispelled all of his fears. We may speculate that it may have been the fact that he was victorious over Esau's angel. In any case, it is clear that Hashem Himself intervened on that night to reassure Jacob and dispel all his fears. This is the meaning of the unusual form בַּלַּיְלָה הוּא, *on that night,* the night of Hashem, the ultimate *He.*

❦ ❦ ❦

וַיִּוָּתֵר יַעֲקֹב לְבַדּוֹ — *Jacob was left alone* (32:24).

Rashi cites the interpretation of the Sages (*Chullin* 91a) that Jacob had forgotten some small earthenware pitchers and returned to fetch them. It is known that Jacob's entourage included a large number of servants, who certainly assisted in packing and transporting his many possessions. Why, then, did he do this seemingly trivial chore himself, when he could easily have sent a servant in his place?

Jacob may have reasoned as follows: My servants are no less my property than these small vessels. Why should I risk one form of valuable property, my servants, just in order to save much less valuable property? Therefore, I must go myself.

If so, we would think that Jacob would have even less reason to risk his own person than his property. However, from this story the Sages (loc. cit.) derived that *to the righteous, their money is dearer to them than their bodies*. This does not mean that the righteous are, Heaven forbid, greedy or miserly. Rather, because they are so concerned to conduct all of their dealings with absolute rock-like integrity, every piece of property that they own is a testimony to their holiness. Not one penny was acquired in a way that left open even the slightest suspicion of dishonesty. Therefore, since every object they own is a testimony to their honesty, which stems from their pure devotion to upholding Hashem's law, they place great value on all of their possessions, even the smallest and least significant.

This explains why Jacob went himself to retrieve the small earthenware pitchers. To send anyone else would be to risk other, more expensive property that also was the fruit of honest hard work and sincere service of Hashem.

❧ ❧ ❧

וַיֵּאָבֵק אִישׁ עִמּוֹ עַד עֲלוֹת הַשָּׁחַר: וַיַּרְא כִּי לֹא יָכֹל לוֹ — וַיִּגַּע בְּכַף־יְרֵכוֹ וַתֵּקַע כַּף־יֶרֶךְ יַעֲקֹב בְּהֵאָבְקוֹ עִמּוֹ:
And a man wrestled with him until the break of dawn. When he perceived that he could not overcome him, he struck the socket of his hip. So Jacob's hip-socket was dislocated as he wrestled with him (32:24-25).

Rashi cites the opinion of the Sages that the "man" who fought with Jacob was really Esau's guardian angel. According to this opinion, we can say that this angel had been given permission by Heaven to fight with Jacob in order to frighten him, and also to find out how Esau would fare in the future in a struggle against Jacob. The result was, as the Torah recounts, that Esau could not defeat Jacob and, indeed, the only weak point he could find was Jacob's thigh. Let us consider what is the significance of the "thigh" in the struggle between Jacob and Esau.

Rashi comments in *Parashas Eikev* (*Devarim* 11:6) that in the "body" of the Jewish people, the "leg" symbolizes the money that supports Torah, which is the mainstay of the nation, just as the body stands on its legs. According to this, we may say that Esau's angel found a deficiency in the financial support of Torah and exploited it to gain a partial victory over Jacob. What does this mean to us?

Malbim comments that Isaac fully realized that Esau was not as righteous and worthy of blessings as Jacob. Isaac knew that Jacob was the one who would uphold the Torah, as we see from the blessings that he gave him later, when he knew that he was talking to Jacob (cf. *Bereishis* 28:3-4). Why, then, did Isaac intend to bless Esau with wealth and dominion over his brother?

Isaac wanted Esau to be wealthy so that, by supporting Jacob's learning of Torah, he could have a share in Jacob's reward, in an arrangement similar to the one which later developed between the descendants of Zebulun and Issachar. Furthermore, Isaac was worried that if Jacob's descendants were to control wealth on their own, they would be more subject to worldly temptations and more in danger of neglecting Torah. Therefore he envisioned an arrangement in which Jacob would be dependent on Esau for his support, to make sure Jacob would be obligated to learn Torah.

Rebecca saw the matter differently. Perhaps, having grown up with her brother Laban, she was more familiar than Isaac with the ways of the wicked and so she deemed it better that Jacob's descendants not be dependent on Esau for anything. This is why she insisted that Jacob "steal" the blessings.

When Esau complained that he had been cheated, Isaac consoled him, saying, as *Rashi* explains, that when Israel transgresses the Torah, so that Esau will have a valid reason to be aggrieved over the blessings that Jacob took from him, he may cast off Israel's yoke from his neck (see *Bereishis* 27:40).

In other words, when wealthy Jews, whom Hashem causes to prosper only so that they can support Torah, do not fulfill their responsibilities, Esau can complain, "The only reason that you took away my blessing was so that you would support Torah instead of me. Now that you are not living up to your obligation, why should you have my money?"

Thus, Esau's angel found Jacob's weak spot by looking forward into Jewish history and seeing times when the "legs" of the Jewish people—the wealth which should have been used to support Torah study—would run after the fleeting pleasures of the world and neglect the eternal Torah. Then he knew just where to attack Jacob.

❧ ❧ ❧

וַיֹּאמֶר אֵלָיו אֲדֹנִי יֹדֵעַ כִּי־הַיְלָדִים רַכִּים וְהַצֹּאן וְהַבָּקָר עָלוֹת עָלָי וּדְפָקוּם יוֹם אֶחָד וָמֵתוּ כָּל־הַצֹּאן: — *He said to him, "My lord knows that the children are tender, and the nursing flocks and herds are upon me; if they will be driven hard for a single day, then all the flocks will die"* (33:13).

After the reconciliation of the two brothers, cemented by Esau's acceptance of Jacob's massive gift, Esau offered to escort Jacob and his entourage to the field of Edom. Jacob, however, still did not trust his brother completely and therefore used the frailty of his children and sheep as an excuse to decline his brother's offer. He told Esau to go home alone and promised to make his way slowly to Esau's home in Seir.

We may ask, why does Jacob mention the children at all? It would seem that the frailty of the sheep would be an adequate reason for him to travel more slowly than Esau would want.

It is now more than three thousand five hundred years later and Jacob's descendants have not yet fulfilled this promise. Still, it has not been forgotten, as we read in this week's *Haftarah* : וְעָלוּ מוֹשִׁעִים בְּהַר צִיּוֹן לִשְׁפֹּט אֶת־הַר עֵשָׂו וְהָיְתָה לַה' הַמְּלוּכָה — *Saviors will ascend Mount Zion to judge Esau's mountain, and the kingdom will be* HASHEM's (Ovadiah 1:21). Even though we may tarry, the prophet assures us that Jacob's descendants will eventually go to Esau's land and exact justice for the wrongs that have been done to them. Then, finally, the two brothers can truly become friends.

In our verse, however, it seems that Jacob once again tricked Esau with an unkept promise. We can understand why Jacob wanted to distance himself from Esau by answering the question we raised earlier. Jacob was really concerned for his children, not because of their physical weakness (after all, shortly afterwards two of his sons killed the whole city of Shechem), but rather because of their spiritual immaturity. Jacob knew that his children were still too impressionable to be exposed to their uncle's wicked ways, and he wanted to shelter them as much as possible, until they could grow and mature.

Unfortunately, three thousand five hundred years later, the time has not yet come for Jacob's descendants to become friends with Esau. Why has it taken so long? The answer is that we are dragging our feet about waking up and realizing our potential as a people. The calls to wake up are not lacking—every time someone predicts that the Messiah's arrival is imminent, it is a reminder that the redemption could come even today, as the Sages said (*Sanhedrin* 98a), הַיּוֹם אִם־בְּקֹלוֹ תִשְׁמָעוּ, *Even today, if we but heed His call!* (*Psalms* 95:7). The voice of Hashem is calling to us constantly to repent and go in His ways — if only we would listen to it, the time would come in an instant.

❋ ❋ ❋

פרשת וישב
Parashas Vayeishev

וַיֵּשֶׁב יַעֲקֹב בְּאֶרֶץ מְגוּרֵי אָבִיו בְּאֶרֶץ כְּנָעַן׃ — *Jacob settled in the land where his father had sojourned, in the land of Canaan* (37:1).

This verse informs us that Jacob became a תּוֹשָׁב, *settler,* a term that indicates a semi-permanent status, in the country in which his father had been a גֵּר, *sojourner,* a wanderer. The Torah calls Isaac a sojourner, rather than a settler, in fulfillment of Hashem's prophesy to Abraham (*Bereishis* 15:13), *You shall surely know that your offspring will be sojourners in a land which is not theirs . . . four hundred years.* If the status of "sojourner" was to continue until the entire nation crossed the Jordan around two hundred eighty years later, why was Jacob referred to here as a settler?

The truth is that as long as Jacob was in his father's home, he had the same status as his father, that of a sojourner. Certainly also, the whole time he lived with Laban he was not settled, as he himself said in the message he sent to Esau (ibid. 32:5), *I have "sojourned" with Laban and have lingered until now.* However, when he came back to Canaan, which would eventually be called *Eretz Yisrael,* a critical change occurred: Hashem gave him the name יִשְׂרָאֵל, *Israel* (see ibid. 35:10). With this name, he could no longer be called a sojourner in the land that was named after him; he had to be a settler. But in accordance with Hashem's decree, it was still far too soon for Abraham's grandson to be a permanent settler in that land. Therefore, as soon as he attempted to achieve some kind of permanent status, events were set in motion which would force him into exile in Egypt.

❦   ❦   ❦

וַיָּבֵא יוֹסֵף אֶת־דִּבָּתָם רָעָה אֶל־אֲבִיהֶם: וְיִשְׂרָאֵל אָהַב אֶת־יוֹסֵף מִכָּל־בָּנָיו כִּי־בֶן־זְקֻנִים הוּא לוֹ וְעָשָׂה לוֹ כְּתֹנֶת פַּסִּים: — *Joseph would bring evil reports about them to their father. Now Israel loved Joseph more than all his sons since he was a child of his old age, and he made him a fine woolen tunic* (37:2-3).

Commonly, when someone has a son in his old age, the older siblings accept their father's extra show of love to him and do not resent this added affection. Knowing this, Jacob was not concerned that he would arouse the hatred of his older sons by showing that Joseph was his favorite. And in the normal course of things, he would have been correct.

In this case, however, there was an unexpected factor that upset Jacob's calculations: *Joseph would bring evil reports about them to their father.* When the brothers perceived that Joseph was trying to turn their father against them, their hatred for him was aroused. Once that happened, they hated him for the favoritism Jacob had shown him as well.

For this reason the Sages taught (*Shabbos* 10b) that one should never show favoritism to one son over the others. Even in a case such as this, where Jacob had good reason to think that Joseph's brothers would not harbor resentment against him, one can never know what additional factors will come into play. As the Sages said (loc. cit.), Jacob's favoritism became the vehicle that carried our fathers down to Egypt.

※ ※ ※

וַיִּשְׁלָחֵהוּ מֵעֵמֶק חֶבְרוֹן וַיָּבֹא שְׁכֶמָה: — *So he sent him from the depth of Hebron, and he arrived at Shechem* (37:14).

It is worth noting that the Torah uses the suffix of destination (ה) in the word שְׁכֶמָה, *to Shechem,* rather than the simple prefix (ל) which means the same thing, but is more direct. The form that is used carries the connotation that what happened there could have been expected, since there was a precedent for unfortunate happenings in the city of Shechem, where Jacob's daughter Dinah was abducted by Shechem, the son of the ruler of the city. The Sages taught (*Taanis* 29a), מְגַלְגְּלִים חוֹבָה עַל יְדֵי חַיָּיב, *a punishment comes through someone who is himself guilty.* Later, in the days of King Rechavam, it was in Shechem that the Ten Tribes seceded from the House of David (see *Melachim I* 12:1), so we see that Shechem was a fitting place for punishments. All these things are implied by the Torah's usage of the word שְׁכֶמָה rather than לִשְׁכֶם. This is also why *Rashi* cites the verse וַיָּבֹא רְחַבְעָם שְׁכֶמָה, *And Rechavam came to Shechem,* from *Divrei HaYamim II* (10:1) rather than from *Melachim I* (loc. cit.), which uses only the simple form of the word, וַיֵּלֶךְ רְחַבְעָם שְׁכֶם, *and Rechavam went to Shechem.*

❧ ❧ ❧

וַיֹּאמֶר אֲלֵהֶם רְאוּבֵן אַל־תִּשְׁפְּכוּ־דָם הַשְׁלִיכוּ אֹתוֹ אֶל־הַבּוֹר הַזֶּה אֲשֶׁר בַּמִּדְבָּר וְיָד אַל־תִּשְׁלְחוּ־בוֹ לְמַעַן הַצִּיל אֹתוֹ מִיָּדָם לַהֲשִׁיבוֹ אֶל־אָבִיו: — *And Reuben said to them: "Shed no blood! Throw him into this pit in the wilderness, but lay no hand on him!" — in order to rescue him from their hand, to return him to his father* (37:22).

Rashi points out that the phrase לְמַעַן הַצִּיל אֹתוֹ, *in order to save him,* is a Divine testimony that Reuben's motivation was purely to save Joseph from the hands of his brothers. It is difficult to understand why *Rashi* thought it necessary to give this explanation. That Reuben's intention was such seems obvious from the later incident (v. 29), when he returned to the pit and found it empty, and was devastated by Joseph's disappearance.

On closer analysis, however, we can see that that incident still does not clarify Reuben's motivation. At that time Reuben says, *"The boy is gone! And I—where can I go?"* As *Rashi* explains, the real meaning of his rhetorical question was, "Where can I flee from my father's grief?" This suggests that his real concern was to avoid causing his father grief rather than for Joseph's well-being.

This is why *Rashi* needed to emphasize in our verse that Reuben's motivation was not just for Jacob's sake, it was also genuinely to save Joseph. According to this interpretation, then, the Torah wanted to stress that Reuben acted to save his brother because, to an outside observer, it would have seemed that he was concerned only about his father's reaction. Reuben himself, however, did not want to take credit for his true motive, and thus when he discovered Joseph's disappearance from the pit, he attributed his dismay solely to his concern for his father. This reluctance to reveal his true reaction shows us Reuben's nobility, which covered up his concern for his brother because no one would believe it. Rather, people would suspect him of bearing resentment against Joseph for having usurped his birthright (see also our commentary on *Parashas Vayeitzei* 29:32). The early commentator *Rashba* (*teshuvah* 981) derives from the Torah's publicizing of Reuben's motive that it is proper to publicly acknowledge and record one who performs a *mitzvah*.

❊ ❊ ❊

וַיְשַׁלְּחוּ אֶת־כְּתֹנֶת הַפַּסִּים וַיָּבִיאוּ אֶל־אֲבִיהֶם וַיֹּאמְרוּ
זֹאת מָצָאנוּ הַכֶּר־נָא הַכְּתֹנֶת בִּנְךָ הִוא אִם־לֹא: —

They dispatched the fine woolen tunic and brought it to their father, and said, "We found this. Recognize, if you please: is it your son's tunic or not?" (37:32).

It seems strange that the brothers sent the message of Joseph's "misfortune" to Jacob in this way. They could simply have said, "We found your son's shirt, here it is." As it is, their message has the tone of a prosecutor cross-examining a witness in court, as if they were trying to ensnare Jacob in a trap of some kind.

We can say, however, that they wanted to make Jacob see that *he* had brought this sorrow on himself by favoring Joseph over his other brothers, as exemplified by the gift of the fine woolen tunic. It is as if they had subtly wanted to say, "Recognize, if you please, that *you* are to blame."

The Sages taught (*Sotah* 10b) that Judah, the leader of the brothers in their plot to sell Joseph, was responsible for this message. As a result, he was later punished measure for measure when Tamar used the same words (38:25): *"By the man to whom these belong I am with child. Recognize, if you please, whose are this seal, this wrap, and this staff."* In other words, she was saying, "Recognize, if you please, that *you* are at fault."

When he received this message from his daughter-in-law, Judah was forced to admit (38:26): *"She is right; it is from me, inasmuch as I did not give her to Shelah my son."* As *Targum Yonasan* interprets Judah's words, "Measure is set against measure. I used the same expression to my father when I asked him to identify his son's tunic, and now I am constrained to hear at my judgment that I should identify my signet, wrap and staff."

❈ ❈ ❈

פרשת מקץ
Parashas Mikeitz

וַיְהִי מִקֵּץ שְׁנָתַיִם יָמִים — *It happened at the end of two years to the day* (41:1).

This verse describes the additional time that Joseph spent in prison with two words: שְׁנָתַיִם, *two years,* and יָמִים, *of days.* At first glance, it is not apparent what the word יָמִים, *of days,* adds to our understanding of the verse, since we have already been told that Joseph had to wait two years.

The Sages taught that the word יָמִים means *a full year* to the day (*Kesubos* 57b). Our translation accords with this interpretation. We can say, then, that this seemingly unnecessary word indicates that Hashem did not reduce the additional two-year term He had decreed for Joseph to spend in prison by even one day, even though a year plus any number of days can be considered two years. Why was it important for the Torah to stress this to us?

At the end of the previous *parashah, Rashi* (40:23) commented that because Joseph, instead of trusting in Hashem, had put his trust in the Chamberlain of the Cupbearers to intercede with Pharaoh to free him from prison, Hashem punished him by making him spend two more years in prison. *Rashi* cites a verse in *Tehillim* (40:5), *Praises to the man who made Hashem his trust and turned not to the arrogant,* which the Midrash applies to this situation. (*The arrogant* refers to the Egyptian people, who were noted for this trait.)

Still, we must ask why Hashem considered this a punishable crime. We are taught that Hashem does not want us to rely on miracles, and therefore we are to manage our affairs in accordance with the normal conduct of the world (see our commentary at the beginning of *Parashas Vayishlach*). By appealing his case to Pharaoh through a direct intermediary, Joseph had simply tried to open an avenue to freedom that would not require Hashem's miraculous intervention. What then was Joseph's sin?

Joseph's strategy would have been correct in any country other than Egypt. Under other circumstances, Hashem would have freed Joseph without performing an obvious miracle, yet in a way that nonetheless showed His control over events. This was, after all, Hashem's method in freeing Joseph: to glorify His Name.

Egypt, though, because of the arrogance of its people, was in a class by itself, as suggested by the Midrash cited above. True, had the Chamberlain of the Cupbearers mentioned Joseph to Pharaoh, undoubtedly Joseph would have been freed and risen to be in charge of all of Egypt, as he eventually was. Then, however, the arrogant Chamberlain would have claimed all the credit for himself, and Hashem's role would have gone unnoticed. Hashem's purpose in freeing Joseph, while publicizing His control over the world, would have been thwarted.

In other words, once Joseph had asked the Chamberlain to intercede on his behalf, the only way for Hashem to accomplish His purpose was to wait long enough so that the Chamberlain could no longer claim that *he* had freed Joseph, that is, until he would normally have forgotten the incident. The combination of the Chamberlain's arrogance and the passage of time convinced him that Joseph had no role in winning his freedom, so he easily forgot him. Then when Pharaoh had his strange dreams two years later, Hashem's role in reawakening his dormant memory was clear to everyone. Even the arrogant Chamberlain himself had to admit that he had failed in his obligation to Joseph, *"My transgressions* [against Joseph] *do I mention today"* (ibid. 41:9).

Thus, the extra two years that Joseph spent in prison was not a punishment, as such. It was merely the time that was required to free him in a way that would make Hashem's role in the sequence of events apparent.

❀ ❀ ❀

וְעַתָּה יֵרֶא פַרְעֹה אִישׁ נָבוֹן וְחָכָם וִישִׁיתֵהוּ עַל־אֶרֶץ מִצְרָיִם — *"Now let Pharaoh seek out a discerning and wise man and set him over the land of Egypt"* (41:33).

Having interpreted Pharaoh's dream as a prediction of seven years of famine, Joseph advised Pharaoh to appoint a man who is נָבוֹן וְחָכָם, *discerning and wise,* to oversee preparations for the famine. As used in the Torah, חָכְמָה, *wisdom,* refers to the possession of a body of knowledge, while בִּינָה, *discernment and understanding,* refers to the ability to build upon that knowledge and expand it.

If so, it would seem more appropriate to describe someone first as *wise,* and then *discerning,* since one must first possess knowledge in order to utilize it. Why, then, did Joseph reverse the "natural" order of these two words in describing the qualities an overseer would need?

Before this dream of Pharaoh, no king of any nation had ever had a dream predicting a famine. Hashem devised this new phenomenon specially in order to bring Joseph into power. Furthermore, no nation had ever had the foresight to prepare for bad years (just as modern governments do not set aside funds during boom years to provide for recessions). In years of bounty, everyone ate well and left nothing over for the next year. No one had ever bothered to stockpile grain to protect against famine. Were it not for Joseph's plan, the people would develop enormous appetites during the seven years of plenty and starve as soon as the famine set in.

Thus, there was no existing חָכְמָה, *wisdom,* as to how to react to this unprecedented situation. Therefore Joseph first had to build up a body of knowledge; for this task he had to be a נָבוֹן, *a person of discernment and understanding.* Only after such knowledge had come into being was it possible to be a חָכָם, *wise man,* in the wisdom of public resource management, to institute a system to prepare for the future.

❧ ❧ ❧

וַיִּקְרָא יוֹסֵף אֶת־שֵׁם הַבְּכוֹר מְנַשֶּׁה כִּי־נַשַּׁנִי אֱלֹהִים
אֶת־כָּל־עֲמָלִי וְאֵת כָּל־בֵּית אָבִי: — *Joseph named the firstborn Manasseh for, "God has made me forget all my hardship and all my father's household"* (41:51).

As viceroy of Egypt, Joseph must have been extemely busy day and night. This left him little time to brood over his exile from his father's household or about the years he had spent in prison, and therefore he forgot these things. Presumably he was referring to this when he explained the significance of his firstborn's name.

Once before we were told that Joseph forgot his exile and his father's house. As overseer in the house of Potiphar, he began to eat, drink, and curl his hair. Hashem said, "Your father is mourning for you, and you curl your hair!" and set in motion the chain of events which would lead to Joseph's fall from his high position and to twelve years of imprisonment.

What is the difference between the two incidents of forgetfulness, that one was praiseworthy, while the other one brought Hashem's punishment on him?

In the case of his stay in Potiphar's house, Joseph allowed himself to be so seduced by the vanities of Egyptian materialism that he forgot about the pure Torah atmosphere in which he had grown up. For this he alone was to blame, and therefore he was punished for it. Now, however, Joseph himself said, *God has made me forget all my hardship.* His forgetfulness this time was Hashem's will (see *Ramban* on why Hashem wanted Joseph to forget his father's house).

In *Parashas Ki Savo*, Hashem warns the Jewish people concerning their future exile, וּבַגּוֹיִם הָהֵם לֹא תַרְגִּיעַ, *You shall not rest among those nations* (*Devarim* 28:65). This phrase can be seen both as a prediction, "You shall not rest," and as an injunction, "Do not rest." The Torah foretells that we will have no rest and it also commands us not to rest nor to forget that we are in exile. If we do allow ourselves to forget, however, this becomes a threat that we will not be permitted to rest or forget that we are Jews in exile, who must never cease longing to return home. We must always bear this in mind until such time as the exiles are gathered in and Hashem's glory is restored to its place in the *Beis HaMikdash.*

However, we may forget that we are in exile because Hashem has kept us so busy with Torah and *mitzvos* (including the struggle for survival, though not the pursuit of material luxuries) that we have no time to remember our true situation. In such situations, we cannot be held responsible, because, like Joseph's, our forgetfulness is in accordance with Hashem's will. We then have no time to think about and bemoan our exile.

❦ ❦ ❦

So — וַיֵּרְדוּ אֲחֵי־יוֹסֵף עֲשָׂרָה לִשְׁבֹּר בָּר מִמִּצְרָיִם:
Joseph's brothers—ten of them—went down to buy grain from Egypt (42:3).

Rashi asks two questions about this verse: Why does it call them *Joseph's brothers?* Had the Torah called them *Jacob's sons,* as is more common, we would perforce know that they were also Joseph's brothers. Further, why does the Torah say that *ten* brothers went down to Egypt? We are told in the next verse that Benjamin did not go, so it must be that only ten brothers went. Clearly the Torah considers the number ten signficant for some reason, but what?

In answer, *Rashi* says that by calling them *Joseph's brothers,* the Torah wants to emphasize that they all regretted having sold Joseph into servitude and therefore went with brotherly affection, determined to find their lost brother and buy his freedom, whatever the price. Their sentiments were not totally uniform in this, however, and some had stronger feelings than others. Therefore we are told that they were *ten,* with ten different levels of concern about their lost brother. Still, they were completely united in their intention *to buy grain from Egypt.*

The word אָח, *brother,* is related etymologically to two other words, one meaning *sorrow* or *worry* (see *Yechezkel* 6:11), and the other meaning *to sew together* (see *Sanhedrin* 56a). We may say that the duty of a brother encompasses both of these concepts. When someone feels sorrow or worry, his brothers have an inborn instinct to share it with him. Likewise, when someone has problems, his brothers are obligated to join together with him and help him.

In light of the above, we may say that the term אֲחֵי־יוֹסֵף, *Joseph's brothers,* in our verse has an additional implication. If the Torah had called them *Jacob's sons,* we might have thought that their desire to redeem Joseph was motivated not by brotherhood, but rather out of concern for the feelings of their father. Now, however, the Torah testifies that they acted as brothers would; they felt genuine concern over Joseph's sorrow and wanted to help him, as brothers should.

At the same time, they were still *ten.* Each of them experienced these feelings of brotherhood to a different degree, with a different level of intensity.

❦ ❦ ❦

וַיֹּאמְרוּ אִישׁ אֶל־אָחִיו אֲבָל אֲשֵׁמִים אֲנַחְנוּ עַל־אָחִינוּ אֲשֶׁר רָאִינוּ צָרַת נַפְשׁוֹ בְּהִתְחַנְנוֹ אֵלֵינוּ וְלֹא שָׁמָעְנוּ עַל־כֵּן בָּאָה אֵלֵינוּ הַצָּרָה הַזֹּאת: — *They then said to one another, "Indeed, we are guilty concerning our brother, inasmuch as we saw his heartfelt anguish when he pleaded with us, and we paid no heed. That is why this distress has come upon us"* (42:21).

To Joseph, who had accused them of being spies, the brothers totally denied all charges and asserted themselves to be upright people. Still, among themselves, they admitted that they were guilty of ignoring their brother's plea for mercy many years earlier. Their confession begins with the word אֲבָל, which is normally translated *but.* Rashi, however, following *Onkelos,* translates it בְּקוּשְׁטָא, *in truth we are guilty.* Why did they mention such an old incident at this time?

Even though they had acted suspiciously in entering the city through ten gates, the brothers never considered that they might be arrested for spying. They assumed that the merit of the *mitzvah* of searching for their lost brother would protect them. They also reasoned that, in their Jewish dress which made them highly conspicuous, no one would suspect them of spying, since spies always try to blend in with their surroundings.

Thus, recognizing that the accusations against them had no logical foundation, they asked themselves why Hashem was sending them this particular form of punishment. They knew that they were not guilty of espionage. But they also knew that if Hashem allows someone to be punished for an offense he did not commit, it is because that person had previously sinned in some similar manner, and therefore deserved this punishment. What similarity was there between their insensitivity to Joseph's pleading and the spying they were accused of?

The word רָכִיל used to describe the gossipmonger is related to the word מְרַגֵּל, *spy* (see *Rashi* to *Vayikra* 19:16). The job of a spy is to analyze a country to discover its weaknesses. Even if he is sent to the loveliest and most powerful country in the world, he has to focus on its bad points. We find the same trait in those who speak *lashon hara* (evil speech)—however many good qualities the person they speak about may possess, they focus only on the bad.

Once the brothers decided to sell Joseph into servitude, they looked for ways to justify their plan. Rather than look at his many good qualities (which caused their father to love him and the Sages to call him Joseph the Righteous), they focused on his bad points. Even though they should have realized that he was incapable of doing such a horrible act, they imagined that he wanted to kill them. They then exaggerated any defect they could find in his character to buttress their inflated accusations.

Now, in response to Joseph's charge of spying, and in response to their sincere desire to repent, they realized what they had really done. "Even though we are not spies as this man accuses us, we were guilty of acting like spies when we spoke against Joseph, and so Hashem's punishment is just." Therefore, "but" is a justified translation.

❈ ❈ ❈

פרשת ויגש
Parashas Vayigash

וַיִּגַּשׁ אֵלָיו יְהוּדָה וַיֹּאמֶר בִּי אֲדֹנִי יְדַבֶּר־נָא עַבְדְּךָ דָבָר
בְּאָזְנֵי אֲדֹנִי וְאַל־יִחַר אַפְּךָ בְּעַבְדֶּךָ כִּי כָמוֹךָ כְּפַרְעֹה:
Then Judah drew near to him and said: "If you
please, my lord, may your servant speak a
word in my lord's ears and let not your anger
flare up at your servant — for you are like
Pharaoh" (44:18).

Why does the Torah inform us that Judah "drew near" to
Joseph? It would seem sufficient to say merely that he
"spoke" to him. In *Parashas Vayeira* (18:23), the Torah
says that Abraham *drew near* to plead on behalf of the cities of
Sodom and Amorah before Hashem. *Rashi* comments there that we
find the expression *to draw close* used in three connections in
Tanach: in reference to war, conciliation and prayer. Each of these
three approaches requires preparation, to ensure that one is in a
clear-headed and rational frame of mind for the task at hand, free
from emotional distortions. Thus the word וַיִּגַּשׁ, *he drew near,* tells
us that Judah first *approached* the task at hand, to put himself in a
suitable frame of mind, and only then וַיֹּאמֶר, *he said.*

Judah knew that his father held him alone responsible for
Benjamin's safety. Now that Benjamin had been caught with
Joseph's "stolen" goblet in his possession, Judah was certainly very
involved emotionally. When the goblet was first discovered in
Benjamin's sack, he and the other brothers rent their garments.

When Joseph confronted them, it was Judah who said (v. 16), *"What can we say to my lord? How can we speak? And how can we justify ourselves? God has uncovered the sin of your servants."* These are emotional words, words of despair.

As Judah approached Joseph in an attempt to negotiate Benjamin's freedom, then, it required a great effort to overcome his emotions and act in a rational, calculating fashion. We may surmise that this was why Jacob had accepted Judah's guarantees of Benjamin's safety in the first place: He knew that Judah, whose offspring would become kings of Israel, would have the ability to act rationally in any circumstances, as a king must; but not so Reuben who acted on emotion.

Thus, once Judah had prepared himself to speak to Joseph, he had a defense ready at hand. He drew near both for war (as the Midrash says, *"For you are like Pharaoh — if you provoke me I will slay both of you"*), as well as for conciliation, in the hope that Joseph would compromise and accept him as a servant in Benjamin's place.

❦ ❦ ❦

וַיֹּאמֶר יוֹסֵף אֶל־אֶחָיו אֲנִי יוֹסֵף הַעוֹד אָבִי חָי וְלֹא־יָכְלוּ אֶחָיו לַעֲנוֹת אֹתוֹ כִּי נִבְהֲלוּ מִפָּנָיו: — *And Joseph said to his brothers, "I am Joseph; does my father still live?" But his brothers could not answer him because they were overwhelmed before him* (45:3).

Together with his startling self-revelation, in the very same breath Joseph asked his brothers if his father is still alive. Ever since the brothers first appeared before Joseph in Egypt, they had made it clear many times that their father was alive. In the discussion that had just transpired in particular, Judah referred to his concern for Jacob in terms which left no question that he was still alive. If so, why did Joesph need to ask this question? And even if we will say it was necessary, why did he choose this time to pose it?

In truth, Joseph's words were meant to be a rebuke to his brothers for the way they had treated their father in selling him into servitude. *Rashi (Bereishis* 37:35) cites the teaching of the Sages that Heaven decrees that the dead be forgotten from the hearts of the living after a year's time. Normal life could not continue without such a decree, since people would mourn forever for their lost ones. This decree does not apply, however, to those who are still alive, as Joseph was.

Thus, Joseph was able to rebuke his brothers as follows: "If I were dead, then my father would have ceased to mourn for me long ago. But since I am alive, as you had suspected all along and can now see with your own eyes, he could not have forgotten me and must still be grieving over me.

"All along, you have been arguing that if Benjamin does not return to his father, the anguish of his loss will kill him. Now I'm asking you, 'Is my father still alive?' After twenty-two years of anguish over me, how you can say my father is still 'living'? Did you not kill him yourselves when you sold me away from him twenty-two years ago?"

This, then, is why Joseph felt it necessary to ask if his father was still alive at that moment, when the shock of realizing who he was and the powerful rebuke his very identity implied to them was still fresh. And indeed, the rebuke made such a strong impression that the Torah tells us that *they were overwhelmed before him,* and had nothing at all to say in their defense.

❧ ❧ ❧

וַיִּפֹּל עַל־צַוְּארֵי בִנְיָמִן־אָחִיו וַיֵּבְךְּ וּבִנְיָמִן בָּכָה עַל־צַוָּארָיו: — *Then he fell upon the neck of his brother Benjamin and wept; and Benjamin wept upon his neck* (45:14).

Rashi cites the Midrashic interpretation that Joseph wept for the two Temples that would be in Benjamin's territory and would suffer destruction, and Benjamin wept for the Tabernacle of Shiloh that would be in Joseph's territory and would likewise be destroyed. What was there about this moment, when they were reunited after twenty-two years' absence, to turn their minds to these tragic far-future events?

Perhaps, the same Divine Spirit which prophesied those events also foretold that they would be caused by baseless hatred among

Jews (cf. *Yoma* 9b). As Joseph and Benjamin embraced, the baseless hatred that the other brothers had felt for Joseph was very much on their minds, since it seemed that they had now repented and admitted their error. It may be that this reminded Joseph of the future baseless hatred which would cause the destruction of the Second Temple. [Possibly the sins that caused the destruction of Shiloh and the First Temple would have eventually led to baseless hatred, and thus the destruction of those Sanctuaries was a pre-emptive action.]

❧ ❧ ❧

וַיַּגִּדוּ לוֹ לֵאמֹר עוֹד יוֹסֵף חַי וְכִי־הוּא מֹשֵׁל בְּכָל־אֶרֶץ מִצְרָיִם וַיָּפָג לִבּוֹ כִּי לֹא־הֶאֱמִין לָהֶם: — *And they told him to say, "Joseph is still alive," also that he was ruler over all the land of Egypt, but his heart rejected it, for he could not believe them* (45:26).

The word לֵאמֹר, *to say,* generally connotes indirect speech, a message to be delivered to a third person. In this context, it may be an allusion to the Midrashic story of the song sung by Serach daughter of Asher, which indirectly planted in Jacob's mind the idea that Joseph might still be alive, and prepared him for the shocking revelation which he was about to receive.

We may ask, however, why the brothers included the word עוֹד, *still,* in their announcement. It would seem that had they said only, "Joseph is alive," without the word "still," the same message would have been conveyed. What does עוֹד signify?

The brothers were worried that the sudden realization that Joseph was still alive might prove too great a shock for someone of Jacob's advanced years and frail constitution (see commentaries on 48:8). They therefore wanted to introduce the news to him gradually, in a way that would not cause him too much sudden excitement.

Had the brothers said directly, "Joseph is alive," it could have had only one meaning. However, "Joseph is still alive" is the kind of expression which is commonly used in eulogizing a righteous person who has passed away, to say that his deeds and his spirit continue to influence those who knew him even though he is no longer alive. This usage is based on the teaching of the Sages (*Berachos* 18a) that even in their death the righteous are called living.

Thus when the brothers said, "Joseph is still alive," they left open the possibility for Jacob to believe that Joseph was not actually physically alive, but alive only in this spiritual sense. Next, they said Joseph was ruler over all the land of Egypt. This could only mean that he was physically alive; but then we may assume that he no longer kept Torah and *mitzvos,* since it was hard to imagine that someone in such a high position could have remained steadfast in his righteousness. Thus, the words *still alive* would be contradicted.

This is precisely what the Torah means in telling us, *Jacob did not believe them*: He did not believe that Joseph was as pious and righteous as ever. It was hard to imagine that a Jew who had been isolated in Egypt for twenty-two years, and now occupied such a high position, could have remained loyal to Torah and *mitzvos.* For this reason also, the Torah does not say that Jacob's "spirit revived" until after he saw the wagons (עֲגָלוֹת, *agalos*) that Joseph had sent him. These were intended as a reminder that he had been learning the laws of *eglah arufah* (the calf that was decapitated in expiation of an unsolved murder) with Joseph at the time of the latter's disappearance. This "message" finally convinced Jacob that his long-lost son was not only physically alive, but was also spiritually alive, and as committed as ever to Torah. It was then that he set off to see him, his spirit revived for the first time in so many years.

❀ ❀ ❀

וַיֹּאמְרוּ אֶל־פַּרְעֹה לָגוּר בָּאָרֶץ בָּאנוּ — *And they said to Pharaoh, "We have come to sojourn in the land"* (47:4).

In stating their intentions to Pharaoh, Joseph's brothers use the term לָגוּר, *to sojourn,* which suggests a temporary stay. However long they remained in Egypt, they wanted to retain their status as sojourners. There is an interesting *gematria* (numerical analysis) associated with this word.

The numerical value of גּוּר is 209. By using this word, the brothers wanted to make the following allusion: "If we wish to remain sojourners, גֵּרִים, we must leave Egypt after 209 years. If we stay longer than that, we may be affected by the corrupting influences of this country." And indeed, 209 years later marked the beginning of the ten plagues, which prepared the way for the Jews' departure from Egypt the following year.

❀ ❀ ❀

פרשת ויחי
Parashas Vayechi

וְעָשִׂיתָ עִמָּדִי חֶסֶד וֶאֱמֶת אַל־נָא תִקְבְּרֵנִי בְּמִצְרָיִם: —
*"And do kindness and truth with me—please
do not bury me in Egypt"* (47:29).

R ashi explains that kindness shown to the dead is חֶסֶד שֶׁל
אֱמֶת, *kindness of truth* (i.e., sincere altruistic kindness),
since there can be no expectation that the beneficiary will
return the favor.

This comment, however, does not seem to explain the meaning
of our verse. The Torah does not say *true kindness,* it says *kindness
and truth,* suggesting that kindness and truth are not the same thing.
Actually, Jacob was demanding *kindness,* which is itself a form of
truth, and not something different.

Hashem created the world and gave it to us to use. The world,
however, is not self-explanatory, and we would not know how to
use it properly just by looking at it. Therefore, Hashem, in His great
kindness, gave us the Torah as a manual so that we can make proper
use of the world to arrive at our destination, the World to Come.

We can understand this allegorically by thinking of someone who
gives his friend a machine as a gift. If the donor is genuinely kind, he
will make sure that the package includes the operating instructions
for the machine so that its new owner will be able to use it properly.
In the same way, along with the world, Hashem gave us the Torah
as a kindness, to enable us to derive the optimum benefit from the
world.

A fundamental principle of the Torah is the requirement to do kindness to our fellows. We should not approach kindness as an optional way of fulfilling the Torah, as merely a way of increasing our reward. Rather, we must look at doing acts of kindness as a fundamental obligation that the Torah, the ultimate Truth, excepts us to fulfill.

However, since we are flawed human beings, we can never know if a kindness we have done was performed sincerely. Perhaps it was done to curry favor, or to earn future benefits. This is the question to which *Rashi* addresses himself in our verse.

Only when one does a kindness without any possibility of receiving reward can we know that his motive is purely to fulfill the Torah. This is why *Rashi* calls the *mitzvah* of burying the dead a *kindness of truth,* because only in such a case is it certain that his kindess was genuinely for the sake of the truth of the Torah. The literal definition is equally exact. It is a kindness *of* truth, because there is no element of insincerity involved.

❀ ❀ ❀

וַאֲנִי בְּבֹאִי מִפַּדָּן מֵתָה עָלַי רָחֵל בְּאֶרֶץ כְּנַעַן בַּדֶּרֶךְ
בְּעוֹד כִּבְרַת־אֶרֶץ לָבֹא אֶפְרָתָה וָאֶקְבְּרֶהָ שָּׁם בְּדֶרֶךְ
אֶפְרָת הִוא בֵּית לָחֶם׃ — *"But as for me—when I came from Padan, Rachel died on me in the land of Canaan on the road, while there was still a stretch of land to go to Ephrath; and I buried her there on the road to Ephrath, which is Bethlehem"* (48:7).

As part of his request to Joseph, Jacob recounts the story of Rachel's death and burial. *Rashi* explains that Jacob wanted to forestall a claim that Joseph might have made that his father had not taken the trouble to bury his mother in the nearby city of Bethlehem. We would like to examine the nature of this claim and Jacob's response to it.

Joseph might have thought that Jacob did not care enough for Rachel to take the trouble to find her a fitting burial site, since she was only one of four wives. This is why Jacob uses the seemingly unnecessary word, עָלַי, *on me,* in his account. This word alludes to a teaching of the Sages (*Sanhedrin* 22b): *A woman dies only to her husband.* They meant by this that a woman's loss is felt most intensely by her life's companion, more so than by other family members, who are hopefully by then settled into lives of their own.

The Sages also taught (*Berachos* 61a) that Adam and Eve were originally created as one organism, like Siamese twins, joined together at their backs. This lasted until Hashem said, *"It is not good for the man to be alone"* (2:18), and split them into two people. At the same time, we can visualize that all future generations were split into two halves, to be born separately and reunited later through marriage.

We see from this that, even though the Torah permits a man to marry a number of times, he has only one "Siamese twin," the one who was Divinely ordained for him before birth and who is his true spiritual partner. The dictum, *A woman dies only to her husband,* refers to this wife, because when she dies, a part of her husband dies with her.

Thus, when Jacob said, *"Rachel died on me,"* he wanted to assure Joseph that Rachel was his true wife, and that he felt her loss most intensely. That he did not take the trouble to bury her in Bethlehem, then, was for a reason other than lack of caring. As *Rashi* points out, "Know, however, that it was by the command of Hashem that I buried her there so that she might be of help to her children." This was to be in the future, when Nebuzaradan, chief general of King Nebuchadnezzar of Babylon, would lead Israel into captivity after the destruction of the First Temple. As the Jews passed along that road, Rachel ascended over her grave, and wept, beseeching mercy upon them (see *Jeremiah* 31:15*ff*).

Said Jacob, "Nothing less than Hashem's direct command would have stopped me from burying Rachel in the cave of the Machpelah field, in the burial place of my fathers, where I am now asking you to bury me. Therefore, do not harbor a grudge against me over your mother's burial."

❅ ❅ ❅

וַיְבָרֲכֵם בַּיּוֹם הַהוּא לֵאמוֹר בְּךָ יְבָרֵךְ יִשְׂרָאֵל לֵאמֹר
יְשִׂמְךָ אֱלֹהִים כְּאֶפְרַיִם וְכִמְנַשֶּׁה — *So he blessed them that day saying, "By you shall Israel invoke blessing, saying, 'May God make you like Ephraim and like Manasseh'"* (48:20).

Jacob blessed his two grandsons that they should serve as models for future generations. When someone wishes to bless his children, he should invoke the blessing of these two: *May God make you like Ephraim and like Manasseh.*

This is a puzzling blessing. Hashem does not give people achievements of righteousness as a gift. Spiritual greatness comes only after years of hard work, of dedication to Hashem and His Torah. How can one ask Hashem simply to *make* his son like these two? A more fitting blessing would seem to be, "May you grow up to be like Ephraim and Manasseh," expressing the hope and prayer that the child will work hard on his own to become as great as they were.

The Sages taught that even the most righteous person needs help from Heaven in overflowing measure. The Evil Inclination is so strong that no one can stand up to it unless Hashem assists him. For example, if someone who until now has kept a store open on the Sabbath decides to mend his ways, he cannot rely on Hashem to repent for him, he himself must take the step of closing the store. If so, what help can he ask from Hashem? He can ask Hashem to make it easier for him to keep the store closed, perhaps by sending him more customers during the rest of the week so that his livelihood will not suffer too much and the temptation to slip back to his old ways will be minimized.

This principle teaches us the intent of the blessing which Jacob suggested for his descendants. We do not ask Hashem to make our children into righteous people; that can be accomplished only by their own hard work. Instead, we ask Hashem to help them in whatever ways He can, operating through the natural processes of the world.

For this blessing, it is more appropriate to invoke the names of Ephraim and Manasseh than of anyone else in that generation because, of all of Jacob's grandchildren, they grew up in conditions least favorable for spiritual greatness. All of their cousins were born and raised in the land of Canaan, under Jacob's powerful spiritual influence. Ephraim and Manasseh, however, grew up in the very immoral land of Egypt, and therefore had many more obstacles to overcome in their spiritual ascent. The fact that they grew up to be people of such stature shows that Hashem must have given them more than the usual help to achieve their aspirations. Therefore, when we bless our children to be like them, we mean that they should make every effort to overcome all the obstacles they face in their spiritual development—and that Hashem should give them as much help as they need, even as much as He gave Ephraim and Manasseh.

❦ ❦ ❦

שִׁמְעוֹן וְלֵוִי אַחִים כְּלֵי חָמָס מְכֵרֹתֵיהֶם: — *"Simeon and Levi are brothers, their weaponry is a stolen craft"* (49:5).

Why does Jacob state the obvious fact that Simeon and Levi are brothers? Furthermore, all of his children were brothers; why does he single out these two to emphasize their relationship?

Of all of Jacob's children, Simeon and Levi had the greatest sense of family attachment. To avenge the honor of their sister Dinah, they killed an entire city. This by itself shows how strong their loyalty to their siblings was.

Recognizing this, Jacob must have wondered what motivated them to sell their brother Joseph. According to *Rashi*, it was they who proposed to kill him, saying (37:20), *So, now, come and let us kill him, and throw him into one of the pits.* How could brothers with such strong family loyalty suggest such a thing about their brother? We would have thought that they would be inclined in the opposite direction, to try to save him.

To answer this question, Jacob says, כְּלֵי חָמָס מְכֵרֹתֵיהֶם, *their weaponry is a stolen craft.* According to *Rashi*, חָמָס could mean something that was stolen. This suggests that the attitude which induced them to sell their own brother was a *stolen craft,* foreign to them and their feelings.

We may also understand מְכֵרֹתֵיהֶם to mean *their sale*. This suggests the following interpretation: Their sale of Joseph was really a stolen weapon in the hands of Simeon and Levi because on their own, they would never have hurt one of their siblings. The fact that they participated in this sale, totally against their natures, is a proof that the sale was not their own plan, but rather Hashem's work, a preparation for the family's descent to Egypt. The brothers were merely tools to accomplish Hashem's purposes.

❧ ❧ ❧

וַיְבָרֶךְ אוֹתָם אִישׁ אֲשֶׁר כְּבִרְכָתוֹ בֵּרַךְ אֹתָם: — *He blessed each according to his appropriate blessing* (49:28).

Rashi explains that even though it appears that Reuben, Simeon and Levi received rebukes from their father, rather than blessings, our verse informs us that, even in their case, Jacob's words were really blessings. The commentators present various interpretations of his words to them to show that they contained hidden blessings, but we will suggest a different approach.

Perhaps the very rebukes that Jacob gave Reuben, Simeon and Levi were themselves blessings. For example, Reuben was told that because he was impetuous like water, he would not be worthy to be king, even though he was the firstborn. Indeed, this was the greatest blessing he could have received. Who knows what disaster and tragedy such an impetuous person could cause, as king, to himself and to his whole people. It was truly a blessing to keep him from power and protect him from himself.

Similarly, Simeon and Levi are rebuked for their anger and told that they would be divided and dispersed throughout Israel. In this way also, such angry people would be protected from harming themselves and the rest of the people. Likewise, Zebulun was told that his descendants would be seafarers. Even though this is a difficult and dangerous occupation, the Sages (*Kiddushin* 82a) said that sailors are very pious, since they are aware how totally dependent they are on Hashem's mercy even to stay alive. (See also our commentary on *Parashas Bamidbar*.)

Thus, even the rebukes Jacob gave several of his sons were really blessings. We should learn from this that everything that happens to us, even if it seems to be an unpleasant rebuke from Hashem at the time, is really a great blessing. (See also our commentary on *Parashas Vaeira, Shemos* 6:10.)

❀　❀　❀

ספר שמות

Sefer Shemos

פרשת שמות
Parashas Shemos

וְאֵלֶּה שְׁמוֹת בְּנֵי יִשְׂרָאֵל הַבָּאִים מִצְרַיְמָה אֵת יַעֲקֹב
אִישׁ וּבֵיתוֹ בָּאוּ: — *And these are the names of
the Children of Israel who came to Egypt with
Jacob. Each man came with his household*
(1:1).

The Torah says אֵת יַעֲקֹב, *with Jacob,* implying that Jacob
was the mainstay and that everyone else was secondary to
him.

However, we do not find this special emphasis on Jacob in the
earlier account of the descent to Egypt contained in *Parashas
Vayigash*. There the Torah says simply (*Bereishis* 46:8), *And these
are the names of the Children of Israel who came to Egypt: Jacob
and his sons* . . . This wording suggests that Jacob and his children
had equal status. How can we explain this shift in Jacob's position
between the two accounts?

To answer this question, we must realize that in *Parashas
Vayigash* the Torah merely related an event as it happened:
Because there was no food in Canaan, Jacob and his children had to
go where there was food, to Egypt. Jacob did not receive special
mention as the elder and leader because he was in the same plight as
the rest of his family.

When the Children of Israel first arrived in Egypt they had no
intention of becoming settled there. As they said to Pharaoh, לָגוּר
בָּאָרֶץ בָּאנוּ, *We have come to sojourn in the land* (ibid. 47:4). This

aloof attitude did not change the entire time they spent in Egypt; never did they aspire to become part of Egyptian society.

If we think about it, this is an amazing phenomenon, almost unparalleled in the history of any people. When has such a powerless subculture ever resisted the enormous pressures to assimilate into a dominant culture during a period of over two centuries? What was their secret?

The answer to this question is one which we need to keep reminding ourselves every day of our lives, even though we all know it very well: Only because of Jacob were the Jews able to sojourn in Egypt for two hundred and ten years without becoming Egyptians. Thanks to Jacob's inspiration, they continued to speak their own language the whole time, they never adopted Egyptian dress or Egyptian names, and they never intermarried with the Egyptians.

For their entire stay in Egypt, these strictures gave the Jews a continual reminder that protected them from the seductive influences of Egyptian culture. And ever since then, through all the difficult exiles we have endured, we have survived only because we have clung firmly to the faith and the tradition our forefather Jacob instilled in us.

This explains why the Torah emphasizes Jacob's role as the leader *after* his descendants already were spending time in Egypt and not when they first arrived. Only after they had survived the trials of exile with their identity and faith intact could it be apparent that Jacob's inspiration was what kept them on the path of truth.

❧ ❧ ❧

וּבְנֵי יִשְׂרָאֵל פָּרוּ וַיִּשְׁרְצוּ וַיִּרְבּוּ וַיַּעַצְמוּ בִּמְאֹד מְאֹד וַתִּמָּלֵא הָאָרֶץ אֹתָם: — *And the Children of Israel were prolific and teemed and became exceedingly great and powerful; and the land was filled with them* (1:7).

It would seem, at first glance, that the blessing that Hashem gave the Jews — their great fertility and success turned out to be in reality a curse. We see that their very greatness intimidated Pharaoh, as he said (v. 9), *"Behold! The people of the Children of Israel are greater and stronger than us."* Had they not been so numerous and powerful, surely Pharaoh would not have imposed the harsh labor and the other cruel decrees. But can it be imagined that Hashem would give His people a curse disguised as a blessing?

There is a story in the Midrash (*Eichah Rabbasi* 3:20) about the Roman emperor Hadrian, who hated the Jews. Once his imperial procession passed a Jew who saluted him and said, "Hail, O mighty Emperor!" When he heard this, Hadrian immediately ordered that the Jew be beheaded for having the audacity to greet the emperor.

A short while later, he passed a second Jew who, having seen what had just happened, remained silent as the emperor went by. Again Hadrian stopped and ordered his soldiers to behead the second Jew also, this time for his insolence in failing to greet the emperor.

One of Hadrian's ministers had the boldness to ask him, "I don't understand. If a Jew greets you, you have him executed. If he fails to greet you, you have him executed. What is a Jew supposed to do?"

Answered the emperor, "Don't tell me how to get rid of this people, whom I hate so passionately. I'll treat them however I want to."

In the same way, Pharaoh's hatred of the Jews was beyond any sense or reason. Whether they were great or small, powerful or weak, he would have found some excuse to make their lives difficult. Therefore, it is wrong to think that Hashem's blessing was in any way a curse.

Nevertheless, it may sometimes seem so on the surface, because our enemies use Hashem's blessings as an excuse to hate us. Thus, Pharaoh would always be able to find an excuse to show his hatred. But there should be no doubt in our minds that whenever Hashem gives a blessing, it is genuinely a blessing. The fact that people like Pharaoh seize on any excuse to abuse and oppress us does not change this; Hashem carries out His plan despite them and His ultimate purpose will be achieved no matter what they do or say.

❦ ❦ ❦

הִנֵּה עַם בְּנֵי יִשְׂרָאֵל רַב וְעָצוּם מִמֶּנּוּ: — *"Behold, the people of the Children of Israel are greater and stronger than us"* (1:9).

Not only were the Jews very numerous but, more importantly, their power and influence was far out of proportion to their numbers. The same is also true today; the power of Jews in the professions and in many aspects of public life far exceeds their numbers in the population at large (though we must always be careful not to flaunt this, as we have learned all too clearly in the course of our history in exile among the nations).

But why should this have worried Pharaoh? Hand in hand with the humility which has always been innate in the Jewish character, there has always been a dedication to serving whatever country they live in. However much power the Jews may have had in Egyptian life, they were still loyal and trustworthy subjects of their masters. Pharaoh knew that the Jewish people were his biggest asset; why was he afraid of them?

The answer to our question may be found in Pharaoh's own words. He warned the Egyptians to be afraid of the Jews פֶּן יִרְבֶּה (v. 10), which is usually translated *lest they become many*. Really, however, these words could also mean *lest they become great*. Pharaoh was worried that the Jews would some day become arrogant about their power and influence and forget their humility. If that happened, they could pose a very serious threat to him. Maybe some day they would realize that they had the power to overthrow him and take the country into their own hands.

Pharaoh understood his people; he knew very well that an Egyptian with even a tenth of the Jews' power would be a great threat to him. As the ruler of a society that was notorious for its treachery, Pharaoh simply couldn't believe that the Jews were fundamentally any different from his own people.

❦ ❦ ❦

וְהִנֵּה הַסְּנֶה בֹּעֵר בָּאֵשׁ וְהַסְּנֶה אֵינֶנּוּ אֻכָּל: —
Behold! The thornbush was burning in fire,
but the thornbush was not consumed (3:2).

There is an interesting symbolism in Hashem's use of a burning thornbush to attract Moshe's attention. At that stage in their history, the Jews were like thorns — they were not of great value because they did not serve Hashem. We can say that Hashem put the Jews into servitude to burn out the "thorns" of the Jews so that the people would be purified. This is the meaning of the phrase, *the thornbush was burning in fire.*

It may be asked, however: If the Jews were like a nation of thorns to be consumed, what would remain of them? This is why the Torah says, וְהַסְּנֶה אֵינֶנּוּ אֻכָּל, *the thornbush was not consumed.* Even during times when there are no worthy Jews to protect the people (Heaven forbid), Hashem will keep the fires of exile burning, but He will not allow them to consume the "thorns," until such time as there are Jews with sufficient merit to bring the redemption. But *never* will He allow total destruction, because the purpose of "punishment" is not to destroy us, but to arouse us to repent. As the Sages expressed it, "My arrows [which I shoot at them] will give out, but the Jewish people will never cease to exist" (see our commentary to *Devarim* 32:23).

❧ ❧ ❧

וַיֹּאמֶר ה' אֶל־מֹשֶׁה עַתָּה תִרְאֶה אֲשֶׁר אֶעֱשֶׂה לְפַרְעֹה
— כִּי בְיָד חֲזָקָה יְשַׁלְּחֵם וּבְיָד חֲזָקָה יְגָרְשֵׁם מֵאַרְצוֹ:
And HASHEM said to Moshe, "Now you will see
what I shall do to Pharaoh, because with a
strong hand he will send them and with a
strong hand he will expel them from his land"
(6:1).

When Moshe delivered Hashem's message that Pharaoh was to allow the Jews to go out into the Wilderness to serve Him, Pharaoh only grew angry and increased the people's workload beyond the point of endurance. Moshe complained to Hashem that, far from helping the people, he, Moshe, had only made matters worse. In our verse, Hashem responded by assuring Moshe that the salvation would definitely come, and that Pharaoh would learn his lesson.

Though it seems like no more than a simple adverb of time, the word *now* is pivotal in this verse. Hashem told Moshe, "Only *now,* that their workload has been so drastically increased, will I be able to show you what I plan to do to Pharaoh. Until now, I could not redeem the Jews because of My decree that they spend four hundred years in servitude. *Now,* however, that the servitude has become harsher, the severity of the oppression will make even a shorter period equivalent to the suffering that would normally have taken much longer. As a result, the four hundred years can be telescoped into a shorter time. Consequently, it is *now* —very soon in fact—that you will see My hand at work."

❈ ❈ ❈

פרשת וארא
Parashas Vaeira

וַיְדַבֵּר אֱלֹהִים אֶל־מֹשֶׁה וַיֹּאמֶר אֵלָיו אֲנִי ה׳: — *And God spoke to Moshe and He said to him, "I am HASHEM"* (6:2).

I t is well known that the name ELOKIM always indicates the quality of judgment, and the name HASHEM indicates the quality of mercy. At the beginning of the verse, Hashem is referred to in His role as a judge, an administrator of strict justice. Then, when Hashem speaks, He identifies Himself with the Name that indicates His mercy.

To understand why this reversal occurs, let us look back to the end of the previous *parashah*. After hearing that he had been ordered by Hashem to allow the Jews to go serve their God, Pharaoh accused them of laziness and ordered their workload drastically increased. Some of the Jews complained to Moshe and Aaron and Moshe said to Hashem, *"Why have You caused harm to this people and why have You sent me? And since my coming to Pharaoh to speak in Your Name, he has wronged them and You have not rescued Your people"* (Shemos 5:22-23).

When Hashem speaks to Moshe at the beginning of our *parashah*, He addresses Himself to this grievance. His answer can be understood as follows: "Originally I decreed that the Jews had to spend four hundred years in exile in Egypt, but so far only two hundred and ten years have gone by. In order to redeem them before their time is up, I have to make their servitude harsher to make it as if they had served the full time of their bondage. That is why I allowed Pharaoh to increase their workload."

Now we can understand why the verse uses two different names for Hashem. It is as if Hashem said to Moshe, "You complain to Me because you think I am acting in My role as a Judge Who metes out strict justice. But really My actions were purely merciful. I only want to redeem My people as soon as possible. Even though at first their lives became harder, I did it entirely for their good."

The above lesson applies in many situations that we encounter all the time. Whenever something seemingly unpleasant happens, we have to keep in mind that it is really for our good. This is why the Gemara (*Berachos* 60b) says that we should be happy when we recite the blessing בָּרוּךְ דַּיַן הָאֱמֶת, *Blessed is the True Judge*, which is said on hearing bad news. Even when a particular event appears to stem from Hashem's attribute of justice, really it is nothing other than pure mercy. We should recognize that it is for our good, and be happy with it.

The prophet Isaiah writes (12:1), אוֹדְךָ ה׳ כִּי אָנַפְתָּ בִּי יָשֹׁב אַפְּךָ וּתְנַחֲמֵנִי, *Thank You, Hashem, for being angry with me. When Your anger disappears, I will be consoled.* The sage Rav Yosef (*Niddah* 31a) explained this verse by telling the story of a man who planned to take a boat journey to complete a business deal which would make him wealthy. Just before he was supposed to sail, the man took ill and was forced to cancel his trip. As he lay in bed, he complained bitterly to Hashem for depriving him of such a great opportunity.

Later he learned that the boat had sunk and everyone on board had perished. Then he cried out in praise to Hashem, "I rejoice that You were angry with me and made me sick so that I missed the boat, because now I see that it was for my good, not to harm me."

In 1940, the Russians sent the many *yeshivah* students to Siberia after the occupation of Lithuania, and the students were all very upset. The war had not yet started in that region and the Jews who remained in Lithuania were still relatively free, while those in Siberia were in forced labor camps. It seemed to them that Hashem had forgotten them.

Only later, when they found out that the Jews who stayed behind had been exterminated by the Nazis, יִמ״ש, may their name be erased, did they realize that Hashem had been taking care of them the whole time, and that they were still alive only because they had been in Siberia.

There is a touching parable about a little boy who gets lost in a crowd and stands hopelessly crying for his father. When his father finally finds him, he gives the boy a slap on the face to punish him for wandering off on his own. As soon as the boy sees that his father has found him, he stops crying and smiles. Even though his face hurts from the slap, he is happy because he knows that his father still cares for him.

So also, when things seem to be going badly for us and we have moments of suffering, we should be happy with the knowledge that Hashem is not ignoring us, and that eventually we will come to see that the things that seem bad to us now are really to our benefit. This is why we have to say the blessing *Blessed is the True Judge*, joyfully.

❧ ❧ ❧

וְגָאַלְתִּי אֶתְכֶם — *I will redeem you* (6:6).

Hashem promised to redeem the Jews from Egypt. The word *redeem* really means to buy someone's freedom with money, as the Torah says (*Vayikra* 25:25), *and he shall redeem his brother's sale*. This implies that the Jews would be ransomed through an exchange of money or other valuables. With what did Hashem intend to buy the Jew's freedom?

The Egyptians deserved all the plagues they received because of the unfair hardships they imposed on the Jews. In other words, the suffering the Egyptians endured from the plagues was a debt they owed. Had they released the Jews when Hashem first told them to, He would not have punished them; in other words, He would have forgiven the debt they owed. This willingness to forgive the debt of the Egyptians was the payment with which Hashem planned to redeem the Jews.

As it was, however, the Egyptians did not let the Jews go willingly until after the last plague, at which time they thought they would all die, as they said (12:33), *"We are all dying."* Had they not freed the Jews then, they may indeed have died, as they richly deserved.

Thus, the sparing of their lives was the "payment" that they received in exchange for the freedom of the Jews.

❈ ❈ ❈

וַיְדַבֵּר ה' אֶל־מֹשֶׁה וְאֶל־אַהֲרֹן וַיְצַוֵּם אֶל־בְּנֵי יִשְׂרָאֵל וְאֶל־פַּרְעֹה מֶלֶךְ מִצְרָיִם לְהוֹצִיא אֶת־בְּנֵי־יִשְׂרָאֵל מֵאֶרֶץ מִצְרָיִם: — *And HASHEM spoke to Moshe and to Aaron, and He commanded them concerning the Children of Israel and concerning Pharaoh, King of Egypt, to take the Children of Israel out from the land of Egypt* (6:13).

We understand what Hashem told Moshe and Aaron to command Pharaoh; namely, to release the Jews. However, the wording of this verse suggests that they were also supposed to command the Jews to do something, but it is not immediately apparent what this was.

It may be that the same command which Moshe and Aaron were to give to Pharaoh was also relevant to the Jews, לְהוֹצִיא, *to take out*. As a command for Pharaoh, this obviously meant to allow Moshe to lead them out of the country. In the case of the Jews, since they were not in control of their comings and goings, the command was simply that they should remain *worthy* to go out, so that Hashem would be willing to effect their release.

❈ ❈ ❈

וַיִּקַּח עַמְרָם אֶת־יוֹכֶבֶד דֹּדָתוֹ לוֹ לְאִשָּׁה — *And Amram took Yocheved his aunt to himself for a wife* (6:20).

In three places in this passage, concerning Amram, Aaron and Elazar, the Torah uses the expression לוֹ לְאִשָּׁה, *to himself for a wife*. We may assume that the Torah wishes to stress to us that the women these men married were wives *for them*, wives who were suited to them. Had the Torah not emphasized this point, we might have thought that Amram was presumptuous in marrying his aunt, or that Elazar was wrong to take a wife who had an ancestor who had, as *Rashi* says (v. 25), "fattened calves for idolatry." Now, however, we have the Torah's testimony that these men took the correct wives for themselves. Similarly, *Rashi* states that Aaron investigated his wife's brother Nachshon, the *Nasi* of the tribe of Judah, and found that it was a suitable family to marry into.

Conversely, nowhere do we find it said that Moshe took his wife Tzipporah לוֹ לְאִשָּׁה, *to himself for a wife*, only that her father Yisro gave her to him (see 2:21). Perhaps the Torah felt that it was not proper for Moshe to marry the daughter of a man who had been the High Priest of the idol-worshiping cult of Midian, even though in her own right she was a most righteous woman and made a fine wife for Moshe.

❧ ❧ ❧

וְאַתָּה וַעֲבָדֶיךָ יָדַעְתִּי כִּי טֶרֶם תִּירְאוּן מִפְּנֵי ה' אֱלֹהִים: — *"And of you and your servants I know that you are not yet afraid before HASHEM, the God"* (9:30).

After the seventh plague, hailstones, had caused further devastation to the land of Egypt, Pharaoh sent for Moshe and Aaron and admitted that Hashem was just and he and his people were wicked. He then asked Moshe to beseech Hashem to end the plague, promising to send the Jews away. To this, Moshe answered that he knew that Pharaoh still did not really intend to comply with Hashem's command. How did Moshe know with certainty that Pharaoh, after being bludgeoned with plagues that had left his country in ruins, was not finally sincere in his promise to send the Jews out? Hashem had assured him that the Jews would leave eventually; how could he know that this was not the time?

According to *Yalkut Shimoni* (173), Moshe's staff, the one which he used to cause most of the plagues, had written on it the acronym included in the Passover *Haggadah* for the names of the ten plagues: דְּצַ"ךְ עַדַ"שׁ בְּאַחַ"ב, *D'tzach, Adash, B'achav.* With this, Moshe was able to keep a count of the plagues as they happened and thus he knew that there were three more to come. He reasoned that if Hashem would find it necessary to bring three more plagues on Pharaoh, it must be that Pharaoh was not yet willing to capitulate, and therefore did not yet sincerely fear Hashem. Had Pharaoh been sincerely fearful, Hashem would not have reinforced his stubborness about releasing the people. But Pharaoh, bolstered by Hashem, found excuses to remain stubborn, which shows that he was not really so fearful.

❊ ❊ ❊

פרשת בא
Parashas Bo

וַיֹּאמְרוּ עַבְדֵי פַרְעֹה אֵלָיו עַד־מָתַי יִהְיֶה זֶה לָנוּ
לְמוֹקֵשׁ — *And Pharaoh's servants said to him,*
"How long will this person be a snare for us?"
(10:7).

Their question is puzzling in two ways. For one thing,
Pharaoh's servants refer to Moshe with the word זֶה, *this*
one. This seems to suggest that Moshe was still present,
even though he had already left.

Also, what did they mean by calling Moshe a מוֹקֵשׁ, *a snare?* Did
they really think that Moshe was responsible for their difficulties and
that if only he would disappear everything would be fine? They
must have known that the source of their problems was the fact that
Hashem was angry with them for not releasing the Jews. If so, why
did they blame him?

In answer to these questions, we can say that when Pharaoh's
servants spoke of Moshe, they really meant to refer to the Jewish
people as a whole. This is why they said in the same verse, שַׁלַּח
אֶת־הָאֲנָשִׁים וְיַעַבְדוּ אֶת־ה׳ אֱלֹהֵיהֶם, *Send the people away and let*
them serve HASHEM their G-d. The solution they proposed reveals
that they saw that their problem lay in their failure to release the
Jews.

There is an allusion to this interpretation in the choice of the word
זֶה, *this one*, to refer to Moshe. The *gematria* (numerical value) of

זֶה is twelve, suggesting that Moshe is nothing more than a representative of the twelve tribes.

In one other place, the Torah hints that Moshe as leader is simply a representative of his followers. In his farewell address at the beginning of *Devarim*, Moshe recounts to the Jews the story of their wanderings through the desert. During this narrative he says (ibid. 2:16-17), *And it was when all the warriors of that generation ceased to die from amongst the people, HASHEM spoke to me . . .* *Rashi* points out that this is the first time in that narrative since he alluded to the incident of the spies (ibid. 1:1) that he mentioned how Hashem had spoken to him with affection and compassion.

According to *Rashi*, this shows us that while the rebellious generation was alive, Moshe never once had the same kind of loving "face to face" dialogue with Hashem that he did before and after. From this we learn that prophets receive their Divine inspiration only in the merit of the people they lead. Because Hashem was angry with the Jews, He did not favor Moshe with the closeness he had otherwise enjoyed. Thus, we have another example of how Moshe as leader personifies his followers.

❧ ❧ ❧

וַיֹּאמֶר מֹשֶׁה בִּנְעָרֵינוּ וּבִזְקֵנֵינוּ נֵלֵךְ בְּבָנֵינוּ וּבִבְנוֹתֵנוּ בְּצֹאנֵנוּ וּבִבְקָרֵנוּ נֵלֵךְ כִּי חַג־ה' לָנוּ: — *And Moshe said, "With our youths and our elders shall we go, with our sons and our daughters, our flocks and our herds shall we go, because it is HASHEM's festival for us"* (10:9).

Pharaoh finally agreed to allow the Jews to bring offerings to Hashem, but he wanted to know which of them would go. Moshe answered that everyone had to go because they were going out to celebrate *HASHEM's festival for us*. Had he said, חַג לַה', *a festival to HASHEM*, it would have meant that the Jews planned to make a festival in Hashem's honor. Then it might not have been so important to bring everyone along; the dignitaries alone would have been enough to honor Hashem. Generally when there is an affair honoring a revered guest, only the most illustrious people are invited.

This, however, was HASHEM's *festival,* meaning that Hashem was the Host, and the Jews were to be His guests. Therefore He wanted *all* of His people to come and everyone, even the children, were invited.

❦ ❦ ❦

וּלְכֹל בְּנֵי יִשְׂרָאֵל לֹא יֶחֱרַץ־כֶּלֶב לְשֹׁנוֹ — *And at all the Children of Israel not a dog will bark* (11:7).

The silence of the dogs on that night, when Hashem smote all of the first-born Egyptians, showed Pharaoh that Hashem did indeed spare the Jews. How did it prove this? The Sages taught (*Bava Kamma* 60b) that dogs always wail when the Angel of Death goes through a town. If the dogs were silent in the Jewish neighborhoods, that was proof that the Angel of Death had passed over them and left them in peace.

❦ ❦ ❦

הַחֹדֶשׁ הַזֶּה לָכֶם רֹאשׁ חֳדָשִׁים רִאשׁוֹן הוּא לָכֶם לְחָדְשֵׁי הַשָּׁנָה: — *This month shall be for you a beginning of months, the first of the months of the year* (12:2).

Astronomically, the month of Nissan is represented by the constellation טָלֶה, *sheep* (commonly called the Ram). The Egyptians worshiped sheep as a symbol of wealth (cf. *Devarim* 7:13, עַשְׁתְּרֹת צֹאנֶךָ, *your flocks of sheep,* on which *Rashi* comments that sheep enrich their owners).

The month of Nissan is also the beginning of spring, the time of new life, when the earth is rejuvenated after the dormancy of winter. This is the season when people dream of the wealth they hope to realize from their new crops and their sheep; as such it is most important in the springtime to denounce the concept that wealth is the primary goal of life. Therefore, the Jews were called upon when the season was most alluring to take the sheep, which they had worshiped together with their Egyptian neighbors, and offer it to the service of Hashem. This is the true wealth, of which

King Solomon said (*Mishlei* 3:15), *It is more precious than jewels.* This is why Hashem used the demonstrative pronoun and said, "הַחֹדֶשׁ הַזֶּה, *'this' month.*" He pointed to the Ram and said, "This is the reason!"

❀ ❀ ❀

לֵיל שִׁמֻּרִים הוּא לַה׳ לְהוֹצִיאָם מֵאֶרֶץ מִצְרָיִם — *It is a night of watching for HASHEM, to take them out of Egypt* (12:42).

The expression לֵיל שִׁמֻּרִים הוּא לַה׳, *it is a night of watching for HASHEM,* suggests that He had been watching and waiting anxiously for the most appropriate time to take the Jews out of Egypt. This implies that there was no fixed time for the redemption; had there been, Hashem would simply have waited patiently until it came, instead of watching anxiously every moment to see if *this* would be the time.

Thus, the four hundred years of exile and servitude that Hashem had foretold to Abraham was not inflexible. As we have seen above, under certain conditions, the time could be shortened. This is why Hashem "watched" for the most propitious time. Since there was a possibility that they would be ready soon, Hashem could not simply relax and wait for the four-hundred-year deadline.

Just as the Egyptian exile was flexible, the duration of our current exile is not fixed (see also our commentary in *Parashas Lech Lecha, Bereishis* 15:8). It is in our power, and is therefore our obligation both as a people and as individuals, to make ourselves worthy to bring the redemption in the near future.

May Hashem bring it soon, in our days.

❀ ❀ ❀

פרשת בשלח
Parashas Beshalach

וַיְהִי בְּשַׁלַּח פַּרְעֹה אֶת־הָעָם וְלֹא־נָחָם אֱלֹהִים דֶּרֶךְ
אֶרֶץ פְּלִשְׁתִּים כִּי קָרוֹב הוּא כִּי אָמַר אֱלֹהִים פֶּן־יִנָּחֵם
הָעָם בִּרְאֹתָם מִלְחָמָה וְשָׁבוּ מִצְרָיְמָה: — *And it was*
when Pharaoh sent the people, and God did
not lead them by the route of the land of the
Philistines, which was close, for God said,
"Lest the people have regret when they see
war and return to Egypt" (13:17).

This verse contains two distinct pieces of information: Pharaoh sent the Jews from Egypt, and Hashem decided not to lead them to the land of Canaan via the most direct route. These two events seem unrelated to each other, yet there must be some connection between them, since the Torah relates them in the same verse.

To understand their connection, let us consider for a moment what would have happened if Hashem had seen fit to take the Jews out of Egypt without Pharaoh's consent. The Jews would have marched away in stunned awe at the sight of Pharaoh and his mighty army watching their departure in powerless frustration. No one could have doubted that Hashem had the power to protect them from any enemy and Hashem could have led them into the midst of the Philistines without concern that they would turn timid and want to return to Egypt.

Hashem's wisdom dictated otherwise, however. He wanted Pharaoh to release the Jews of his own volition. Therefore He inflicted plague after plague on the Egyptians until, finally, Pharaoh gave in and said he wanted them to go. As a result, the Jews could err and imagine that Hashem's power was sufficient only to cause plagues, but not to overcome an armed enemy. In such a state of mind, the Jews could easily have panicked in the face of a Philistine attack and fled back to Egypt. That is why Hashem thought it best not to expose the Jews to the threat of armed battle with the Philistines and therefore led them in a circuitous route through the desert.

To understand why Hashem found it best to do things in this way, we should consider the deep spiritual darkness in which the Jews lived at that time and how weak was their appreciation of Hashem's power in the world. To attain each new level of awareness they had to overcome the influence of two centuries of exposure to Egyptian idol worship and denial of Hashem. Each realization was so hard won that they could not be expected to go any further on their own.

We see this illustrated many times in the course of their wanderings through the desert. As King David recounts (*Tehillim* 78:19-20), *And they spoke against God. They said, "Can God prepare a table in the wilderness? True, He struck a rock and water flowed and streams flooded forth — Can He give bread also? Can He supply meat for His nation?"* Every step of the way, they doubted that Hashem was capable of doing more than He had shown until then.

Hashem, on His side, chose not to show the Jews too much of His power at once, in order to introduce them gradually to a new way of looking at the world — that every minute detail of everything that happens is under His control. But that learning process would take time and require carefully measured doses. This is why Hashem arranged for them to leave *with* Pharaoh's consent. The function of the plagues was to demonstrate conclusively — even to Pharaoh — that Hashem controls every aspect of "nature." This process came to a climax at the Splitting of the Sea, when the Torah says (14:31) that the Jewish people *believed in HASHEM and in His servant Moshe.*

❧ ❧ ❧

וַיַּרְא יִשְׂרָאֵל אֶת־הַיָּד הַגְּדֹלָה אֲשֶׁר עָשָׂה ה' בְּמִצְרַיִם
— *And the Jews saw the great hand that*
HASHEM *inflicted upon Egypt* (14:31).

This verse describes the awed reaction of the Jews to the sight of the Splitting of the Sea of Reeds. Similarly, in the next *parashah*, upon hearing Moshe's account of how Hashem saved the Jews from the Egyptians, Yisro says (18:11), *Now I know that* HASHEM *is greater than all the gods*. In both cases, it would seem more appropriate to talk about Hashem's power and might rather than His "greatness." What is the greatness that is referred to in these two places?

To explain this, we will propose that greatness is the ability to control oneself and not do more than one should. Normally, someone who has been hurt finds it difficult to control his anger and will punish the person who harmed him far out of proportion to the wrong suffered. The great person is the one who is able to control his natural impulse and react to a wrong done in a way that is just and logical, not to exact retribution from an enemy but rather to try to correct the situation and prevent further wrongdoing.

This is the greatness the Jews saw in Hashem, and that so impressed Yisro. When Hashem drowned all the Egyptian soldiers, it was in retribution for the Egyptian plan to drown all the Jewish male offspring. King Solomon said, וְהָאֱלֹהִים יְבַקֵּשׁ אֶת־נִרְדָּף, *And God always seeks the pursued* (*Koheles* 3:15). This means not only that Hashem protects those who are persecuted, but also that He examines each situation carefully to untangle all the complications and determine who is really being persecuted and to exactly what extent.

Other cultures and religions teach that might makes right and emphasize that power is to be worshiped. The Torah teaches us that Hashem's greatness lies in the fact that He is just and gives to everyone exactly what he deserves.

❧ ❧ ❧

וַתִּקַּח מִרְיָם הַנְּבִיאָה אֲחוֹת אַהֲרֹן אֶת־הַתֹּף בְּיָדָהּ וַתֵּצֶאןָ כָל־הַנָּשִׁים אַחֲרֶיהָ בְּתֻפִּים וּבִמְחֹלֹת: — *And Miriam the Prophetess, the sister of Aaron, took the tambourine in her hand. And all the women went out after her with tambourines and dancing* (15:20).

The Torah here calls Miriam a prophetess. *Rashi* comments that since this verse describes her as *the sister of Aaron*, ignoring the fact that she was also the sister of Moshe, the prophesy referred to was before Moshe was born, when she was the sister of only Aaron. At that time, she predicted that her mother would give birth to a son who would rescue the Jews from Egyptian bondage. Therefore, it is especially appropriate that the Torah call her a prophetess *now*, when her prophesy was finally confirmed with the destruction of the Egyptian army. This explains also why it was she who led the women in praising Hashem, since the salvation they had just witnessed was the fulfillment of the prophesy she had had over eighty years earlier.

※ ※ ※

שָׁמַעְתִּי אֶת־תְּלוּנֹת בְּנֵי יִשְׂרָאֵל דַּבֵּר אֲלֵהֶם לֵאמֹר בֵּין הָעַרְבַּיִם תֹּאכְלוּ בָשָׂר וּבַבֹּקֶר תִּשְׂבְּעוּ־לָחֶם וִידַעְתֶּם כִּי אֲנִי ה' אֱלֹהֵיכֶם: — *"I have heard the complaints of the Children of Israel; speak to them to say, 'In the afternoon you shall eat meat and in the morning you will be satiated with bread, and you shall know that I am* HASHEM, *your God'"* (16:12).

The meaning of the word לֵאמֹר, *to say,* in this verse is not immediately apparent. Normally in the Torah this word introduces a statement which the listener is expected to repeat to others, yet to whom were the Jews supposed to repeat Hashem's words in this verse?

We may say, however, that they were being instructed to tell their offspring in all future generations of Hashem's might in supplying them with food in the Wilderness. This is why later in this *parashah* (v. 33), Moshe tells Aaron to preserve a specimen of manna, so that future generations will be able to see with their eyes that Hashem provided for all of their needs. Although we no longer have this specimen in our days, many people have the practice of reading this whole *parashah* every day, as a constant reminder of Hashem's ability to care for our needs (see *Shulchan Aruch Orach Chaim* 1:5 with *Mishnah Berurah*). By renewing our faith in Hashem's goodness and power to provide for all our needs, we become more deserving of His abundance.

❈ ❈ ❈

וַיֹּאמְרוּ אִישׁ אֶל־אָחִיו מָן הוּא כִּי לֹא יָדְעוּ מַה־הוּא — *And they said, each to his brother, "It is manna," because they did not know what it was* (16:15).

Rashi explains that the word מָן, *manna*, means *a preparation of food*. We may ask why they called their Heavenly bread by such a general name. Why did they not call it a more specific name that would identify its nature?

The Jews in the Wilderness had difficulty deciding exactly what it was since, as the Sages taught (*Yoma* 75a), it tasted to each individual like the food he most liked. Imagine, then, the following conversation between two Jews on one of the first mornings it fell:

"This is the best cake I've ever had. I've never tasted anything so sweet and dainty."

"What do you mean, cake? It tastes like rich, juicy carrots, just like the ones I used to get in the market in late summer."

Because they could not agree on what manna tasted like, they gave it a name that everyone could agree on: *food*.

❈ ❈ ❈

פרשת יתרו
Parashas Yisro

וַיִּקַּח יִתְרוֹ חֹתֵן מֹשֶׁה אֶת־צִפֹּרָה אֵשֶׁת מֹשֶׁה אַחַר
שִׁלּוּחֶיהָ: — *And Yisro, Moshe's father-in-law,
took Tzipporah, the wife of Moshe, after he
had sent her away* (18:2).

Why does the Torah stress that it was *after he [Moshe] had
sent her away* that Yisro took his daughter back to her
former husband? Also, how could Yisro be so confident
that Moshe would want to take her back now since, as *Onkelos*
interprets this verse, he had already given her a *get* (divorce)?

Yisro realized that the only reason Moshe had divorced Tzipporah was for her benefit, so that she would not remain tied to him
while he was forced to be separated from her. As *Rashi* comments
on our verse, when Aaron came out to meet Moshe in the
Wilderness, he advised Moshe not to take his wife and children with
him to Egypt. Since the Jews there were suffering great burdens, it
would be wrong to expose more people to such danger. Moshe
therefore sent her back to her father, but first gave her a *get* so that
she would be free to remarry if she did not wish to remain
husbandless for a long period.

Now, however, the danger was over and Tzipporah wanted to
return to her husband. Therefore, since Yisro knew that Moshe had
all along been concerned only for her benefit, he was confident that
Moshe would want to take her back.

For this reason, the Torah makes a point of calling our attention
to the divorce. The very fact that Moshe had divorced her out of

consideration for *her* interests was proof to Yisro that Moshe would now want to take her back and remarry her.

❧ ❧ ❧

וַיִּחַדְּ יִתְרוֹ עַל כָּל־הַטּוֹבָה אֲשֶׁר־עָשָׂה ה' לְיִשְׂרָאֵל אֲשֶׁר הִצִּילוֹ מִיַּד מִצְרָיִם: — *And Yisro rejoiced over all the good which HASHEM did to Israel, that He rescued them from the hand of Egypt* (18:9).

ashi says that "all the good" refers to the manna, the well the Torah, and, a still greater manifestation of God's goodness, "that He rescued them from the hand of Egypt." He goes on to explain that Egypt was such a tightly sealed land that no servant had ever been able to escape from it, but now Hashem had rescued millions of Jews.

Why did the escape from Egypt make a stronger impression on Yisro than any of the other good things Hashem had done for the Jews? The giving of the Torah at Mount Sinai was no less awe inspiring, and the daily provision of food directly from Heaven in a barren desert to millions of hungry people must also have impressed him. Why is the Exodus from Egypt singled out as the most important?

To answer this question, let us first look back to the four different terms that Hashem uses in his promise to redeem the Jews at the beginning of *Parashas Vaeira*: *And I will take you out* (וְהוֹצֵאתִי) *from the burdens of Egypt, and I will rescue* (וְהִצַּלְתִּי) *you from their servitude, and I will redeem* (וְגָאַלְתִּי) *you with an outstretched hand and with great judgments. And I will take* (וְלָקַחְתִּי) *you to Me for a people . . .* (6:6-7).

The last of these expressions, in which Hashem promises to make the Jews His people, seems to be in a completely different realm from the first three, which relate to freeing them from the Egyptians. We must, however, understand that the last promise is the keystone of the whole process. If the Jews had simply left the land of Egypt and gone elsewhere, there would be nothing to keep them from slipping back into the spiritual morass they had sunk into in Egypt, the bondage to the physical world, with its pleasures and demands.

Therefore they needed something to keep them on the high spiritual level they had attained when they witnessed the miracles that had been done to the Egyptians. The physical freedom they achieved by leaving Egypt had no power to keep them on that high level. To the contrary, all physical pleasures quickly reach a point of diminishing returns: The more ice cream you eat, the less you enjoy it. They needed something higher to keep them from going back to the Egyptian way of life.

Let us return now to our original question. Yisro's conviction that Hashem's greatest kindness to the Jews was taking them out of Egypt really referred to the spiritual aspect of Egypt. Only because of that could they continue to be safe from any lingering effects of the cultural and spiritual influence of Egypt. Otherwise, sooner or later they would have slipped back to the level they had started from.

This is what *Rashi* meant when he explained that no servant had ever been able to escape from Egypt; that no one had ever been able to free himself from Egyptian-style hedonism without Torah. This remains true even in our times.

The other kindnesses *Rashi* mentions, the manna that fell from Heaven and the well that followed the Jews through the desert, were only intended to sever their attachment to the physical world so they would be better prepared to receive the Torah. Hashem's greatest kindness, however, was giving the Jews the Torah and *mitzvos* so they would truly become *His* people and would never want to return to Egypt, or to the Egyptian way of thinking.

Following the four expressions of redemption mentioned above, Hashem makes a fifth promise: וְהֵבֵאתִי אֶתְכֶם אֶל־הָאָרֶץ, *And I will bring you to the land* (6:8). This also follows from the fourth promise, to make the Jews Hashem's people by giving them the Torah, which could be fulfilled in its entirety only in *the land*. During the forty years that the Jews spent in the desert on their way to *Eretz Yisrael,* Hashem took care of all of their physical needs so they were able to devote themselves exclusively to reviewing the Torah they had learned at Mount Sinai. This assured them that the Torah would stay with them and would serve as an everlasting protection against returning to Egypt, in any sense of the word.

❦ ❦ ❦

וַיַּרְא חֹתֵן מֹשֶׁה אֵת כָּל־אֲשֶׁר־הוּא עֹשֶׂה לָעָם וַיֹּאמֶר
מָה־הַדָּבָר הַזֶּה אֲשֶׁר אַתָּה עֹשֶׂה לָעָם מַדּוּעַ אַתָּה
יוֹשֵׁב לְבַדֶּךָ וְכָל־הָעָם נִצָּב עָלֶיךָ מִן־בֹּקֶר עַד־עָרֶב:
And Moshe's father-in-law saw everything
that he was doing to the people and he said,
"What is this thing which you are doing to the
people? Why do you sit by yourself and the
entire people stand over you from morning to
evening?" (18:14).

The common interpretation of this verse is that Yisro was concerned that his son-in-law was overexerting himself by trying to answer all the questions that were brought before him and would eventually wear himself out. However, from the wording of his question, we can see that he had something else in mind.

Yisro does not ask, "What are you doing to yourself?" but rather, "What are you doing to the people?" He was concerned that by making himself the sole *halachic* authority, to whom all the Jews had to come with their problems, he was preventing other gifted Jews from realizing their own potential.

It is as if Yisro was saying, "If you keep on like this, everyone will think that you are the only person capable of being a judge, since you're the only one who has learned directly from Hashem. No one else will ever bother to try since everyone knows he can never achieve your level of greatness. You're not being fair. Even though no one can be just like you, you shouldn't discourage them from trying to attain at least some part of your achievements."

In this way we can also understand another statement Yisro makes (18:18), נָבֹל תִּבֹּל גַּם־אַתָּה גַּם־הָעָם הַזֶּה, *You will surely wither away, you and also this people*. In this warning, Yisro tells Moshe that if he doesn't prepare qualified subordinates and encourage others to learn Torah on their own, then there will be no one left to transmit the Torah to future generations when Moshe is gone.

There is an important lesson in this for all of us. We should not depend solely on the great scholars and leaders of our people to pass Torah knowledge to the present generation. Each of us must learn and teach Torah to the full extent of his abilities, as if our people's future knowledge of Torah depends on him alone.

❈ ❈ ❈

בַּחֹדֶשׁ הַשְּׁלִישִׁי לְצֵאת בְּנֵי־יִשְׂרָאֵל מֵאֶרֶץ מִצְרַיִם בַּיּוֹם הַזֶּה בָּאוּ מִדְבַּר סִינָי: — *In the third month from the departure of the Children of Israel from the land of Egypt, on this day, they came to the Wilderness of Sinai* (19:1).

Rashi comments that the Jews arrived at the Wilderness of Sinai on Rosh Chodesh Sivan, six days before they were to receive the Torah there. Astronomically, the month of Sivan is represented by תְּאוֹמִים, *Twins*.

There is an interesting symbolism in the fact that the Torah was given under the sign of the Twins. The Torah is called *Toras Chessed,* the Torah of Kindness (cf. *Mishlei* 31:26), as the sage Rabbi Simlai taught, "the Torah begins with *chessed* and ends with *chessed"* (*Sotah* 14a). In order to keep the Torah properly, the Torah of Kindness, a Jew must relate to his fellow Jews in the same way that one twin relates to another. The Torah wants us to strive for twin-like sensitivity to each other's joys and sorrows, pleasures and frustrations.

This was the level that the Jews attained at Mount Sinai, under the sign of the Twins. In the next verse, the Torah says, וַיִּחַן־שָׁם יִשְׂרָאֵל נֶגֶד הָהָר, *Israel encamped there, opposite the mountain.* From the fact that the word "encamped" is in the singular form, *Rashi* concludes that the Jews at that time were as one man with one heart.

This is a goal to which we should aspire in all of our dealings with our fellow Jews. Even though we are separate individuals, with differing needs and personalities, we are still closely tied to all our fellow Jews with bonds of love and responsibility for one another. As Rabbi Akiva taught: וְאָהַבְתָּ לְרֵעֲךָ כָּמוֹךָ, *Love your fellow as yourself* (*Vayikra* 19:18), is a cardinal rule of the Torah (see *Rashi*).

❈ ❈ ❈

וְגַם־בְּךָ יַאֲמִינוּ לְעוֹלָם — *And in you also they will believe forever* (19:9).

Hashem told Moshe that He would appear in a cloud and speak to him in the presence of the people, so that they would hear and obey the Torah, and would believe in Moshe forever. We can interpret the phrase, *in you also*, as a promise that they would believe in the precepts Moshe derives from his own interpretation of the Torah and his own insights into it, based on the Torah he learned from Hashem, just as they would believe in the Torah which he passed on to the Jews directly from Hashem. That this promise was given *forever* implies that no one would ever question any of the prophets who assumed Moshe's role in later generations. Presumably this applies, even after the end of prophecy, to those leaders who presided over the Sanhedrin, as well as to the leaders of all the later generations, until the present. As the Sages taught, Gideon, Samson and Yiftach in their generations were like Moshe in his generation (*Rosh Hashanah* 25b).

❧ ❧ ❧

פרשת משפטים
Parashas Mishpatim

וְאֵלֶּה הַמִּשְׁפָּטִים אֲשֶׁר תָּשִׂים לִפְנֵיהֶם: — *And these are the statutes which you shall place before them* (21:1).

The word *these* in our verse suggests that only these and no other statutes are to be placed before the Jews. It follows logically that the Torah means that certain other statutes were not to be placed before the Jews. We must ask ourselves which statutes our verse excludes from our consideration.

As each person grows up, he acquires from his parents or his friends a sense of what is right and wrong, what is just and unjust. For example, almost everyone today knows that it is wrong to kill, or to make someone a slave. Yet in this week's portion, the Torah gives legitimacy, in certain circumstances, to both killing and servitude. Thus the Torah's concept of justice and people's "innate" sense of right and wrong seem to be in conflict.

This is why the Torah specifies that *these* statutes and no others represent true justice; we are not allowed to make up concepts of right and wrong for ourselves. However reasonable our own ideas may seem to us, only the Torah's sense of right and wrong is correct.

We sometimes hear people saying, or perhaps even catch ourselves saying, something along the following lines: "I think it's cruel to kill someone, even if he's a convicted murderer. But what can I do? The Torah disagrees with me and I know that the Torah is always right."

While it is good that this person recognizes that the Torah is right, this is still not the best way to think. The goal of a Torah Jew should be to align his thinking with that of the Torah and not to allow any thoughts inconsistent with the Torah to enter his mind. The best way to do this is to review the Torah that one has learned over and over again until he comes to understand the logic behind it on its own terms.

We must realize that we have a tendency to accept basic principles of justice not necessarily because they are right, but because we have grown up with them. For example, Americans cannot conceive of justice without a jury system, while most European legal systems rely on panels of judges. The justice of the Torah, because it embodies Hashem's wisdom, is inherently just, compassionate and correct—it is for us to condition our thought processes to assimilate and understand it.

This approach can often lead to very desirable consequences. For example, sometimes one person injures another under circumstances that do not allow the injured party to collect damages in court. However, if the party at fault sincerely wants to act in accordance with Torah values, he will pay for the damages anyway, because he knows that the Torah wants him to do what is just, even when the strict letter of the law does not require him to do so. Thus, supressing one's own values in favor of Torah values causes more justice to be done in the world.

At the same time, we should not think that there is no place in Torah for the individual's ability to reason. The verse under consideration actually says, "וְאֵלֶּה, and these . . ." According to the principles of Torah exegesis, the word *and* indicates that in addition to the statutes mentioned in this portion, there are still other statutes included in the discussion.

This refers to the statutes which we deduce ourselves. Once we have understood the basic laws and concepts of the Torah, then we are allowed and even encouraged to use our reason to derive the laws which apply in specific instances.

❈ ❈ ❈

וְשַׂמְתִּי לְךָ מָקוֹם אֲשֶׁר יָנוּס שָׁמָּה: — *And I shall make for you a place to which he may flee* (21:13).

I n this verse, Hashem says He will designate cities of refuge, to which someone who kills unintentionally may flee and find protection from the vengeance of his victim's relatives. It is curious that Hashem says He will make these cities *for you,* implying that they are for everyone, when they would seem to be of benefit only to those who happen to commit accidental murder.

We may say, however, that there is a deep message to all of society in these words. If someone kills "unintentionally," it is only because the whole society has been lax in demonstrating respect for human life. Therefore, we may say that these cities are for the benefit of everyone, since the atmosphere that fostered carelessness is a social problem, common to everyone. Thus, because the murder was a product of our behavior, the safety of the murderer will protect us from harm also.

❦ ❦ ❦

אִם־בַּמַּחְתֶּרֶת יִמָּצֵא הַגַּנָּב . . . אִם־אֵין לוֹ וְנִמְכַּר בִּגְנֵבָתוֹ: — *If a thief is caught in a tunnel [breaking into a house] . . . if he does not have [money to pay], he shall be sold for his theft* (22:1-2).

S omeone who has been caught stealing and cannot pay for what he has stolen is sold as a slave. In ancient times, people understood the seriousness of the crime of stealing. They understood that a thief deserves to be sold into slavery, as we see from the story of Benjamin's being caught with Joseph's goblet in his possession (*Bereishis* ch. 44). In Judah's eloquent plea to Joseph to accept him as a slave in Benjamin's place, Judah never even suggested that servitude was an unjust punishment for stealing, even though he could easily have paid for the goblet.

By decreeing that a thief deserves to be sold into slavery, even though such a thing rarely happened in practice since the thief can usually afford to buy his freedom, the Torah means to impress on us how serious an offense theft is. If the penalty were any less, a thief might think that if he sincerely intends to pay back what he has stolen when he has more money, then what he is doing is not really wrong. But the Torah makes it clear to him that this is not so, that really any thief deserves to be a slave and nothing better.

Lest we think that this equation, slavery for stealing, is unjustified, let us look into the matter a bit further. If someone finds a burglar in the process of breaking into his home to steal, the Torah gives the owner the right to kill the burglar without being punished for it. This is because it is assumed that the thief expects the home-owner to protect his property and would not break into a house unless he were willing to kill to steal.

Thus, to such a person, who is willing to risk his life for money, the Torah gives a clear message: "If you think that money is so important that you're willing to give up your life for it, we'll show you how wrong you are by taking away from you something even more important — your freedom. Once you become a slave, then you'll know how important your freedom was."

However, the Torah is merciful even in its punishments. Because of the humane conditions of employment the Torah places upon the master of a Jewish slave, only a wealthy person would buy a slave. Thus, the offender is likely to live a better life in servitude than he did as a free man. Furthermore, someone who buys a slave must be willing to take on the responsibility of rehabilitating this person who can't manage on his own and giving him a new apprenticeship in the art of living in the world, because otherwise the slave is not worth his cost. Still, a slave knows better than anyone else what a precious thing freedom is, and undoubtedly will learn to take his life more seriously in the future.

❦ ❦ ❦

אִם־כֶּסֶף תַּלְוֶה אֶת־עַמִּי אֶת־הֶעָנִי עִמָּךְ לֹא־תִהְיֶה לוֹ כְּנֹשֶׁה לֹא־תְשִׂימוּן עָלָיו נֶשֶׁךְ: — *When you lend among My people to a poor person who is with you, you shall not be to him as a usurer, you shall not place upon him interest* (22:24).

In *Parashas Re'eh* (*Devarim* 15:7-10), the Torah goes to some length to stress the *obligation* to lend money to those in need. For this reason, *Rashi* comments that the word אִם in our verse means *when*, rather than its more common meaning, *if*. If so, why does the Torah in this case use a word which nearly always means *if*?

The phrase *if you lend money* suggests a situation in which a wealthy person, on his own, takes the initiative to approach someone whom he knows to be in need and offers him a loan. Such a lender is surely doing it for the sake of the *mitzvah* involved, and would never think of burdening his borrower with interest, since his motive is sincerely to help someone in a difficult situation.

Thus, by saying *if* when it really means *when* in our verse, the Torah is telling us that we should always take this approach to lending money. Even if we are doing it only because the Torah requires it (for example, when we lend to someone whom we are not friendly with and may even dislike), we should act as if our motives are purely altruistic. Therefore, we should never think of taking interest or exerting pressure on the borrower. The desire to perform this *mitzvah* (or any other *mitzvah,* for that matter) should be so ingrained in us that we should do it in exactly the same way we would do any other matter of personal choice—*if you lend*—rather than because it is the decree of the King.

❧ ❧ ❧

לֹא־תְבַשֵּׁל גְּדִי בַּחֲלֵב אִמּוֹ: — *You shall not cook a kid in the milk of its mother* (23:19).

Why does the Torah phrase the prohibition against cooking milk and meat together in terms of a kid being cooked in its mother's milk, instead of simply stating, *You shall not cook milk and meat together?*

We may say that the Torah wants to teach us an important lesson about parenthood. It is clearly against the nature of a mother to cook her own child, and difficult even to imagine that such a thing would ever happen. Yet, a mother who, trying to be "good" to her child, fails to rebuke him and teach him when he has done wrong, is surely "cooking" her child's whole personality, as King Solomon said (*Mishlei* 13:24), *One who withholds his staff hates his son.*

This, perhaps, is the allegorical meaning of the verse (*Eichah* 4:10), *The hands of merciful mothers cooked their children.* By being too "merciful," parents can do their children a great injustice, as if they were actually "cooking" them. By emphasizing the obvious point that a mother should not "cook" her child, the Torah shows that it is not always obvious that she is doing so. She must therefore exercise great caution and care to raise her children properly.

※　※　※

פרשת תרומה
Parashas Terumah

דַּבֵּר אֶל־בְּנֵי יִשְׂרָאֵל וְיִקְחוּ־לִי תְּרוּמָה — *Speak to the Children of Israel that they should take for Me terumah* (25:2).

W hy does Hashem say that they should *take terumah?* Doesn't the word *give* seem better suited to the context of this verse?

In *Parashas Tzav* (*Vayikra* 8:2), Hashem tells Moshe to *take* Aaron and his sons to be *Kohanim. Rashi* comments that *take Aaron* means to take him with words, to draw him into agreement of accepting the position of *Kohen.* Similarly, in *Parashas Beha'alosecha* (*Bamidbar* 8:6), Hashem tells Moshe to *take* the Levites and purify them for the special service they are to do in the *Mishkan* (Tabernacle). There also *Rashi* says that *take* means to take them with words: "How fortunate are you to have the privilege of being Hashem's servants!"

We may therefore assume that here also, when Moshe was instructed to tell the Jews to *take terumah,* the word *take* means to persuade them to give their offerings for Hashem's sake (as *Rashi* comments, *to Me* means *for My sake*): "How fortunate are you to be Hashem's people, whom He has commanded to give of your possessions to make a dwelling place for His Presence in the world. Know, however, that Hashem has commanded you to give your offerings *for His sake,* for His dwelling, and not because *you* want the honor of having such a structure in your midst." Thus, Moshe was to convince them to give with the most noble motive, that they would understand that it is an honor to serve Hashem. Thus before performing a *mitzvah,* we recite the blessing אֲשֶׁר קִדְּשָׁנוּ בְּמִצְוֹתָיו, *Who has made us holy with His mitzvos;* He made us holy by giving us His *mitzvos,* and that is our honor.

It was important for Moshe to make this fact clear to them. If the Torah had written וְיִתְּנוּ לִי, *they shall give Me,* instead of *take for Me,* then the emphasis would have been on the *gift* rather than on the intention of the giver. Each individual would have had the choice of giving his offering for Hashem's sake or for his own pleasure, as we said above. Even if he had given generously, out of the free volition of his heart, his intention might still have been selfish. However, since they were told in advance that they must give only for Hashem's sake, then they would certainly be careful to give only in the fashion which Hashem desired, purely for the sake of observing His command.

❀ ❀ ❀

וְעָשׂוּ אֲרוֹן עֲצֵי שִׁטִּים . . . וְצִפִּיתָ אֹתוֹ זָהָב טָהוֹר מִבַּיִת וּמִחוּץ — And they shall make an Ark of shitim wood . . . And you shall cover it with pure gold from within and without (25:10-11).

The main body of the *Aron* (Ark) was made of wood and, while it appeared golden to the beholder, everyone knew that the gold was no more than a veneer. At first glance, it would seem more appropriate for the Tablets of the Covenant to be housed in a solid gold *Aron* rather than in one which was primarily wood. Surely gold would more clearly have reflected the power and grandeur of the Creator and His Torah, which represented His special relationship with His people.

We should not think that Hashem commanded the Ark to be made of wood because of the practical obstacles involved in making it of gold. Even made of wood as it was, with its golden castings and the golden cover and cherubim, it has been calculated that the Ark weighed on the order of eight tons, far too heavy for four Levites to carry without Divine assistance. We can assume that they would have had similar help in bearing a still heavier *Aron* of solid gold.

Nor can we say that the gold was not available. The Sages tell us that the jewels needed for the *Kohen Gadol's* breastplate were lacking in the desert until Hashem caused them to rain down from Heaven. So also it would have been within His power to provide enough gold for a solid gold Ark.

Hashem could certainly have commanded the construction of a solid gold Ark and there must be some reason why He did not do so. What is the important lesson that a wooden Ark teaches us that we would not learn from a golden one?

Wood is a living substance: it grows and reproduces itself. Gold, on the other hand, while it has much more inherent beauty than wood, is inert and lifeless. Which one makes a more appropriate container to house the Torah?

The Torah was given not to angels, who are not subject to the same imperfections and desires as human beings, but rather to living flesh and blood. The Torah is not meant to be a display piece and sit lifelessly on a shelf; it is meant to be used. A set of the Talmud which still looks new and shiny after twenty years in someone's home has no beauty at all. The beautiful set, which does true honor to the Torah, is the one that looks old and used, that has worn itself out to make human beings into living repositories of the Torah.

Thus a wooden Ark teaches us that the Torah, which is the Tree of Life, which is life itself, was given not to cold, inert gold, however stunning it is. The Torah was given to living, growing human beings to give them true eternal life.

Why then, in the terms of our image, was the *Aron* covered with gold *from within and without*? The answer is that while a Torah scholar is of course only flesh and blood, subject to the same weaknesses and desires as everyone else, he must nevertheless try to purify himself as much as possible to look like a gold-covered person in the eyes of the world. This is why the gold covering had to be *from within*, as well as on the outside, to teach us that scholars of the Torah should become as much like angels as they possibly can. Even the innermost parts of his private life that no one can see have to be pure, like the Torah.

❀ ❀ ❀

וְנִשָּׂא־בָם אֶת־הַשֻּׁלְחָן: — The Table shall be carried by them (25:28).

Hashem instructed Moshe that long wooden staves should be inserted into rings at the sides of the *Shulchan* (Table), and used to carry it. The wording of this verse in the passive voice, *shall be carried,* instead of the active "to carry," suggests that the staves were intended primarily for some other use, but could also be used to carry the *Shulchan.* In *Parashas Vayakhel* (37:15) however, the Torah uses the active voice, לָשֵׂאת אֶת־הַשֻּׁלְחָן, *to carry the Shulchan,* suggesting that the main purpose of the staves was for carrying the *Shulchan,* and not for anything else. Why, then, does our verse suggest that they were meant for some other purpose?

If the Torah had said only לָשֵׂאת, *to carry,* it would have meant that the staves had no function other than the utilitarian one of transportation. If so, we might have thought that the staves must be removed from their rings once the Table had been set down in its place in the *Mishkan.* The expression וְנִשָּׂא־בָם, *it shall be carried by them,* however, indicates that the staves need not be removed but may remain constantly available to carry the *Shulchan* at any time.

We may interpret this allegorically to teach an important lesson. *Rashi* comments (v. 24) that the *Shulchan* represented wealth and greatness, as is implied by the common expression, "a king's table." The staves could be left in the *Shulchan* to symbolize that the wealth which the *Shulchan* represented was not meant only for the *Mishkan.* Just as the *Shulchan,* like all the furnishings of the *Mishkan,* brought atonement and elevation to Israel, so too, we must "carry" the concepts they represent into our homes. The Sages teach (*Berachos* 55a) that the table in our homes can bring atonement—if we use it to help the poor and those in need of hospitality.

❧ ❧ ❧

וְנָתַתָּ עַל־הַשֻּׁלְחָן לֶחֶם פָּנִים לְפָנַי תָּמִיד: — *And you shall place the show bread in front of Me continually* (25:30).

The phrase, **לֶחֶם פָּנִים**, which is normally translated as *show bread*, literally means "the bread of faces," and our Sages said that its two ends faced upward, so that they were like two faces looking at each other. What moral lesson can we draw from this unusual shape?

The Sages meant to teach us that, even when we eat, we should not think primarily of satisfying our own needs, but rather of serving Hashem. The two faces looking at each other teach that as we eat we should have the needs of others continually in mind.

This means that if we see someone who doesn't have what to eat, we must share our food with him, even though we may be depriving ourselves. Furthermore, we should do this for the sake of pleasing Hashem and not just because we feel it is the right thing to do. To give away all of one's food because he has no appetite is a lower level of righteousness than to give away a small amount that one wants to eat because Hashem wants him to be generous to others.

The real measure of someone's commitment to Torah is not how he learns but rather how he eats. Someone who can master his human, physical desires for the sake of Heaven is the highest kind of *tzaddik*.

One test of whether one's eating is really for the sake of Heaven is whether he is capable of putting aside a particularly tasty food for Shabbos. After all, Shabbos is the one day when there is a special *mitzvah* to enjoy the pleasures of the world.

The Talmud (*Beitzah* 16a) relates that when Shammai the Elder found a choice piece of meat, he would save it for the coming Shabbos. If he found a better piece later in the week, he would eat the first one and save the better one for Shabbos.

Hillel the Elder had a different approach. If he found a choice piece of meat at the beginning of the week he would eat it right away, in order to demonstrate his *confidence* that Hashem would send him another worthy piece of meat in time for Shabbos.

We see from these stories that both Shammai and Hillel sought ways to serve Hashem in their eating habits, each in his own way. So also, each of us should look continuously for ways to make our eating part of our service of Hashem.

❀ ❀ ❀

וְשַׂמְתָּ אֶת־הַשֻּׁלְחָן מִחוּץ לַפָּרֹכֶת וְאֶת־הַמְּנֹרָה נֹכַח הַשֻּׁלְחָן עַל צֶלַע הַמִּשְׁכָּן תֵּימָנָה וְהַשֻּׁלְחָן תִּתֵּן עַל־צֶלַע צָפוֹן: — *And you shall place the Table outside the Paroches; and the Menorah opposing the Table, on the south side of the Tabernacle, and put the Table on the north side* (26:35).

From the perspective of the Holy of Holies, at the western end of the *Mishkan* where Hashem's Presence "rested," the south side of the *Mishkan* (Tabernacle) was on the *right* side, and the north was on the *left* side.

King Solomon said (*Mishlei* 3:16), *Length of days on her right hand, and on her left hand wealth and honor. Length of days* refers to the World to Come, which is represented by the Menorah on the south or right side, and *wealth and honor* are represented by the *Shulchan* (Table) on the north or left side. This is fitting, since we find that the Torah always assigns greater importance to the right.

To someone entering the *Mishkan* at the eastern end, however, this perspective is reversed, as *Rashi* says (*Bereishis* 48:13), someone who approaches his friend has his right side facing the friend's left side. Thus, to the one entering the *Mishkan*, Torah (symbolized by the Menorah) would be on the left, while prosperity (represented by the *Shulchan*) would be on the right.

There is a lesson for us in this. A human being in this world, bound up by his flesh and blood as he is, cannot understand clearly that the Menorah (length of days in the World to Come obtained by adherence to the Torah) is more important than the *Shulchan* (wealth and honor in this world). Even if he knows intellectually that his perspective is wrong, his body prevents him from genuinely feeling it, and he must remind himself constantly that his perspective is the result of his material environment. The true scale of values, however, is exactly the reverse of the illusionary values of this world.

❀ ❀ ❀

פרשת תצוה
Parashas Tetzaveh

וְאַתָּה תְּצַוֶּה אֶת־בְּנֵי יִשְׂרָאֵל וְיִקְחוּ אֵלֶיךָ שֶׁמֶן זַיִת זָךְ כָּתִית לַמָּאוֹר לְהַעֲלֹת נֵר תָּמִיד: — *And you will command the Children of Israel and they shall take for you pure olive oil, beaten for light, to fuel the eternal light* (27:20).

The opening phrase of this week's portion, וְאַתָּה תְּצַוֶּה אֶת־בְּנֵי יִשְׂרָאֵל, is normally understood to be a command: Hashem instructs Moshe to command the Jews to make oil for the Menorah. Grammatically, however, the word תְּצַוֶּה is not an imperative form expressing a command, but rather a future declarative making a statement about a future event: Hashem informs Moshe that at some later time he will issue such a command, but for the present he is not required to do anything. And, indeed, at the end of *Parashas Emor* (*Vayikra* 24:1), Hashem instructs Moshe, this time using the imperative form צַו, *command,* to order the Children of Israel to prepare olive oil for the Menorah.

This is a singular occurrence: Nowhere else in the Torah does Hashem give a similar forewarning of His intention to give a later command. What was it about the *pure olive oil, beaten for light,* that merited this special treatment?

The Torah uses pure olive oil to symbolize a whole approach to Torah study. In order to be acceptable for the eternal light, olive oil had to be pure from the moment it emerged from the press. Oil that had once contained impurities, however thoroughly refined and purified it later became, could not be used.

Similarly, Torah must be learned in a way that minimizes the possibility of impurities from the very beginning, not in a way that might allow impurities which would later require cleansing. What does this mean?

The study of Torah must be approached with a conviction that the Torah is pure truth, the words of the living God. This does not mean that questions are forbidden; throughout the generations scholars have learned Torah by asking questions and searching for answers to them. However, the questions of genuine Torah scholars are never directed at the basic validity of the Torah. Their purpose is only to clarify what the Torah says about a particular matter.

Another feature of the true outlook on Torah relates to how one approaches other fields of study, such as science, mathematics, and the like. The Torah does not prohibit or even discourage these studies, provided they are put in proper perspective. For example, a Torah Jew who studies medicine in order to be able to perform the great *mitzvah* of healing the sick fulfills Hashem's will in his studies. He is not likely to be influenced by those ideas and values he may encounter in his studies that are opposed to the Torah. On the contrary, in everything he learns he will find testimony to Hashem's infinite power and wisdom.

If, however, someone studies medicine as part of general culture, in terms that are almost certain to be colored by the values of the secular culture from which they emerged, his learning is not pure. Such a person is likely to absorb many ideas and values antithetical to the Torah and will someday be faced with the arduous task of filtering out impurities after they have been absorbed in the "lamp" of his accumulated wisdom.

Now we can understand why the *mitzvah* of preparing the pure olive oil merited a special announcement that it would be given in the future. Hashem was saying, "You, Moshe, who are committed to pure Torah with every fiber of your being, *you* will command the Jewish people concerning this *mitzvah* which is so vital to the very essence of Torah. *You* are the most qualified to do so." And because the commandment would come from Moshe, who practiced this concept in his personal life, the people would accept it from him.

❧ ❧ ❧

בְּאֹהֶל מוֹעֵד מִחוּץ לַפָּרֹכֶת אֲשֶׁר עַל־הָעֵדֻת יַעֲרֹךְ אֹתוֹ אַהֲרֹן וּבָנָיו מֵעֶרֶב עַד־בֹּקֶר לִפְנֵי ה' — *In the Tent of Meeting outside of the Paroches which is on the testimony shall Aaron and his sons establish it, from evening until morning, in front of Hashem* (27:21).

The word עֵדֻת, *testimony,* normally refers to the Torah, represented by the stone Tablets on which Hashem had inscribed the Ten Commandments and which were kept in the Ark in the Holy of Holies. In our verse, however, the Sages (*Shabbos* 22b) understood that it referred to the Menorah, which gives testimony that the *Shechinah* (Divine Presence) dwells among the Jewish people. How was this testimony conveyed?

There was a particular miracle connected with the Menorah in the *Mishkan* (Tabernacle). Every day before sunset, the *Kohen* would light the seven lamps of the Menorah that were filled with just enough oil to last through the night. Six of them burned until the following morning and then went out for lack of fuel. One of the lamps, however, continued burning until just before sunset the following afternoon, when the time came to re-kindle the others, even though it had no more oil than the rest of them. This was the נֵר תָּמִיד — the Eternal Light. It was called the נֵר מַעֲרָבִי, *the Western Lamp,* because its flame leaned toward the Holy of Holies in the west, while all the others leaned toward it.

The miracle of the Western Lamp was testimony that the *Shechinah* was present in the Tabernacle. It burned in this way continuously from the inauguration of the Tabernacle in the Wilderness until the destruction of the First Temple, and again in the Second Temple until the time of Simon the Righteous (cf. *Avos* 1:2). After his death, the miracle would sometimes be suspended and the flame would go out, to indicate Divine displeasure with the Jews.

The Menorah's light was never needed for illumination — surely not by Hashem, and not even by a *Kohen.* By the time the first *Kohen* entered in the morning to light the incense, it was already daylight and, even then, the light had already gone out. Thus, its sole purpose was to testify to Hashem's Presence.

It is very hard to see the hand of Hashem at work in the physical world. Even though we know rationally that Hashem is alone "the Creator and Guider of all creatures," there are many temptations that distract us from applying this knowledge to specific situations. For example, when we succeed at something, as much as we pay lip service and thank Hashem, we still want to take some of the credit for ourselves, to claim that our own talents and efforts brought about our success.

Such is the case with material endeavors. In the realm of Torah achievements, however, it is more difficult. Any sensible person has to recognize that his own abilities are inadequate to accomplish much and that all of his successes come only from Hashem. The Sages teach (*Bava Basra* 12a) that the wise are gifted with some measure of prophecy. Without an infusion of Divine wisdom, how could anyone ever give a correct answer to a complicated question on the spot, without taking time to analyze all of its facets? Yet we find that great rabbis and scholars do this all the time.

These very rabbis are the first to admit that their success comes solely through סִיַעְתָּא דִּשְׁמַיָּא, *help from above*. Obviously Hashem does not impart His wisdom to those who are unworthy of it, to those who claim credit for themselves. This is why we would never believe that a gentile has attained genuine Torah wisdom, even though he may be capable of great technical or philosophical knowledge.

This quality of Torah learning is symbolized in the light of the Menorah, which burned beyond the power of the oil that fueled it. Just as it was impossible to claim that the Western Lamp burned its oil in the normal way, without Divine assistance, so also it is impossible to deny that a Torah scholar has Divine assistance in his accomplishments.

❀ ❀ ❀

וְאֵלֶּה הַבְּגָדִים אֲשֶׁר יַעֲשׂוּ חֹשֶׁן וְאֵפוֹד וּמְעִיל וּכְתֹנֶת תַּשְׁבֵּץ מִצְנֶפֶת וְאַבְנֵט — *And these are the garments which they shall make: Choshen, Ephod, Robe, checkered Tunic, Turban and Sash* (28:4).

In this verse, the Torah lists six garments that the artisans were to make for the *Kohen Gadol*. In the following verses, however, instructions are given for the fabrication of a total of *eight* garments, including two not mentioned here: the *Tzitz* (Headplate) and the *michnasayim* (breeches). Why were these garments left out of the list in our verse?

Even though these two garments were not included in the list, it is obvious that they are required. It would be unthinkable for the *Kohen Gadol* to go without breeches, since this would leave his nakedness exposed. Indeed, he had to put this garment on before any of the others, to show that he recognized he was an imperfect human being, with nakedness to cover. Only then could he put on the other garments to elevate himself to serve Hashem. (According to *Ramban*, even though Moshe was commanded to dress Aaron and his sons in their priestly garments, this did not apply to the breeches. Those they had to don themselves, for the sake of modesty.)

The *Tzitz*, on which was inscribed קוֹדֶשׁ לַה', *Holy to Hashem*, was the last item the *Kohen Gadol* put on. This was the culmination of his attire, and showed that he had brought himself up to the highest level which a human being can attain.

Thus, our verse leaves out the first and last garments which the *Kohen Gadol* donned, because they were in a different category from the others. The breeches formed a foundation which prepared him for the other garments, and the Headplate was the apex of his attire, giving meaning to everything else. Although the Torah later explains how they should be, it was not necessary to say that the *Kohen Gadol* should have such garments. Every person must begin with elementary decency and aim for a spiritual peak, and then he will surely be crowned.

※ ※ ※

וְנֹעַדְתִּי שָׁמָּה לִבְנֵי יִשְׂרָאֵל וְנִקְדַּשׁ בִּכְבֹדִי: — *And I shall meet there with the Children of Israel and I shall be made Holy in My Glory* (29:43).

The *Mishkan* (Tabernacle) had *kedushah* (holiness) only because of the *Shechinah* (Divine Presence) which dwelt there. Beautiful and elegant as this structure was by itself, without the *Shechinah* it had no feeling of holiness.

When one builds a beautiful house, he can appreciate its beauty, but the four walls of a building cannot impart an atmosphere of holiness in and of themselves. When the *Shechinah* rests there, however, anyone who enters it feels the awe and reverence which are due to Hashem. This is the implication of our verse: Even the *Mishkan* becomes holy *only* when it contains the glory of Hashem. This tells us that we must strive to inject an awareness of Hashem's glory into all our activities, whatever and wherever they are.

❧ ❧ ❧

וְהִקְטִיר עָלָיו אַהֲרֹן קְטֹרֶת סַמִּים בַּבֹּקֶר בַּבֹּקֶר בְּהֵיטִיבוֹ אֶת־הַנֵּרֹת יַקְטִירֶנָּה: — *Aaron shall burn upon it [the Incense-Altar] the incense-spices every morning; when he cleans the lamps he is to burn it* (30:7).

The Torah commanded Aaron to burn the incense-spices at the same time that he cleaned the lamps of the Menorah. What is the connection between these two seemingly unrelated aspects of the Temple Service, that they were required to be performed together?

The Sages teach that the incense was given to atone for the sin of *lashon hara,* slander (*Arachin* 16a). And, as we said at the beginning of our *parashah,* the Menorah is a symbol for the learning of Torah. The Torah requires that these two activities be done together in order to teach us that Torah is an infallible remedy for *lashon hara* (see *Arachin* 15b): When one sanctifies his organs of speech by reciting the words of Hashem's Torah, he can hardly contaminate those same organs by using them for *lashon hara*. Thus, the Sages teach (*Sanhedrin* 106b) that when Doeg slandered David, a Heavenly voice exclaimed, "What right have you to indulge in the study of My Torah!"

❀   ❀   ❀

פרשת כי תשא
Parashas Ki Sisa

כִּי תִשָּׂא אֶת־רֹאשׁ בְּנֵי־יִשְׂרָאֵל לִפְקֻדֵיהֶם וְנָתְנוּ אִישׁ כֹּפֶר נַפְשׁוֹ לַה' בִּפְקֹד אֹתָם — *When you will raise up [count] the heads of the Children of Israel, each man shall give a redemption for his soul to HASHEM in their counting* (30:12).

The phrase *When you will raise up the heads of the Children of Israel* arouses a lovely image in our minds. The Jews were lifted up to a very high level of holiness by the census that was taken. (See also our comments in *Parashas Bamidbar*.) Indeed, their level was so high that the census took the form of a tax of half a shekel per person, to be used in the construction of the *Mishkan* (Tabernacle) and, in later years, for the purchase of communal offerings in the *Beis HaMikdash*. This was an atonement for any impure motives that may have crept into their actions.

This has implications for all of us in our daily affairs. When someone undertakes a particular project, he should declare from the very beginning that his purpose is purely for the sake of Heaven and pray for help on that basis: "I'm doing this only for You, Hashem, therefore please grant me success." One should be wary of undertaking projects simply because he feels enthusiasm about them, because it is easy to deceive oneself about whether a project is really necessary or worthwhile. Also, one has to realize that his own abilities are never adequate, and that he will accomplish his goals only with help from Above. This process of involving Hashem and directing all of one's activities to His purposes is what the Torah refers to as *redemption for his soul*.

This is what our Sages meant in the Mishnah (*Avos* 4:14): *Every assembly that is dedicated to the sake of Heaven will have an enduring effect, but one that is not for the sake of Heaven will not have an enduring effect.* If the leaders of the assembly have pure intentions, Hashem will grant them success at what they set out to accomplish. But if they allow personal goals, such as building reputations or gaining personal power, to color their actions, then they will not benefit from Divine help.

We must realize, however, that it is nearly impossible for flesh and blood to achieve such high standards of behavior. Even the Vilna Gaon said that when he stood to benefit personally from a particular undertaking, he could never be entirely sure that his motives were purely for the sake of Heaven. How much more so must we, in our generation, confess that, however lofty we may set our sights, personal goals often influence our actions. Monetary gain is not the only kind of benefit we have to worry about: The desire for power and a good name often distorts people's thinking.

For this reason the Torah levies a tax of half a shekel on each individual, in order to redeem that part of his activities which is not purely motivated. From this we learn that if we want to do something for the sake of Heaven, we must always suspect that we may be influenced by self-interest, in ways which may be hidden even from ourselves. For example, the Sages (*Eruvin* 13b) taught that when someone runs away from greatness, greatness runs after him. Therefore someone who runs away from honor must distrust himself: Maybe deep down inside, he really wants the honor to catch up with him. One can never judge himself objectively.

To avoid such difficulties, one should always search out ways to limit the personal benefit that he derives from his activities and to give more than he is required to, as a "redemption" for those rewards that he cannot avoid. This may require subtle judgments, and in certain situations it is worthwhile to undertake a project for the sake of Heaven even though one stands to gain from it personally. However, if one makes a sincere effort to avoid personal gain, he may feel assured of special help from Heaven to purify his motives and to bring his undertakings to successful fruition.

❀ ❀ ❀

הֶעָשִׁיר לֹא־יַרְבֶּה וְהַדַּל לֹא יַמְעִיט מִמַּחֲצִית הַשָּׁקֶל לָתֵת אֶת־תְּרוּמַת ה' לְכַפֵּר עַל־נַפְשֹׁתֵיכֶם: — *The wealthy man shall not increase and the poor man shall not decrease from half a shekel to give Hashem's offering, to redeem your souls* (30:15).

ashem commanded that every Jew contribute the exact same amount for the foundations of the *Mishkan* (Tabernacle), so that no one would be able to say that his contribution was more important than someone else's. The person who is blessed, either in money or in Torah scholarship, cannot claim that he serves Hashem more than an ordinary person who conducts himself scrupulously according to the *Shulchan Aruch,* any more than the worker who assembles the frame of an automobile can claim that he does more than the worker who makes the little screws that hold the body together. Just because people serve in different capacities does not mean that any one gives more than the others.

What counts in Hashem's eyes, however, is not how much *total* time one devotes to His service, but rather how much each individual gives from the time he has *available.* Hashem also looks at how sincerely one performs that service which he is able to.

Thus Moshe, the greatest scholar and leader the Jewish people has ever known, did not hold himself to be any more important than even the lowliest of his followers. The only distinction he saw was that he had a greater load to carry.

This is why Moshe says, at the beginning of *Parashas Nitzavim* , אַתֶּם נִצָּבִים הַיּוֹם כֻּלְּכֶם לִפְנֵי ה', *You are standing this day, all of you, before Hashem* (*Deuteronomy* 29:9). In his eyes, all those who served Hashem to their utmost ability stood together as equals, from the greatest leaders down to the smallest children. Someone who is less gifted cannot say that Hashem expected less from him, because Hashem expects everyone to give as much of the twenty-four hours in a day, in quantity and quality, as he has strength for. Different people may vary in the amount that they are capable of accomplishing in those twenty-four hours, but they are ultimately judged according to the quality and sincerity of their efforts.

❈ ❈ ❈

וְאַתָּה קַח־לְךָ בְּשָׂמִים רֹאשׁ מָר־דְּרוֹר . . . — *And you, take for yourself select spices, mar-dror . . .* (30:23).

Why does the Torah emphasize the word *you* in describing the anointing oil — *you* take for *your*self?

The anointing oil had the power to elevate people and objects, such as the *Kohanim* or the vessels of the *Mishkan* (Tabernacle), to a state of *kedushah* (holiness). It would seem more appropriate that these forms of instilling *kedushah* should come directly from Heaven, rather than through human agency. Why did Hashem want this *kedushah* to come through us by means of oil made and administered by people, rather than directly from Him?

We may say that *kedushah* Hashem imposes on us does not make as much of an impression as the *kedushah* we create through our own efforts. For example, if someone is told that a particular *tzaddik* is holy, it does not make as powerful an impression on him as if he meets the *tzaddik* himself and senses personally how he struggled to achieve his high level of *kedushah* through unremitting personal effort. Similarly, even though a maidservant who witnessed the Splitting of the Sea of Reeds saw Hashem's hand at work in a clearer fashion than the Prophet Ezekiel ever did, she did not attain as high a level of *kedushah* as he did. The reason is that her *kedushah* was a gift from Heaven; since she had not worked for it, it did not leave a lasting impression. On the other hand, Ezekiel's *kedushah* was the fruit of long years of diligent application to Torah and the service of Hashem, and therefore it became a genuine part of him and stayed with him.

With this in mind, we can better understand the allusion to the Purim story that the Sages saw in this verse (*Chullin* 139b). Based on *Onkelos'* translation of the name of the spice מָר־דְּרוֹר, *mar-dror*, which he renders מֵירָא דַכְיָא, *meira dachya*, they find in this spice an allusion to Mordechai, whose name is similar to this translation. What is the significance of this allusion to these words?

Until the miracle that saved the Jews from Haman's machinations, the Torah that the Jews had accepted at Mount Sinai was, in a sense, external, a *kedushah* that came to them as a gift. Therefore, it did not leave a lasting impression, and the Jews of that period did not fully appreciate that it truly taught them the best way to live. We can see this from the events which led to the destruction of the First Temple.

In the Purim story, they were saved through a miracle whose miraculous nature was not obvious on the surface. Nevertheless, the Jews of the time saw Hashem's hand at work behind the veil of "natural" events. With this perception, they imparted a human *kedushah* to this miracle, which led them to a renewed acceptance of the Torah with a stronger commitment than previously, since it came through their own effort and realization. Thus we read (*Esther* 9:27), קִיְּמוּ וְקִבְּלוּ, *they upheld and they accepted.* According to Rava (*Shabbos* 88a), this means that they accepted the Torah anew, as it were, with a fervor even greater than they had had at Sinai.

This, then, is the meaning of our verse, *take for YOU:* The *kedushah* which the anointing oil imparted, because it came through human effort and understanding, was felt much more strongly than those forms of *kedushah* which Hashem gave directly as gifts.

❁ ❁ ❁

שֶׁמֶן מִשְׁחַת־קֹדֶשׁ יִהְיֶה זֶה לִי לְדֹרֹתֵיכֶם: — *This will be a holy anointing oil to Me for your generations* (30:31).

Rashi remarks that the Sages (*Horayos* 11b) derived from this verse that all of the original anointing oil made by Moshe lasted through all the generations and will still be available when the *Beis HaMikdash* is rebuilt (may it be soon). In other words, even though the oil was used to anoint all the vessels and utensils of the Tabernacle and every *Kohen Gadol* through the generations, the original twelve *luggin* (from the numerical value of the word זֶה, *this*) remained intact, no matter how many times it was used.

Why did Hashem see fit to perform such a miracle with the anointing oil? It cannot be said that He wanted only the batch compounded by Moshe to be used. If that were His reason, He could have simply commanded that enough be made up at once to suffice for all future *Kohanim Gedolim*. Without question, He would know the correct amount. For this purpose alone, there would have been no need for the oil to remain undiminished with use.

We may say, however, that this miracle was intended to teach us an important lesson about the nature of *kedushah*. If the anointing oil had been expended with each use, one might have thought that the oil imparted some of its own *kedushah* to the person or object being anointed. As it is, however, none of the oil was used up. We are therefore forced to conclude that it did not *impart* anything to the recipient; rather, it aroused and kindled the *kedushah* which already existed inside the person so that the pre-existing *kedushah* was now revealed and became dominant.

This, then, is the inner meaning of the miracle of the anointing oil, which remained a full twelve *luggin* however many times it was used, just as the flame of a candle is not diminished, however many other candles are lit from it. This is also a fundamental principle of education at any level, that a parent or teacher cannot "impart" wisdom or skills to anyone, but rather can only arouse and develop the skills and wisdom which lie dormant inside the person. King Solomon referred to the same principle in the well-known verse (*Mishlei* 22:6), *Educate the child according to **his** way.* Only when one attempts to bring out the way which is already imbedded in the child will his education truly be for *him*.

❧ ❧ ❧

וַיֹּאמֶר ה' אֶל־מֹשֶׁה כְּתָב־לְךָ אֶת־הַדְּבָרִים הָאֵלֶּה כִּי עַל־פִּי הַדְּבָרִים הָאֵלֶּה כָּרַתִּי אִתְּךָ בְּרִית — *And* HASHEM *said to Moshe, "Write for yourself these words, for according to these words have I made a covenant with you"* (34:27).

Hashem told Moshe to write *these words*, which suggests that this term refers to תּוֹרָה שֶׁבִּכְתָב, the Written Torah. On the other hand, the expression עַל־פִּי, which is translated *according to* but literally means "through the mouth of," seems to be a reference to תּוֹרָה שֶׁבְּעַל פֶּה, the Oral Torah. In light of this, our verse takes on a new meaning: Hashem explained to Moshe the process of the covenant He was making with the Jewish people through him. The phrase *according to these words* means that this covenant was based on the Written Torah, but only as it is interpreted through the Oral Torah. Thus, the "Thirteen Rules by Which the Torah Is Expounded" constitute a pivotal element in this covenant that Hashem forged with Moshe.

❦ ❦ ❦

פרשת ויקהל
Parashas Vayakhel

שֵׁשֶׁת יָמִים תֵּעָשֶׂה מְלָאכָה וּבַיּוֹם הַשְּׁבִיעִי יִהְיֶה לָכֶם
קֹדֶשׁ שַׁבַּת שַׁבָּתוֹן לַה' כָּל־הָעֹשֶׂה בוֹ מְלָאכָה יוּמָת:
— *Six days shall work be done and on the seventh day it will be holy for you, a day of complete rest for HASHEM; whoever does work on it will die* (35:2).

At the beginning of this *parashah,* Moshe called the Jews into assembly, having just returned from his third stay on Mount Sinai, during which Hashem commanded him concerning the construction of the Tabernacle. As a preface to talking about the *Mishkan* (Tabernacle), which is the main topic of this *parashah,* he cautioned them not to do *melachah* (work) on the Sabbath. The Sages learned two things from this juxtaposition: first, that even work on the *Mishkan* had to cease on the Sabbath; and second, that the *melachos* (work processes) which the Torah forbids on the Sabbath are precisely those which were required for the construction of the *Mishkan,* no more, no less. But why should we say that there are no other *melachos* forbidden on Shabbos than those required for the *Mishkan?* Perhaps there are other *melachos* that were not needed for the *Mishkan* but are nevertheless forbidden on Shabbos.

We know that Hashem created the world with *melachos,* as we saw in *Parashas Bereishis* (2:2), *On the seventh day God completed His melachah which He had done.* Had the *Mishkan* been built with fewer *melachos* than the world, it would have been possible to think that Hashem was able to cause His Presence to dwell in the *Mishkan* only because the *Mishkan* was less "earthly" than the rest of the world, since it had been built with fewer *melachos.*

The purpose of the Tabernacle is to teach us that Hashem's Presence *can* dwell anywhere in the world. If the Tabernacle had been constructed with any fewer *melachos* than the rest of the world, it would not have accomplished this purpose. Now, however, that we know that Hashem's Presence can dwell anywhere in the world, it becomes an essential part of our task to bring that Presence into our homes and every aspect of our lives.

Another way of understanding this is through a metaphor. The *Mishkan* can be understood as Hashem's embassy in our physical world. When one country builds an embassy in a foreign capital, it hires local contractors to build the structure using the materials and methods of the host country. So also, when Hashem ordered Moshe to construct a physical representation of His spiritual Presence in this world, He specified that the same processes (i.e., *melachos*) be used as He had used to create the world in the first place.

This metaphor gives us a better understanding of the connection between the *melachos* used in the building of the *Mishkan* and the *melachos* forbidden on the Sabbath. The Sabbath is an affirmation that Hashem created the physical world for His glory in six days. Because Hashem rested from his "labors" on the seventh day, so we also rest from those same labors once every seven days as a testimony to that rest. Of course, these *melachos* were not done in the sense that we do them, but were done by an uttered command that they be done (see *Avos* 5:1).

It is possible, however, for us to study the processes by which the *Mishkan* was built, since we not only witnessed its construction, but actually took part in it. This is how our Sages, in their wisdom, were able to determine which *melachos* Hashem used to create the world and instructed us that those are precisely the same *melachos* that are forbidden on the Sabbath.

❦ ❦ ❦

וַיָּבֹאוּ הָאֲנָשִׁים עַל־הַנָּשִׁים — *And the men came with the women* (35:22).

This verse, which describes the offering of the women's jewelry toward the building of the *Mishkan* (Tabernacle), is ambiguous. It is not clear from the phrasing whether the men and women came as equals or, if not, who took precedence. *Rashi* says that the word עַל, which literally means *on*, can also be translated *with*.

We propose that these two meanings refer to different attitudes, both of which are relevant in this context. If the meaning is *with*, it indicates that the men and women came together, though not as equals. (We find a similar usage in the description of the tribal formations in the Wilderness — וְעָלָיו מַטֵּה מְנַשֶּׁה — even though Manasseh camped and traveled *with* or *next to* Ephraim, Ephraim was the leader of the formation and Manasseh was subordinate.) Thus it seems that the initiative to contribute the jewelry to the construction of the *Mishkan* came from the women. The men came along to show their consent to the women's gift, since they also had a share in the ownership of the jewelry, which the women used to make themselves attractive to their husbands.

On the other hand, the word עַל also suggests that the men were *over* the women in this matter and superior to them. According to this interpretation, it was the men who took it upon themselves to urge their wives to give up their jewelry, in expiation for the fact that they, the men, had given their ornaments for the construction of the Golden Calf.

It may be that the Torah phrased this verse ambiguously in order to indicate that both interpretations are correct, and both the men and the women came to bring the offerings for the construction of the *Mishkan* with equal enthusiasm, but with differing motivations.

❈ ❈ ❈

וְהַנְּשִׂאָם הֵבִיאוּ אֵת אַבְנֵי הַשֹּׁהַם וְאֵת אַבְנֵי הַמִּלָּאִים
לָאֵפוֹד וְלַחֹשֶׁן: — *And the Nesi'im brought the*
onyx stones and the stones to be set, for the
Ephod and for the Choshen (35:27).

Rashi cites the question of R' Nassan (*Sifri Bamidbar* 7:3):
Why did the *Nesi'im* (tribal princes) bring their offering first
on the occasion of the inauguration of the Altar, while in
contributing to the *Mishkan* (Tabernacle) they did not bring their
offerings first?

The *Nesi'im* said, "Let the people contribute whatever they want
to and then we will make up whatever they fail to bring."

Then, when the people brought everything, as it says, *And the*
work was sufficient for them, the *Nesi'im* said, "What can we do?"
and so they brought the stones. Because the *Nesi'im* procrastinated
at first, a letter was taken out of their name and the word נְשִׂאָם is
spelled without a *yud* [נְשִׂאָם instead of נְשִׂיאִם].

Thus Rashi strongly implies that there was something improper in
the conduct of the *Nesi'im* , yet at first glance it is difficult to see what
it was. It would seem a praiseworthy attitude for the wealthier
members of a community to promise to make up any shortfall in a
collection after everyone else has contributed. Why was this wrong
on the part of the *Nesi'im*?

The Mishnah (*Avos* 5:16) lists four types of donors to charity.
One of these is the *one who wishes to give himself, but wants others*
not to give — he begrudges others. By promising Moshe that they
would make up any shortfall in the contributions required for the
Mishkan (Tabernacle), the *Nesi'im* seem to have put themselves in
this category. Realistically speaking, the average person is not likely
to give as much to an appeal if he knows for sure that the goal will
be achieved even without his contribution. Thus, the attitude of the
Nesi'im was likely to discourage many potential donors from having
a share in the construction of the *Mishkan.*

There is another way of looking at this situation. By putting off
giving until everyone else had contributed, it could have been
thought that the *Nesi'im* hoped that the rest of the people would
give so much that there would be little lacking for the *Nesi'im* to

give. This would leave them in the category of the *one who wishes that others should give but that he should not give,* who, according to the Mishnah, *begrudges himself.*

Either way we look at it, the *Nesi'im* did not behave in a way befitting their role as leaders. It was incumbent on them to set an example to their followers by being the first to give. Then they would be among those who wish that *he should give and others should give,* whom the Mishnah calls "pious." As *Rashi* points out, it was their delay in contributing until the collection was completed that caused the Torah to record their shortcoming for posterity by leaving a letter out of the word נְשִׂאָם *(Nesi'im).*

※ ※ ※

וַיַּעַשׂ אֶת־שֶׁמֶן הַמִּשְׁחָה קֹדֶשׁ וְאֶת־קְטֹרֶת הַסַּמִּים טָהוֹר מַעֲשֵׂה רֹקֵחַ: — *And he made the holy anointing oil, and the pure incense-spices, the handiwork of an expert spice-compounder* (37:29).

The continuity of the subjects discussed in this verse requires explanation. Following the account of the construction of the Incense Altar, we are told that they first made the anointing oil, and then the incense-spices. The order of these two mixtures seems to be the reverse of what we would expect: First should come the compounding of the incense-spices, which have a natural connection with the Incense-Altar, and then the anointing oil, which has less of a relation to the other items mentioned. Why does the Torah interject the anointing oil *between* the Incense Altar and the spices that were used on it?

The academy of Rabbi Yishmael (*Arachin* 16a) taught that the incense-spices atoned for the sin of *lashon hara* (evil speech). One of the functions of the anointing oil was to sanctify the *Kohanim* who performed the service of the incense. By interrupting the account of the incense service with a mention of the anointing oil, the Torah teaches us how debased is someone who speaks *lashon hara.* This type of person feels he can raise himself only by bringing someone else down. The anointing oil has no effect on such an individual; it cannot elevate him because he looks good only in comparison with the shortcomings of others, not because of his own qualities.

(Lest there be any misunderstanding, we must clarify that this is only a homiletic interpretation intended to convey a moral lesson. While we cannot overemphasize the seriousness of the sin of *lashon hara,* we do not mean to imply that a *Kohen* who speaks *lashon hara* is ineligible to perform the incense service. This question is the subject of another discussion.)

❀ ❀ ❀

וַיַּעַשׂ אֵת הַכִּיוֹר נְחֹשֶׁת וְאֵת כַּנּוֹ נְחֹשֶׁת בְּמַרְאֹת הַצֹּבְאֹת אֲשֶׁר צָבְאוּ פֶּתַח אֹהֶל מוֹעֵד: — *And he made the laver of copper and its base of copper, with the mirrors of the legions, which they gathered at the opening of the Tent of Appointment* (38:8).

Rashi explains that the mirrors were called *mirrors of the legions* because the women used them in Egypt to arouse their husbands, worn out from the hard labor, to produce the legions who served Hashem. We may say that the Torah here gives testimony that the women acted purely for Hashem's sake, and not to gratify their own personal desires.

If so, it seems likely that they had not used the mirrors since then; once the mirrors had been put to this holy purpose, how could they be used for anything less holy? They were therefore left unused until this opportunity presented itself to use them in the *Mishkan* (Tabernacle), where they would bring holiness to the very nation that these same mirrors had been instrumental in creating in Egypt.

❀ ❀ ❀

פרשת פקודי
Parashas Pekudei

אֵלֶּה פְקוּדֵי הַמִּשְׁכָּן מִשְׁכַּן הָעֵדֻת אֲשֶׁר פֻּקַּד עַל־פִּי מֹשֶׁה — *These are the accounts of the Tabernacle, the Tabernacle of the Testimony, which was reckoned by order of Moshe* (38:21).

The *Mishkan* (Tabernacle) is called the *Tabernacle of the Testimony,* but it is not made clear which "testimony" is meant. We find in *Parashas Pinchas* that Hashem added the letters *hei* and *yud* from His Name to the names of the families that He took out of Egypt. In this way He testified that the tribes were free from Egyptian contamination in spite of the years of servitude (see *Rashi* on *Bamidbar* 26:5 and our commentary on *Parashas Lech Lecha, Bereishis* 12:15).

We may say that the *Mishkan* is called the *Tabernacle of the Testimony* for the same reason. This title informs us that the awesome holiness of the *Mishkan* was itself a testimony to the sanctity of those who made its construction possible. We know, therefore, that the silver that came from the half-shekels used to count the Jews was certainly given by people who were truly "Kosher" Jews, the sons of their mothers' husbands.

❅ ❅ ❅

עַל־שְׁמֹת בְּנֵי יִשְׂרָאֵל: — *On the names of the Children of Israel* (39:6).

This phrase, *on the names of the Children of Israel,* appears in two verses, one describing the onyx stones on the *Ephod* and the other describing the stones of the *Choshen* (v. 14). However, the use of the word עַל, *on,* in these verses is ambiguous. (See our discussion of this word in *Parashas Vayakhel* 35:22.) It could mean that the stones were subsidiary to the names and existed only as a medium on which the names could be written. Alternatively, it could mean that the stones were more important, and the names only secondary. According to this, the precious stones reveal the importance of these garments which Hashem designed to accomplish various aspects of His service in the *Mishkan.*

This is more than just a question of semantics. Do we say that the tribes, represented by the names on the stones, aspire to the *kedushah* (holiness) of the *Choshen* and the *Ephod,* but can never fully achieve it, or do we say that their *kedushah* was greater than that of these garments, and elevated them to a higher level?

Both answers are correct, and the very ambiguity of this verse indicates a mutual interaction between the *kedushah* of the priestly garments and the *kedushah* of the Jewish people. *Kedushah* has the potential to elevate us, and at the same time, when we show sufficient devotion to achieving *kedushah,* we can actually elevate *kedushah* itself to a higher level. In other words, *kedushah* is not an end in itself, but rather a product of our deeds. The nobler our deeds, the higher the level of our sanctity and the sanctity of the One Whom we serve.

To understand how this process works, let us examine the Sages' dictum (*Yoma* 35b), נִמְצָא הַלֵּל מְחַיֵּיב אֶת הָעֲנִיִּים, *It emerges that Hillel set an example which obligated even poor people.* It is difficult to say exactly how great is the obligation of poor men to learn Torah, since they have a valid claim that the burden they bear in supporting themselves and their families is greater than that of people whose livelihood is more secure. Once Hillel came along, however, and showed that even someone who lived in abject poverty could become a great Torah scholar, the standard expected of all poor people was raised.

Thus, the devotion of one man to raise himself to a higher level of *kedushah* raised the standard applied to everyone, and with it the level of *kedushah* in the entire world. This is the true meaning of the interaction of the *kedushah* of the Jewish people and the *kedushah* which Hashem imbued in the physical representations of His Presence in the world.

❅ ❅ ❅

וַיִּרְכְּסוּ אֶת־הַחשֶׁן מִטַּבְּעֹתָיו אֶל־טַבְּעֹת הָאֵפֹד בִּפְתִיל תְּכֵלֶת לִהְיֹת עַל־חֵשֶׁב הָאֵפֹד וְלֹא־יִזַּח הַחשֶׁן מֵעַל הָאֵפֹד כַּאֲשֶׁר צִוָּה ה' אֶת־מֹשֶׁה: — *And they attached the Choshen by its rings to the rings of the Ephod with a thread of techeiles to be on the cheishev of the Ephod; the Choshen shall not budge from the Ephod, as* Hashem *commanded Moshe* (39:21).

This verse seems to imply that once the *Choshen* and the *Ephod* were connected to each other, they were never allowed to be separated. Therefore, each time Aaron put them on, it was as a single, connected garment which had to be slipped over his head. In *Parashas Tzav*, however, it appears that Aaron donned the two garments separately (see *Vayikra* 8:7-8). It may be, though, that in *Parashas Tzav*, the Torah meant that the threads which connected the two garments were tightened or loosened to fit the *Kohen Gadol* properly.

In any case, there is an interesting symbolism in this commandment not to separate the *Choshen* from the *Ephod* once they were first connected. The Sages (*Arachin* 16a) teach that the *Ephod* represented מִצְוֹת בֵּין אָדָם לַמָּקוֹם, *mitzvos between man and Hashem,* and specifically atoned for the sin of idolatry. The *Choshen*, on the other hand, represented מִצְוֹת בֵּין אָדָם לַחֲבֵרוֹ, *mitzvos which govern relations among men.* Specifically, the *Choshen* atoned for perversion of justice.

Generally, we say that these two categories of *mitzvos* are of equal importance and that it is impossible to separate them. Thus, one cannot serve Hashem properly unless his relations with his fellows are in order, and, conversely, the only basis of proper human relations is the fear of Hashem. The fact that the *Kohen Gadol* never donned the *Choshen* without the *Ephod* symbolizes this inextricable connection between these two types of *mitzvos*.

Nevertheless, the connection between them had to be evaluated and adjusted regularly, just as the relative weight given to human relations as compared to the service of Hashem is a continually shifting equilibrium requiring constant re-evaluation. This, then, is the meaning of the seeming conflict between our verse and the procedure described in *Parashas Tzav*: The Torah is a living organism in the hands of the *Kohen Gadol,* which at varying times may demand an entirely different response to what seems to be the same set of circumstances. In certain situations, it is necessary to place greater weight upon service of Hashem, while other times we must stress relations with our fellows.

❧ ❧ ❧

כְּכֹל אֲשֶׁר־צִוָּה ה' אֶת־מֹשֶׁה כֵּן עָשׂוּ בְּנֵי יִשְׂרָאֵל אֵת כָּל־הָעֲבֹדָה: — *According to everything which HASHEM commanded Moshe, so the Children of Israel did all of the work* (39:42).

The word כֵּן means *so,* or *in that manner,* but it also means *correctly.* In this sense, our verse tells us that the Jews' performance of their work was correct. What does this mean? The Jews did not only *what* they were supposed to, but also for the exact reason they were supposed to, namely, because Hashem commanded it. As Hashem commanded at the beginning of *Parashas Terumah,* the gifts for the Tabernacle were to be given לִי, *for Me,* which, as *Rashi* explains, meant that they must be given purely for the sake of Hashem. It is in this sense that the Torah tells us here that they acted *correctly.* However eager the people were to have the *Shechinah* come and dwell in their midst, they suppressed their personal desires and acted purely for the sake of fulfilling Hashem's command. (See also our commentary on *Parashas Noach, Bereishis* 6:22.)

❧ ❧ ❧

— וְאִם־לֹא יֵעָלֶה הֶעָנָן וְלֹא יִסְעוּ עַד־יוֹם הֵעָלֹתוֹ:
And if the cloud would not go up, and they would not travel until the day that it went up (40:37).

In the phrase וְלֹא יִסְעוּ, *and they would not travel,* it is not clear why there is a conjunctive *vav*, *and they would not travel.* This word *and* seems totally unnecessary; what does it add to our understanding of the verse?

The word *and* tells us that not only would the Jews not travel if Hashem did not command it, they would not even *want* to travel without Hashem's command, so difficult was it for them even to contemplate separating themselves from the Divine Presence in their camp. This is a higher level than the one we spoke of above; not only did they *do* what they were told, they *wanted* to do it in that way. This is part of Hashem's great kindness, that He makes *mitzvos* out of things that give us so much pleasure that we want to do them.

Thus, delighting in the delicacies which we eat on Shabbos is undoubtedly a much easier and more pleasurable *mitzvah* than eating *marror* on Passover. Still, Jews do both of these *mitzvos* equally לִשְׁמָה, for the sake of fulfilling Hashem's commandments, and not for the pleasure we have in doing them.

❦ ❦ ❦

ספר ויקרא

Sefer Vayikra

פרשת ויקרא
Parashas Vayikra

וַיִּקְרָא אֶל־מֹשֶׁה — *And He called to Moshe* (1:1).

Accorrding to the Masoretic tradition, the letter *aleph* in the word וַיִּקְרָא, *and He called,* is written in miniature, generally less than a third of the size of a normal *aleph*. *Baal HaTurim* says that Moshe would have wanted the word written without an *aleph* at all, וַיִּקָר, *and He happened upon.* This is how the Torah disparagingly describes Hashem's meeting with Bilam, suggesting that Hashem's meetings with Bilam were always happenstance, on a casual basis, and not because Hashem wanted to speak with Bilam at all (see *Rashi* on *Bamidbar* 23:4). In his great humility, Moshe did not want the Torah to suggest that Hashem considered him more worthy than that.

Hashem, however, wanted the Torah to publicize his great regard for Moshe and therefore said וַיִּקְרָא, *and He called,* showing that Moshe was so important that Hashem made a point of calling to him. The miniature *aleph* was a "compromise" between these two preferences.

According to the Sages (*Chagigah* 14a), Moshe knew that the Torah was supposed to be given to the twenty-sixth generation after Adam. (The numerical value of Hashem's name is twenty-six.) Thus he was able to argue to Hashem, "You were committed to give the Torah now, so Your choices were limited. If You could have waited for future generations, You would certainly have found someone more worthy than myself through whom to give the Torah. Therefore, וַיִּקָּר, it just *happened* to be through me the Torah was given, not because of my own merit. I happened to be in the right place, at the right time."

Hashem answered, "That is not true. Had I wanted to, I could certainly have found a way to postpone giving the Torah. The Sages said that Ezra was worthy of having the Torah given through him, but you happened to come before him (*Sanhedrin* 21b). Had you not been qualified, I would have waited until Ezra came. But I gave it through you because you are worthy of it. Therefore it is appropriate that I show you the respect of writing that I called you intentionally, not by happenstance."

❦ ❦ ❦

וַיְדַבֵּר ה' אֵלָיו מֵאֹהֶל מוֹעֵד לֵאמֹר: — *And HASHEM spoke to him from the Tent of Meeting, saying* (1:1).

Rashi comments that Hashem's voice stopped at the doorway of the Tent of Meeting. However, we should not think that He spoke in a low or soft voice, but as it says in *Tehillim* (29:4-5), *The voice of HASHEM in power! The voice of HASHEM in majesty! The voice of HASHEM breaks the cedars, HASHEM shatters the cedars of Lebanon!*

Why did Hashem see fit to create such a miraculous effect, to speak in a supernaturally loud voice, yet not permit it to be heard any farther than the limits of the tent, a voice whose power could be heard only by one man?

In answer, we know that the Torah was given three times in its entirety: first at Mount Sinai, then in the *Mishkan* (Tent of Meeting), and finally on the Plains of Moab (*Chagigah* 6b). Each of these times, it was conveyed in the exact same voice, to show that all three times were of equal importance.

If the exact same Torah was given all three times, with the same importance, why was it necessary to repeat it? Because each time it was given with a different emphasis, corresponding to the three pillars on which the world stands (see *Avos* 1:2): תּוֹרָה עֲבוֹדָה וּגְמִילוּת חֲסָדִים, *Torah, the service of Hashem, and kind deeds*.

The first giving, at Mount Sinai, represented the pillar of Torah. There, in the midst of the Wilderness, the Jews were provided with all their needs (manna, water, shelter, etc.) so that they could rise above the physicality of the world and focus on the pure learning of Torah. The *Mishkan,* where the service of the offerings and the incense took place, was the appropriate place to emphasize the pillar of service of Hashem. And on the Plains of Moab, where the Jews entered into a covenant to be responsible for each other, the pillar of generosity and kind relations among humans was highlighted.

Of course, these three aspects of Torah are mutually interdependent, and each of them is necessary to reinforce the others. Thus, every commandment has within its observance all of these three facets. For example, Torah learning must be purely *lishmah,* for its own sake, and at the same time it must be directed to serving Hashem and to finding ways of expressing kindness to others, as King Solomon wrote (*Mishlei* 31:26), *The Torah of kindness is on her tongue.*

❧ ❧ ❧

אָדָם כִּי־יַקְרִיב מִכֶּם קָרְבָּן לַה׳ — *When a man shall bring from you an offering to* HASHEM (1:2).

Why does the Torah include the seemingly unnecessary words, *from you,* in this verse? It is to teach us that someone who brings an offering should feel as if he had brought *himself* as the offering, rather than an animal, i.e., when you shall bring [it shall be] from you [yourself]. Objectively speaking, when someone sins, Hashem would be justified in taking the sinner's life in atonement for the sin, and only because of His great mercy does He allow the sinner to bring an offering instead.

This verse deals with *olos* (elevation-offerings), the purpose of which was to atone for transgression of or failure to perform a positive commandment. Even though such offerings were brought voluntarily, in fact, those who brought them needed the atonement they afforded.

Clearly, if someone who brought a *korban olah* had the conviction that he himself, rather than the animal, deserved to be sacrificed, it would impress on him much more strongly the seriousness of his lapse.

This, therefore, is the meaning of מִכֶּם, *from you.* Everyone who brought an offering should really have brought it literally *from himself,* and not just an animal surrogate. This was precisely the attitude needed to accomplish the purpose of the offering, to make him realize what a serious thing he had done and do his utmost to avoid such lapses in the future.

❧ ❧ ❧

אִם הַכֹּהֵן הַמָּשִׁיחַ יֶחֱטָא לְאַשְׁמַת הָעָם — *When the anointed Kohen shall sin for the guilt of the people* (4:3).

This passage talks about the sin-offering brought by a *Kohen Gadol* who had unintentionally committed a sin the penalty for which, had he done it intentionally, would have been *kareis,* premature death. If so, why does the Torah describe it as *the guilt of the people,* which seemingly has no connection with the sin committed by the *Kohen Gadol?*

We can say that the Torah is informing us in this verse that a leader is nothing more than a reflection of his followers. When people see the leader doing wrong it gives them an excuse to do wrong also, since they can think, "He is much more powerful and exalted than we are—if even he cannot control his base urges, how can we be expected to do better?" Similarly, when the people sin it is very difficult for their leader to rise above them and perfect his ways.

This is what the Torah was hinting at in the words *for the guilt of the people.* If the *Kohen Gadol* has sinned, either it is because the people sinned and influenced him, or eventually his sin will influence them and make it harder for them to restrain themselves. Thus, the *guilt of the people* is inseparable from his own guilt; either they influenced him or he will influence them.

❧ ❧ ❧

אֲשֶׁר נָשִׂיא יֶחֱטָא וְעָשָׂה אַחַת מִכָּל־מִצְוֹת ה׳ אֱלֹהָיו אֲשֶׁר לֹא־תֵעָשֶׂינָה בִּשְׁגָגָה וְאָשֵׁם: — *That a Nasi shall sin and do one of all the commandments of HASHEM his God which should not be done, unintentionally, and shall be guilty* (4:22).

his verse describes the offerings required of a *Nasi* (king) who unintentionally transgresses certain commandments. *Rashi* comments that the first word of the verse, אֲשֶׁר, *that*, is similar to the word אַשְׁרֵי, *fortunate*. Says *Rashi*, fortunate is the generation whose leader has regret for the wrongs he did unintentionally. How much more so must he regret his intentional transgressions.

Rashi is calling our attention to the positive side of the matter. A *Nasi* is a very public figure and has a strong influence on the people. When the people see that their *Nasi*, in spite of the pride and glory of his lofty position, is not afraid to admit his sin and publicly ask Hashem for forgiveness, it sets a powerful example for them how to repent for own their wrongdoings.

In this light, the Sages taught (*Avodah Zarah* 4b) that King David was too great to have sinned in the normal course of events. The only reason he came to sin was in order to set an example for the nation, to teach the people the proper way to regret one's sins and repent.

❈ ❈ ❈

פרשת צו
Parashas Tzav

צַו אֶת־אַהֲרֹן וְאֶת־בָּנָיו לֵאמֹר זֹאת תּוֹרַת הָעֹלָה הִוא
הָעֹלָה עַל מוֹקְדָה עַל־הַמִּזְבֵּחַ כָּל־הַלַּיְלָה עַד־הַבֹּקֶר
*— Command Aaron and his sons saying: This
is the teaching of the elevation-offering, it is
the elevation-offering that stays on the pyre
on the Altar all night until morning* (6:2).

The first word of this verse, צַו, after which the *parashah* is
named, is a very strong expression — *Command!* It is used
only when the speaker feels that the listener will be lax in
fulfilling the order.Why was Moshe told to give this particular topic,
the burning of the *korban olah* (elevation-offering) on the Altar, so
much stress when he taught it to the *Kohanim* (priests)?

From the *Kohen's* perspective, this law is not easy to understand.
The *olah* was one of the offerings that was completely consumed by
the fire, except for its hide. No one, not even a *Kohen,* was allowed
to eat or receive any other benefit, from it. The *Kohanim* might
have thought that it was a waste of a good animal to burn it on the
Altar. Certainly Hashem did not need it for nourishment.

We said in *Parashas Vayikra* (1:2) that someone who brought an
offering had to have the attitude that he *himself* deserved to be
offered on the Altar, and it was only because of Hashem's mercy
that he was allowed to bring an animal instead. Now, we know that,
practically speaking, one who could afford to bring an animal-

offering was to some degree a person of means. The very poor would more likely bring a *minchah,* an offering of flour and oil, of which the major portion is eaten by the *Kohanim.* To the pauper, even this small amount was a sacrifice. It was food that he had actually deprived himself of. But the animal-offering of the well-off wasn't that much of a sacrifice. He still had what to eat in abundance. So if the *Kohanim* were allowed to eat the *korban olah,* the man who brought it might think, "It's not so bad that I have to bring this. After all, at least I am providing the *Kohanim* with a good meal." This attitude would make it difficult for him to feel that he himself should have been the offering. This is one of the reasons why Hashem insisted that the *korban olah* had to be completely consumed by the fire.

The *Kohanim,* however, might not fully understand this reasoning. They could claim that nothing will influence someone who needs such a strong lesson, and therefore the animal might as well be given to them to eat. This is why Hashem told Moses to *command* the *Kohanim* that this offering must be burned in its entirety. Because they had a personal interest in it, they needed special urging to motivate them to be diligent in observing this particular law.

❦ ❦ ❦

הָעֹלָה עַל מוֹקְדָה — *The olah-offering on the pyre* (6:2).

This term refers specifically to the part of the Altar upon which the fire burned. This indicates that the main purpose of the fire is to burn the *olah,* and that the main purpose of the *olah* is to be burnt. From this we see the distinction between the *olah* and the other offerings. Whereas all of them are burned in part, being consumed on the Altar is only a part of their function. In the case of the *olah,* however, as we described above, the fact that it is burned completely is precisely how it conveys its message to the person seeking atonement.

❦ ❦ ❦

וְאֵשׁ הַמִּזְבֵּחַ תּוּקַד בּוֹ: — *And the fire of the Altar should be kept burning on it* (6:2).

The last word of this verse, בּוֹ, *on it,* seemingly refers to the Altar. If so, however, it is redundant because obviously the fire of the Altar will be kept burning *on it,* i.e., on the Altar itself. Therefore, we must look for another interpretation.

The word בּוֹ could also be translated *in him,* referring to the person who brings the offering. In this sense, it means that someone who has committed a sin requiring an atonement-offering should feel as if the fire of the Altar is actually burning *on him,* and purifying him of the stains the sin left on his soul.

❈　❈　❈

חָלְקָם נָתַתִּי אֹתָהּ מֵאִשָּׁי — *I have given it as their portion from My fire-offerings* (6:10).

This passage deals with the laws and procedures of meal-offerings. It is noteworthy that the expression חֶלְקָם, *their portion,* is used only in connection with meal-offerings, which were brought by those who were so poor that they could not afford to bring animal, or even bird, sacrifices. Earlier we said that it was forbidden to eat any part of the *korban olah* so that the sinner who brought it would appreciate the seriousness of his sin. However, this reason does not apply in the case of a meal-offering; it was so difficult for a poor person just to purchase the flour and oil required for his offering that he would learn his lesson even though the *Kohanim* ate most of it. Therefore, Hashem required only an אַזְכָּרָה, *remembrance,* that the offering was really for Him. As for the share of the *Kohanim,* Hashem calls it *their portion,* because this is the intention in the first place: It should be eaten and not destroyed, for it does not have to convey a message to the person that he needs atonement.

❈　❈　❈

וַיָּשֶׂם עָלָיו אֶת־הַחֹשֶׁן וַיִּתֵּן אֶל־הַחֹשֶׁן אֶת־הָאוּרִים וְאֶת־הַתֻּמִּים: — *And he placed the Choshen on him and he put the Urim and the Tumim on the Choshen* (8:8).

The *Urim* and *Tumim* was a parchment on which was written Hashem's ineffable, four-letter Name. Only after Moshe placed the *Choshen* (breastplate) on Aaron did he insert the *Urim* and *Tumim,* which gave the *Choshen* its supernatural ability to convey Hashem's will to the *Kohen Gadol,* and to the nation. Why was it done in this order? Surely it would have been easier to insert the Name before placing the *Choshen* on the *Kohen Gadol's* breast.

Let us remember, however, that the *Choshen* symbolized fairness in monetary dealings, which is why it was also called the *Choshen Hamishpat* (breastplate of justice). Let us also remember that the *Choshen* had to be connected to the *Ephod,* an apron-like garment which symbolized service to Hashem (*Arachin* 16a). This shows us that true justice can exist only in relation to Hashem's will and under His direction and guidance.

Therefore, the first requirement was to attach the symbol of justice, the *Choshen,* to the symbol of service, the *Ephod,* in order to affirm the nation's commitment to the concept of God-given justice. Only then could the *Choshen* be a fitting setting for the Divine Name, which provided the power needed to bring Hashem's justice into the world through the vehicle of the *Choshen.* But if the *Urim* and *Tumim* were to be put on the *Choshen* before it was attached to the *Ephod,* it would seem to sanction "justice" without considering God's will.

❀   ❀   ❀

פרשת שמיני
Parashas Shemini

וַיְהִי בַּיּוֹם הַשְּׁמִינִי — *And it was on the eighth day* (9:1).

The Sages taught (*Megillah* 10b) that the word וַיְהִי, *and it was*, connotes sadness and asked why the *eighth* day was sad. They explained that since Aaron's two older sons Nadav and Avihu died during the inauguration of the *Mishkan* (Tent of Meeting), the sadness of the day outweighs the joy of the happy event that took place on it.

The questions abound. For one thing, our verse took place before the death of Nadav and Avihu, when the day was still a happy one, so why does the Torah hint at sadness so soon? Secondly, it is obvious to everyone why the day was sad; why did the Sages even have to ask? Thirdly, why did the Sages consider that the sadness of the day outweighed the joy of the inauguration of the Tabernacle? Surely this was one of the most joyous and important events in the history of the Jewish people, the day on which Hashem first established a permanent dwelling place for His Presence which was to last — in this and later Tabernacles and in the Temple — until the destruction of the First Temple, many centuries later.

At the inauguration of the Tabernacle, Hashem wanted the people to feel joy that they had merited a clear and strong perception of His holiness. The best thing would be for them to come to this perception on their own; that would truly have been unblemished joy, like the joy of a bridegroom on his wedding day who sees no clouds darkening the horizon. But Hashem saw that the people were not at a high-enough level to experience that pure enthusiastic joy, so He arranged an event which would cause them to perceive His holiness in a way that would make them understand and take pride in their special connection with Him.

This is why Nadav and Avihu were punished for their sin by death. As Moshe said to Aaron (ibid. 10:3), הוּא אֲשֶׁר־דִּבֶּר ה׳ לֵאמֹר, בִּקְרֹבַי אֶקָּדֵשׁ וְעַל־פְּנֵי כָל־הָעָם אֶכָּבֵד, *"This is what* HASHEM *spoke, saying, 'I will be made holy through those who are close to Me and I will be given honor before the whole people.' "* Rashi explains that when Hashem renders judgment on the righteous, He is elevated and made more awesome and more worthy of praise.

Now we can understand the question of the Sages better. From the word וַיְהִי, *and it was,* they knew that even the beginning of the day was sad, but they did not understand why. They concluded that Hashem knew already, at the start of the day, that the joy was not complete because the people could not yet perceive the full spiritual grandeur of the day. Therefore it would be necessary to give them a powerful demonstration of Divine judgment, by taking away two of the greatest men of the nation (see *Rashi* on *Shemos* 29:43 and *Zevachim* 115b).

Thus, the sadness started even before their death, which is why the Sages considered in retrospect that the sadness of the day outweighed the joy. The joy of that day was never complete, like the joy of a bridegroom who knows that a tragedy lies in wait for him at the end of the day.

❧ ❧ ❧

וַיְהִי בַּיּוֹם הַשְּׁמִינִי — *And it was on the eighth day* (9:1).

Why does the Torah stress that this was the *eighth* day of the setting up of the *Mishkan*? True, it was the culmination of the preceding seven days, which Moshe spent in preparation for the official inauguration. Yet it would seem more appropriate to emphasize that it was the *first* day of the functioning of the *Mishkan*, as we find in the account of the offerings of the *Nesi'im* (tribal princes) in *Parashas Naso*. In this light, it seems that the first seven days were merely "practice" sessions, as it were, which became insignificant once the *Mishkan* and the *Kohanim* assumed their full sanctity. If so, why is the *eighthness* of the day given such prominence, to the extent that even the name of the *parashah* stresses it?

The Torah wants to teach us that the preparations one makes for doing a *mitzvah* have nearly as much importance as the *mitzvah* itself, that they are really part of the *mitzvah* itself. For example, even though the *Seder* lasts only a few hours on Pesach evening, it can require weeks of preparations, including learning many laws and customs. One might think it a waste to spend all that time preparing for such a short affair. In reality, however, the preparations are part of the *mitzvah* because without them it would be impossible to do the *mitzvah* properly.

Similarly, one is allowed to pronounce the blessing *Shehecheyanu* (Who has kept us alive) as soon as one completes building a *succah,* even though one cannot perform the *mitzvah* of dwelling in the *succah* until the first night of the festival.

This is why the Torah stresses the fact that the inauguration of the *Mishkan* took place on the *eighth* day of the preparations, rather than calling it the first day of the *Mishkan* itself. The seven days which preceded the consecration, even though they were not the ultimate *raison d'etre* of the *Mishkan,* had an importance nearly equal to that of the days that followed.

❧ ❧ ❧

וַיִּקְחוּ בְנֵי־אַהֲרֹן נָדָב וַאֲבִיהוּא אִישׁ מַחְתָּתוֹ וַיִּתְּנוּ בָהֵן אֵשׁ וַיָּשִׂימוּ עָלֶיהָ קְטֹרֶת וַיַּקְרִיבוּ לִפְנֵי ה' אֵשׁ זָרָה אֲשֶׁר לֹא צִוָּה אֹתָם: — *And the sons of Aaron, Nadav and Avihu, each took his incense pan; they put fire on them, placed incense on it, and they offered before HASHEM a foreign fire which He had not commanded them* (10:1).

There is a strange switching of number in this verse: *they put fire on "them" and they placed incense on "it".* They had two pans, yet they placed the incense on *it*. What is the meaning of this anomaly?

Nadav and Avihu attempted to devise a new way of serving Hashem, which they thought would be an improvement over the old way, so each one prepared a fire to bring incense. Then they realized that if they were to bring two separate offerings of incense, there would surely be some slight difference between the two offerings. This would signify that there were *two* leaders, each representing a different mode of service. This would defeat their purpose, for the spiritual health of the nation requires unity of purpose under a single leader. They therefore decided that one of them should take the lead, and so they offered their incense on that one's pan and with his fire.

❧ ❧ ❧

וַיְדַבֵּר מֹשֶׁה אֶל־אַהֲרֹן וְאֶל אֶלְעָזָר וְאֶל־אִיתָמָר בָּנָיו הַנּוֹתָרִים — *And Moshe spoke to Aaron and to Elazar and to Ithamar, his remaining sons* (10:12).

Rashi comments that the death punishment had been decreed against all four of Aaron's sons at the time of the sin of the Golden Calf, but Moshe had beseeched Hashem not to wipe out Aaron's children and his prayers had succeeded in saving these two. In light of this, we understand that strict adherence to Moshe's instructions was essential for the survival of Aaron and his remaining sons: "If you do not want to be killed like your brothers, be careful to do everything that I tell you; do not devise your own means of service."

Later, when Moshe was angry with them because he thought they had disobeyed his instructions, we would expect that they might be in renewed danger. However, the Torah nonetheless refers to them as the *remaining* sons, implying that, despite his anger, Moshe still entreated Hashem to spare them.

❧ ❧ ❧

וְלֹא תְטַמְּאוּ אֶת־נַפְשֹׁתֵיכֶם בְּכָל־הַשֶּׁרֶץ הָרֹמֵשׂ עַל־
הָאָרֶץ: כִּי אֲנִי ה' הַמַּעֲלֶה אֶתְכֶם מֵאֶרֶץ מִצְרַיִם
And do not defile your souls with any vermin
which crawls on the earth. For I am Hashem,
Who brought you up from the land of Egypt
(11:44-45).

Normally when the Torah reminds us that Hashem freed us from Egyptian servitude, it uses the term הַמּוֹצִיא, *Who brought you out.* Here, however, the Torah says הַמַּעֲלֶה, *Who brought you up,* to teach us that abstaining from forbidden foods, and especially from the forbidden species of vermin, has an uplifting effect on a Jew.

The Sages (*Yoma* 39a) gave a homiletic interpretation of the previous verse (11:43), וְנִטְמֵתֶם בָּם, *and you will be defiled by them [if you eat them].* The defilement referred to is that the heart would be blocked, as it were, resulting in insensitivity to spiritual concerns.

On the other hand, someone who is careful about what he eats will have an open heart and find it easier to develop a benevolent outlook toward his fellow man. This is the "bringing up" that Hashem spoke of in our verse, an elevation of the spirit from the pride, selfishness and cruelty that characterized the Egyptian mentality.

❧ ❧ ❧

פרשת תזריע
Parashas Tazria

אִשָּׁה כִּי תַזְרִיעַ וְיָלְדָה זָכָר — *When a woman pro-duces seed and gives birth to a male* (12:2).

In talking about a woman who bears a male child, the Torah mentions that she produces seed. A few verses later, however, concerning the birth of a female child, there is no mention of the seed. What is the reason for this discrepancy?

According to Torah law, a male remains associated with the family of his parents throughout his whole life. This has implications as far as his *halachic* status (*Kohen, Levi, Yisrael*) is concerned, as well as his rights of inheritance.

On the other hand, a woman passes into the family of her husband when she marries. Thus, when the daughter of a *Kohen* marries a *Yisrael,* she loses the right to eat from the priestly portions. And, of course, her children are *Yisraelim* and derive no benefit from their maternal grandfather's priestly status.

It is to this arrangement that the Torah alludes when it mentions the woman's seed in connection with the birth of a son but not the birth of a daughter.

❧ ❧ ❧

וְטָמְאָה שִׁבְעַת יָמִים כִּימֵי נִדַּת דְּוֹתָהּ תִּטְמָא: — *She shall be contaminated for a seven-day period, as during the days of her separation pain shall she be contaminated* (12:2).

This verse compares the *tumah* (ritual uncleanliness) of a woman after the birth of a male child to that of a woman experiencing menstrual pains. A few verses later, in discussing a woman after the birth of a female child, the same comparison is made but then there is no mention of pain, only of נִדָּתָהּ, *her menstrual cycle*. Why is pain mentioned in one context but not in the other?

The word נִדָּה (*niddah*) literally means "separation," but it is used to refer to a woman's menstrual cycle, because at that time she feels pain and wants to *separate* herself from her husband. A woman suffers a similar kind of pain upon giving birth, and also wants to be separate from her husband.

In verse 5, the Torah decrees that the mother of a baby girl is *tamei* for two weeks. During the second week, however, the pain of childbirth has generally subsided so that she no longer feels compelled to be separate for this reason. Because her pain is no longer a factor in her separation, the Torah does not mention it in connection with the mother of a female child. Her abstention now is only because of the Torah's commandment, not because of her feelings.

During the first week after birth, a husband who complies with the injunction to separate himself from his wife is rewarded for the consideration he shows *her*; at this time it is both a commandment *bein adam laMakom* (between man and Hashem) and a commandment *bein adam lachaveiro* (between fellow humans). During the second week, however, this second factor no longer exists, and separation becomes a commandment only *bein adam laMakom*.

❋ ❋ ❋

שְׂאֵת . . . בַּהֶרֶת — *S'eis . . . baheres* (13:2).

This verse speaks of two forms of *tzaraas* afflictions that are different shades of white. Each one comes as punishment for conduct on a personal level, and each indicates a slightly different attitude toward faulty behavior. A *baheres* is a clear, glistening white, indicating that the victim regards his behavior as so pure and beyond reproach that his conscience is completely clear. A *s'eis* is not quite as white and clear. Such a person is not as complacent and smug as the one suffering from a *baheres*.

Nevertheless, the affliction came because he regards himself as better, on a higher level, than his fellows. This affliction symbolizes his arrogance and selfishness.

❧ ❧ ❧

הַשְּׁחִין . . . מִכְוַת־אֵשׁ — *The boil . . . a burn* (13:23-24).

In the cases of *tzaraas* listed earlier in the chapter, the Torah provides for two separate seven-day quarantine periods to determine whether or not the victim is definitely contaminated. In the cases of an affliction that formed on a boil or a burn, there is only a single period of quarantine. What is the reason for this difference?

Tzaraas is not an ordinary, physical malady, but rather a Divine punishment for one of seven sins between man and his fellow men. The purpose of *tzaraas* is to shock the victim into recognizing that he has sinned, so that he will be moved to repent. If he does so, the *tzaraas* will disappear and the *Kohen* will pronounce him cured.

If, however, the symptoms of contamination are not conclusive at the beginning, the *Kohen* proclaims a period of quarantine, which is a probationary period for the sinner. This indicates to him that he is not so evil that he must be declared contaminated, but he is nonetheless in danger and needs to repent. If the affliction appeared without any prior condition, he is given two quarantine periods as opportunities to repent.

If, however, the affliction was preceded by a boil or a burn, that prior condition itself constituted notice of sorts to the victim that something was amiss in his conduct. He should have taken that condition as a warning to examine his deeds and correct them. Therefore, the one quarantine period he is given is, in his case, already a "second chance," and if he fails to utilize it, he is not given another opportunity, but is immediately declared *tamei*.

❧ ❧ ❧

וְהַבֶּגֶד — And the garment (13:47).

tzaraas that afflicts a garment indicates another kind of personal flaw. Sometimes one knows that his behavior is lacking and that he must seek ways to improve himself, but instead of trying to correct his failings, he tries to hide them. His hypocrisy is like a garment one wears to conceal a blemish, or like the facade pasted on a building to conceal structural flaws. The only way to induce such a person to repent is to make him strip away the facade and expose the underlying defects so that they may be repaired. This is why a *tzaraas* affliction strikes his garment.

❊   ❊   ❊

פרשת מצורע
Parashas Metzora

זֹאת תִּהְיֶה תּוֹרַת הַמְּצֹרָע — *This will be the law of the metzora* (14:2).

The numerical value of the Hebrew word מְצֹרָע, *metzora,* is 400. Coincidentally, this is also the number of years of servitude which Hashem decreed on the descendants of Abraham (*Bereishis* 16:13). There is an interesting symbolism in this coincidence.

It is possible to view a *metzora* as someone so completely subservient to his desires that he needs a strong warning that his ways are leading him to total spiritual oblivion. The affliction Hashem gives him is precisely this warning. Through it he is shown that he must repent and cure himself.

Thus, the numerical value of the word *metzora* contains an allusion to servitude, as if to declare that the *metzora* was put into this condition by his servitude to his desires.

❧ ❧ ❧

וְצִוָּה הַכֹּהֵן וְלָקַח לַמִּטַּהֵר שְׁתֵּי־צִפֳּרִים חַיּוֹת — *And the Kohen shall command, and he shall take for the one being purified two live birds* (14:4).

The process of purifying a *metzora,* which involves taking two live birds and following a detailed procedure with each of them, vividly illustrates the spiritual purification which the *metzora* requires for the sin of *lashon hara* (evil speech). The chattering birds symbolize that the *metzora* had committed the sin of chattering meaningless gossip and slander, as if he were a bird.

The *Kohen* ordered one bird to be slaughtered over an earthenware vessel containing a *revi'is* of spring water, so that the redness of the blood would be easily noticeable in the water. At this point, the person being purified would surely get the message that one must never speak *lashon hara*.

Then, lest he be tempted to go to the other extreme, by avoiding the company of others altogether to deny himself further opportunities to sin, he was given a reminder that he had to go on living in the world: The remaining live bird was set free to fly out over an open field, symbolizing that normal life must continue. Beforehand, however, the live bird was dipped in the blood of the slaughtered one, so that the *metzora* would remember constantly that he had done wrong and that he had to guard his words very carefully in the future.

❧   ❧   ❧

כִּי תָבֹאוּ אֶל־אֶרֶץ כְּנַעַן אֲשֶׁר אֲנִי נֹתֵן לָכֶם לַאֲחֻזָּה וְנָתַתִּי נֶגַע צָרַעַת בְּבֵית אֶרֶץ אֲחֻזַּתְכֶם: — *When you arrive in the land of Canaan that I give you as a possession, and I will place a tzaraas affliction upon a house in the land of your possession* (14:34).

Why is it only in *Eretz Yisrael* that a house can be afflicted with *tzaraas*? The prophet says וְשָׁבֶיהָ בִּצְדָקָה, *and its returners shall be in [shall be redeemed through] charity* (*Yeshayahu* 1:27), meaning that only through charitable behavior are Jews allowed to return to and continue to live in the land (*Rambam, Matnos Ani'im* 10:1). The affliction of *tzaraas* comes as punishment for sins which reflect selfishness and disdain for others, the opposite of charity. It comes as a warning to the Jews to mend their ways before, Heaven forbid, the land is destroyed and they are sent into exile.

❧   ❧   ❧

וּבָא אֲשֶׁר־לוֹ הַבַּיִת וְהִגִּיד לַכֹּהֵן לֵאמֹר כְּנֶגַע נִרְאָה לִי
בַּבָּיִת: — *The one to whom the house belongs*
shall come and declare to the Kohen, saying:
Something like an affliction has appeared to
me in the house (14:35).

In talking about someone who has an affliction on his body, the
Torah says וְהוּבָא אֶל־הַכֹּהֵן, *he shall be brought to the Kohen*
(ibid. 14:2), whereas here it says that he shall *come* to the
Kohen. Why does the Torah change its terminology from one case
to the other?

Someone with an affliction, indicating that he is himself flawed,
has a natural tendency to deny the existence of his personal
shortcomings, even to himself, as long as possible. He will seize
upon any rationalization to avoid confronting the realization that he
has sinned and must mend his ways. Therefore, since he may resist
admitting to the reality of his affliction, he *has to be brought* to the
Kohen for a ruling as to whether or not he is a *metzora*.

However, when the affliction affects his house, that means that
his whole household has followed his bad ways and is in danger of
being punished. In this situation, where the well-being of his loved
ones is at stake, he requires no encouragement and will *come* on
his own to the Kohen to look for ways of protecting his family from
harm.

❀　❀　❀

וְאִישׁ כִּי־תֵצֵא מִמֶּנּוּ שִׁכְבַת־זָרַע . . . וְאִשָּׁה כִּי־תִהְיֶה
זָבָה דָם — *A man from whom there is a*
discharge of semen . . . And a woman when
there will be a discharge of blood (15:16,19).

Among the events that contaminate someone are the
discharge of semen from a man and the menstrual flow of
a woman. Unlike the discharges of a *zav* or a *zavah*, these
are part of the natural processes of life and are necessary for
continuing life. Why then does the Torah consider that they have
the power to contaminate?

We may say that by declaring that these natural events contaminate the man or woman who experiences them, the Torah wants to cleanse them from the contaminated thoughts that might be associated with these phenomena. The contamination reminds them that the process of creating life is a *mitzvah* no different from other *mitzvos,* and must therefore be undertaken from a pure motivation to observe the will of the Creator, and not from any other motives. When they are able to achieve that level of purity, the offspring they produce will also be on a pure road and will be better able to achieve great heights in the service of Hashem.

❧ ❧ ❧

פרשת אחרי מות
Parashas Acharei Mos

וּמְלֹא חָפְנָיו קְטֹרֶת סַמִּים דַּקָּה — *And his cupped handful of finely ground incense-spices* (16:12).

Rashi, citing the interpretation of the Sages, asks why this verse specifies that the incense of *Yom Kippur* was finely ground, even though all of the incense brought in the *Beis HaMikdash* every day of the year was finely ground. They conclude that the incense for *Yom Kippur* had to be ground exceptionally fine, and was therefore ground again on the day before *Yom Kippur.*

This procedure suggests an interesting symbolism. Every day there were two incense-offerings, one in the morning and one in the afternoon, which atoned for the sin of *lashon hara,* evil speech, a sin people transgress very often.

On *Yom Kippur,* however, when there is a general atonement for all sins, something more is needed. Therefore, exceptionally fine incense must be brought to atone for the more subtle form of *lashon hara,* which is called *avak lashon hara* (literally, the *dust* of *lashon hara*).

Atonement for this sin is especially appropriate on *Yom Kippur,* since *avak lashon hara* is the root of most wrongdoing. Many sins originate when someone says, or even just hints at, derogatory information about someone else. From such a small beginning there can arise the grossest and most despicable forms of behavior.

❧ ❧ ❧

וְסָמַךְ אַהֲרֹן אֶת־שְׁתֵּי יָדָו עַל־רֹאשׁ הַשָּׂעִיר הַחַי
וְהִתְוַדָּה עָלָיו אֶת־כָּל־עֲוֹנֹת בְּנֵי יִשְׂרָאֵל וְאֶת־כָּל־
פִּשְׁעֵיהֶם לְכָל־חַטֹּאתָם וְנָתַן אֹתָם עַל־רֹאשׁ הַשָּׂעִיר
— *Aaron shall lean his two hands upon the*
head of the living he-goat and confess upon it
all the willful sins of the Children of Israel, and
all their rebellious sins among all their errors,
and place them upon the head of the he-goat
(16:21).

The word יָדָו, *his hands,* is written missing a *yud,* as if it were pronounced יָדוֹ, *his hand.* This indicates that in the *Kohen Gadol's* confession over the he-goat, both hands functioned in unison, with a common purpose. What does this mean to us?

The right hand represents sins done knowingly and the left hand represents sins done by mistake. Normally one sins first by mistake, without intending to do so or without knowing that the action was forbidden. However, once one has tasted sin, his will becomes weakened and it becomes easier afterwards for the evil inclination to tempt or trick him into committing willful sins. Then, after he is accustomed to sinning willfully, he no longer considers it important to avoid sin, and will therefore be careless and more likely to commit even unintentional sins.

Thus, the two kinds of sins bolster each other and require a unified confession, symbolized by the *Kohen Gadol's* two hands, functioning as one, in order to effect the needed atonement.

❧ ❧ ❧

כִּי־בַיּוֹם הַזֶּה יְכַפֵּר עֲלֵיכֶם לְטַהֵר אֶתְכֶם מִכֹּל
חַטֹּאתֵיכֶם לִפְנֵי ה' תִּטְהָרוּ: — *For on this day he*
shall atone for you to cleanse you, for all your
sins before HASHEM shall you be cleansed
(16:30).

The Torah specifies that the cleansing from sin, which occurs on Yom Kippur, takes place *before HASHEM.* This is because we do not understand the mechanism by which repentance cleanses someone and grants him forgiveness. Only

Hashem, Who sees into people's hearts and knows that a sincere penitent is actually an entirely new person, can appreciate the cleansing which has taken place. Thus if he slips and sins again, Hashem knows that it was really a new person who has sinned, rather than a confirmed sinner who is adding new transgressions to his already soiled slate.

❧ ❧ ❧

כְּמַעֲשֵׂה אֶרֶץ־מִצְרַיִם אֲשֶׁר יְשַׁבְתֶּם־בָּהּ לֹא תַעֲשׂוּ וּכְמַעֲשֵׂה אֶרֶץ־כְּנַעַן אֲשֶׁר אֲנִי מֵבִיא אֶתְכֶם שָׁמָּה לֹא תַעֲשׂוּ וּבְחֻקֹּתֵיהֶם לֹא תֵלֵכוּ: — *Do not imitate the practice of the land of Egypt in which you dwelled; and do not imitate the practice of the land of Canaan to which I bring you, and do not follow their traditions* (18:3).

It is noteworthy that the Torah says not to imitate the practice of the *land* of Egypt or the *land* of Canaan, rather than cautioning against the practices of the Egyptians or the Canaanites. From this we see that it was the prosperity of the lands themselves that led the inhabitants to their abominable practices. Those who lived in less fertile lands, and therefore had to work harder for their livelihoods, were less likely to go astray. (Before the Jews arrived, the land of Canaan was lush and fruitful, and it remained that way until they were exiled. From then on, Hashem made it barren and desolate, in fulfillment of His earlier warnings.) Thus, this verse is a warning not to be led astray by the fecundity of the land they were about to possess.

❧ ❧ ❧

אֶת־מִשְׁפָּטַי תַּעֲשׂוּ וְאֶת־חֻקֹּתַי תִּשְׁמְרוּ — *Carry out My laws and safeguard My decrees* (18:4).

"Laws" are practices that would be dictated by reason even if they were not commanded by the Torah. "Decrees" are those that are unfathomable by human intelligence. What is the purpose of the decrees, if we are incapable of understanding them?

Perhaps the decrees are a safety feature, to teach us the necessity of unquestioning, trusting obedience to all the laws of the Torah. This is similar to the strictness of military training, in which soldiers are required to comply with many seemingly meaningless and unimportant regulations, such as cutting the hair short or polishing shoes to a high gloss. Even though they may not see the value of such inflexible rules, by being conditioned to follow "decrees" unthinkingly, they will learn to obey serious orders in situations where lives are at stake.

At the end of the *parashah* the Torah says, וּשְׁמַרְתֶּם אֶת־מִשְׁמַרְתִּי לְבִלְתִּי עֲשׂוֹת מֵחֻקּוֹת הַתּוֹעֵבֹת אֲשֶׁר נַעֲשׂוּ לִפְנֵיכֶם, *You shall keep My safeguard not to do any of the abominable traditions that were done before you* (18:30). From our verse we see that מִשְׁמַרְתִּי, *My safeguard*, refers to the חֻקִּים, *decrees*. Thus, if you will keep My safeguard, whose purpose you do not understand, you will not come to do abominations, transgressions of the laws which normal reasoning alone would forbid.

❧ ❧ ❧

פרשת קדשים
Parashas Kedoshim

**אִישׁ אִמּוֹ וְאָבִיו תִּירָאוּ וְאֶת־שַׁבְּתֹתַי תִּשְׁמֹרוּ אֲנִי ה׳
אֱלֹהֵיכֶם:** — *Every man: You shall revere your
mother and father, and you shall observe My
Sabbaths — I am HASHEM your God* (19:3).

Rashi comments that these two commandments were placed
together in the same verse to teach us that if one's parents
tell him to desecrate the Sabbath (or to violate any other
commandment of the Torah), one should not listen to them.

We will suggest another connection between the two commandments in this verse. It is as if Hashem is saying, "Just as you are to
revere your parents because they brought you into the world, so was
I a partner in your birth. You can show your reverence for Me by
keeping My Sabbath, which is a sign that I created the world, and
since you are a part of the world, your observance of the Sabbath will
be a sign that I created you as well."

❧ ❧ ❧

הוֹכֵחַ תּוֹכִיחַ אֶת־עֲמִיתֶךָ — *Reprove your fellow*
(19:17).

In this verse the Torah repeats the word for reproof, *hoche'ach
tochi'ach*. This is a device commonly found in the Torah to
emphasize a point, in this case the requirement to give reproof —
you shall surely reprove. We will suggest, however, that the double
expression implies constant reproof, meaning that before one
reproves someone else, he must first chastise himself repeatedly for

all of his misdeeds, to ensure that his own behavior is above reproach. Only then will he be able to rebuke his friend properly, in a way that will be accepted and make a lasting impression on the recipient.

This principle was exemplified in the person of Aaron the *Kohen*, who was beloved by everyone, even those whom he admonished for their wrongdoings. The Torah testifies that his own behavior was completely correct, as is written (*Malachi* 2:6), בְּשָׁלוֹם וּבְמִישׁוֹר הָלַךְ אִתִּי, *he went with Me in peace and righteouness*, and therefore וְרַבִּים הֵשִׁיב מֵעָוֹן, *he turned back many from sin*. Because his ways were so righteous before Hashem, just by seeing his personal example many sinners were influenced to change their ways for the better. [On this theme, someone told me recently that he had become a *baal teshuvah* through reading the biography of my father, זצ"ל.]

❧ ❧ ❧

לֹא־תִשְׂנָא אֶת־אָחִיךָ בִּלְבָבֶךָ הוֹכֵחַ תּוֹכִיחַ אֶת־עֲמִיתֶךָ וְלֹא־תִשָּׂא עָלָיו חֵטְא: — *Do not hate your brother in your heart; reprove your fellow and do not bear a sin because of him* (19:17).

Why does the Torah include in the same verse the commandment not to hate another Jew secretly and the commandment to give him reproof? We may suggest two possible answers.

One is that when one person reproves another, he sometimes has to speak harshly or engage in arguments to overcome the recipient's natural human tendency to deny that he has done wrong. In the course of doing so, it may often seem that one hates the other. Therefore the Torah commands that, however heated the discussion may become and however harshly one may speak in order to convey his message, in his heart he should not come to hate the other person.

In addition, the Torah is telling us that even though it is a *mitzvah* to reprove someone, one must not offer reproof with hatred in his heart. Such reproof would be given with the intention of degrading its recipient. It will then be a sin instead of a *mitzvah*.

This is why the verse ends with the warning *and do not bear a sin because of him.*

❀ ❀ ❀

לֹא־תִקֹּם וְלֹא־תִטֹּר אֶת־בְּנֵי עַמֶּךָ וְאָהַבְתָּ לְרֵעֲךָ כָּמוֹךָ אֲנִי ה': — *Do not take revenge and do not bear a grudge against the members of your people; you shall love your fellow as yourself — I am* HASHEM (19:18).

The Torah includes these three commandments, which are fundamental to the Torah's approach to human relations, in the same verse in order to make us realize how the first two depend on the third. לֹא־תִקֹּם, *Do not take revenge,* forbids retaliating in any manner against someone who has displeased you. It includes not only attempting to do him harm, but even refusing to do him a favor that you would normally have done, for example, refusing to lend someone a tool because he once refused to make you a similar loan. וְלֹא־תִטֹּר, *and do not bear a grudge,* applies even when no retaliating action is taken. For example, one may not say, "I will lend you the tool you need, even though you refused me when I asked for yours."

If you do not love your fellow, then everything he does to you will make you feel that he has taken advantage of you and will cause you to bear grudges and take revenge.

However, if you love someone, as the Torah requires you to love every Jew, then you will not feel that he has taken advantage of you, but you will understand that he had a good reason for refusing your request. This is analogous to a loved one who is, Heaven forbid, seriously ill, and his family takes care of his needs day and night without feeling burdened. On the contrary, they want only for the person to stay with them forever, in spite of the hardships his care imposes on them.

❀ ❀ ❀

וּבַשָּׁנָה הַחֲמִישִׁת תֹּאכְלוּ אֶת־פִּרְיוֹ לְהוֹסִיף לָכֶם
תְּבוּאָתוֹ אֲנִי ה' אֱלֹהֵיכֶם: — *And in the fifth year
you may eat its fruit — so that it will increase
your crop — I am HASHEM, your God* (19:25).

In this section, the Torah prohibits eating or otherwise benefiting
from *orlah,* any fruit of the first three years after a tree has been
planted. The fruit of the fourth year, which is called *neta revai,*
must be taken to Jerusalem and eaten there in a state of purity.

Then, in our verse, the Torah says that the fruit of the fifth year
and onwards may be eaten normally and it promises that if we
observe the restrictions of *orlah,* we will be blessed with abundant
crops. *Rashi* comments that the verse ends with the words *I am
HASHEM, your God,* to remind us that Hashem can be trusted to
fulfill His promises.

Why would someone need a special assurance on this point? If he
once observed these commandments and thereafter reaped tangible
results of the promise, that in itself would be the best assurance.
Conversely, if he failed to see any positive results, all assurances
would be meaningless to him.

However, it is not always possible to recognize the results of a
special blessing. Even if one's trees seemed to produce abundant
fruit, one might think that they were doing so naturally. It could also
happen that for a year or two one's crops would not be very good,
even though he observed the commandments. Or one might notice
that a neighbor who had not observed the laws of *orlah* also seemed
to have an exceptionally good crop.

In all of these situations, the Torah tells us not to harbor doubts
about Hashem's promises. Even if Hashem's blessings come in ways
that are not clearly obvious, Hashem never fails to keep every
promise that He makes.

❧ ❧ ❧

פרשת אמר
Parashas Emor

וַיֹּאמֶר ה' אֶל־מֹשֶׁה אֱמֹר אֶל־הַכֹּהֲנִים בְּנֵי אַהֲרֹן
וְאָמַרְתָּ אֲלֵהֶם לְנֶפֶשׁ לֹא־יִטַּמָּא בְּעַמָּיו: — **HASHEM**
*said to Moses: Say to the Kohanim, the sons of
Aaron, and tell them: No one may contaminate himself to a [dead] person among his
people* (21:1).

ashi often comments that the word וַיֹּאמֶר, *and he said,*
indicates a soft kind of speech, one which will be easy to
receive, while וַיְדַבֵּר, *and he spoke,* expresses harshness,
such as a rebuke or a command that will be difficult to accept.

The root *emor* appears three times in this verse, in three different
grammatical forms, and the whole *parashah* takes its name from it.
Why does the Torah phrase this set of commandments, which place
severe limitations on the activities of *Kohanim,* in such soft tones?
Wouldn't it be difficult for the *Kohanim* to accept these commandments; and therefore shouldn't Hashem have used the stronger
expression *dabeir?*

The answer is that even though the *Kohanim* were restricted
regarding whom they could marry and in practices of mourning, we
may assume that they were happy to forgo these things in exchange
for the privilege of participating in the Temple service and the right to
eat the holy portions of various offerings. Whatever sacrifices they
had to make in their personal lives were far outweighed by the
spiritual elevation and closeness to Hashem they received in return.

Later, the *parashah* says, וַיְדַבֵּר ה' אֶל־מֹשֶׁה לֵּאמֹר: דַּבֵּר אֶל־אַהֲרֹן לֵאמֹר אִישׁ מִזַּרְעֲךָ לְדֹרֹתָם אֲשֶׁר יִהְיֶה בוֹ מוּם לֹא יִקְרַב לְהַקְרִיב לֶחֶם אֱלֹהָיו: — *HASHEM spoke to Moshe, saying: Speak to Aaron, saying: Any man of your offspring throughout the generations in whom there will be a blemish shall not come near to offer the food of his God* (ibid. 21:16-17). There follows a list of physical defects or conditions which disqualified a *Kohen* from participating in the Temple service or from eating from the holy portions.

Here Hashem uses the harsh expression *dabeir* (speak) because it was hard for those *Kohanim* to withdraw themselves from the closeness to Hashem which these privileges would have brought them, and therefore they needed to be commanded in a stronger language.

To stress this further, Moshe repeats these instructions not only to Aaron and his sons but also to the whole congregation, since the courts might have responsibility to make sure that the *Kohanim* abided by all these restrictions. Here again, Moshe uses the word *dabeir*: וַיְדַבֵּר מֹשֶׁה אֶל־אַהֲרֹן וְאֶל־בָּנָיו וְאֶל־כָּל־בְּנֵי יִשְׂרָאֵל — *Moshe spoke to Aaron and to his sons, and to all the Children of Israel* (ibid. 21:24).

❧ ❧ ❧

. . . אֵלֶּה הֵם מוֹעֲדָי: שֵׁשֶׁת יָמִים תֵּעָשֶׂה מְלָאכָה וּבַיּוֹם הַשְּׁבִיעִי שַׁבַּת שַׁבָּתוֹן מִקְרָא־קֹדֶשׁ — *These are My appointed festivals: For six days labor may be done, and the seventh day is a day of complete rest, a holy convocation* (23:2-3).

Rashi says that the Sabbath is listed together with the festivals in order to teach us that if someone desecrates the festivals, it is as if he desecrated the Sabbath, and if someone upheld the festivals, it is as if he upheld the Sabbath. What does this mean?

The Torah repeats many times that the Sabbath is a sign that Hashem created the world. Similarly, the festivals are testimony that He continues to rule over the world forever, and does not simply allow the world to continue without direction.

Thus, if one observes the Sabbath but not the festivals, he is in effect declaring that Hashem created the world but no longer pays attention to it and leaves it to run automatically. Indeed, such a person must think that since Hashem cannot control the world according to His purposes there was no value in creating it in the first place. In other words, it is as if Hashem did not even create the world, since He has no control over it. Creating such a world is not a show of greatness. This is why *Rashi* says that if someone keeps the Sabbath but not the festivals, it is as if he had not kept even the Sabbath.

By keeping the festivals, however, one asserts not only that Hashem created the world, but also that He continues to rule it and to control every event that occurs. If so, the continued existence of the world becomes a tribute to Hashem's glory, and Creation is shown to have been worthwhile. This is precisely the message of the Sabbath, and thus someone who observes the festivals also fulfills the purpose of the Sabbath, just as *Rashi* said.

This is what the Sages meant by the saying (*Avos* 6:11), *All that the Holy One, Blessed is He, created in His world, He created solely for His glory.* Hashem not only created the world, but by continuing to rule it, He is glorified by His association with it.

❈ ❈ ❈

וּבְקֻצְרְכֶם אֶת־קְצִיר אַרְצְכֶם לֹא־תְכַלֶּה פְּאַת שָׂדְךָ בְּקֻצְרֶךָ וְלֶקֶט קְצִירְךָ לֹא תְלַקֵּט לֶעָנִי וְלַגֵּר תַּעֲזֹב אֹתָם אֲנִי ה' אֱלֹהֵיכֶם: — *When you reap the harvest of your land, you shall not remove completely the corners of your field as you reap and you shall not gather the gleanings of your harvest; for the poor and the proselyte shall you leave them; I am HASHEM, your God* (23:22).

The placement of this verse seems very peculiar. It comes in the middle of the description of the festivals, sandwiched in between Shavuos and Rosh Hashanah, and yet it does not seem to have any connection with them.

However, the Torah had a reason for placing the commandment to leave a portion of the harvest for poor people immediately after the commandment to keep the festival which celebrates the giving of the Torah. The Torah wants to stress to us that one cannot receive the Torah, which is called *Toras Chessed,* the Torah of Kindness, without accepting upon himself the obligation to attend to the needs of the poor.

For the same reason, Purim, which is also a festival of accepting the Torah with joy — as it says (*Esther* 9:27), קִיְּמוּ וְקִבְּל הַיְּהוּדִים, *the Jews upheld [at that time] what they had accepted [previously, at Mount Sinai]* (*Shabbos* 88a) — also carries with it a special commandment to give *matanos la'evyonim*, gifts to the poor.

❧ ❧ ❧

בַּחֹדֶשׁ הַשְּׁבִיעִי בְּאֶחָד לַחֹדֶשׁ יִהְיֶה לָכֶם שַׁבָּתוֹן זִכְרוֹן
תְּרוּעָה מִקְרָא־קֹדֶשׁ: — *In the seventh month, on the first of the month, there shall be a rest day for you, a remembrance of shofar blasts, a holy convocation* (23:24).

In *Parashas Pinchas,* the Torah says simply (*Bamidbar* 29:1), יוֹם תְּרוּעָה יִהְיֶה לָכֶם, *a day of shofar blasts it shall be for you,* while here it says "remembrance of shofar blasts." Why is there this difference between the two verses?

We can say that these two verses refer to two different aspects of the shofar. On the one hand, the shofar that we blow on Rosh Hashanah is a *remembrance* of other shofar blasts: the shofar that was blown at Mount Sinai to call the Jews to accept the Torah (*see Shemos* 19:19), and the great shofar that will be blown to herald the final redemption, may it come soon. The shofar blown on Rosh Hashanah reminds us of the great love Hashem displayed (or will display) for us on these other occasions, and thus it inspires us to repent out of love for Him and awe of His greatness and might.

These motives are not always adequate, however, so the Torah also has to appeal to our fear of Hashem's punishment. This is the purpose of the shofar mentioned in *Parashas Pinchas,* where the Torah describes the offerings to be brought on Rosh Hashanah. These offerings were intended to arouse us to repent by showing us that just as living animals are slaughtered to atone for our sins, so we ourselves deserve the same treatment if we don't repent. In this sense, the shofar blast of Rosh Hashanah is an anguished cry to awaken us to the present reality of the damage which our sinning has caused, and to remind us of the unescapable judgment which awaits us, as the Sages said (*Avos* 4:29), *Against your will you are destined to give an account before the King Who rules over kings, the Holy One, Blessed is He.*

Thus, the *remembrance of shofar blasts* of our verse is just that, a reminder of occasions when a shofar was blown as a sign of Hashem's great love for us. In *Parashas Pinchas*, however, the Torah refers to the shofar blasts sounded every Rosh Hashanah to remind us of the inescapable, pressing need for immediate repentance, while there is still time.

❊ ❊ ❊

וְיִקְחוּ אֵלֶיךָ שֶׁמֶן זַיִת זָךְ כָּתִית לַמָּאוֹר לְהַעֲלֹת נֵר
תָּמִיד: — *They shall take to you clear olive oil, pressed for lighting, to kindle a continual lamp* (24:2).

Baal HaTurim comments that the commandment to press pure olive oil for the Menorah immediately follows the commandments of the festival of Succos to make a comparison between Succos and Chanukah, the festival which commemorates the pure olive oil which burned for eight days in the Menorah.

We may say that this juxtaposition is an allusion to the fact that Chanukah, which was added after the Torah was given, follows Succos in the yearly calendar.

This allusion may be extended even further, however. In the next paragraph, the Torah says וְלָקַחְתָּ סֹלֶת וְאָפִיתָ אֹתָהּ שְׁתֵּים עֶשְׂרֵה חַלּוֹת, *you shall take fine flour and bake it into twelve loaves* (ibid. 24:5). This alludes to the festive meal which we make on Purim, the festival which comes after Chanukah in the calendar. Let us consider the significance of these allusions.

The Torah gave us the festivals to raise us up so that we can serve Hashem on a high spiritual level. As the generations grew weaker in their resolve, however, Hashem in His wisdom decided that we needed two additional festivals to strengthen us even further. This is why we have Chanukah and Purim.

It is worthwhile to note that even though the events which Purim celebrates occurred earlier than the Chanukah story chronologically, the two festivals are reversed in the calendar of the year. In the light of our explanation of why we were given these two festivals, this reversal can be easily understood.

Chanukah commemorates a miracle which occurred in the physical world, the flame which burned for eight days on one day's worth of oil. Thus the purpose of Chanukah is to publicize the fact that Hashem controls nature and conducts it according to His will.

Purim, however, celebrates an even deeper level of Hashem's conduct of the world, His ability to direct even the seemingly "natural" events of the world to accomplish His design, even without performing open miracles. The events of the Purim story can all be explained naturally and logically, and yet the discerning eye can see Hashem's hand in them at every step of the way.

This is why Purim comes last in the cycle of the festivals of the year, because it is the culmination of a twelve-month process, which started with Passover, of raising us to higher levels in our perception of Hashem's sublime might.

❀ ❀ ❀

פרשת בהר
Parashas Behar

וַיְדַבֵּר ה' אֶל־מֹשֶׁה בְּהַר סִינַי לֵאמֹר: דַּבֵּר אֶל־בְּנֵי
יִשְׂרָאֵל וְאָמַרְתָּ אֲלֵהֶם כִּי תָבֹאוּ אֶל־הָאָרֶץ אֲשֶׁר אֲנִי
נֹתֵן לָכֶם וְשָׁבְתָה הָאָרֶץ שַׁבָּת לַה': — *HASHEM*
spoke to Moshe on Mount Sinai, saying:
Speak to the Children of Israel and say to
them: When you come into the land that I give
you, the land shall observe a Sabbath rest for
HASHEM (25:1-3).

The Torah makes a point of mentioning that the commandment of resting the land on the Sabbatical Year was given
on Mount Sinai. Now, we know that all of the commandments were given there, so why does the Torah pick out this one to
stress the place where it was given?

We can say that the Torah wants to point out to us that this
commandment required a clearer faith in Hashem than most of the
others, the kind of faith that was instilled in those who were
privileged to witness the giving of the Torah at Mount Sinai.
Consider what an act of faith it is for a farmer, someone totally
dependent on the land for his food, to forgo planting and tending his
crops for a year.

However, to those who were present when Hashem revealed
Himself in all of His might and glory, such confidence in Hashem's
ability to care for their needs and such devotion to do His will came
easily. The sight of Hashem's Presence was sufficient nourishment
for them, as the Torah says in *Parashas Mishpatim* (*Exodus 24:11*),

וַיֶּחֱזוּ אֶת־הָאֱלֹהִים וַיֹּאכְלוּ וַיִּשְׁתּוּ, *and they beheld HASHEM and they ate and they drank.* Kli Yakar comments that the mere sight of Hashem's radiance sustained them better than food and drink, like Moshe, who spent forty days on the mountain without eating or drinking. Someone who had witnessed that sight, or even heard about it from his forefathers, would find it easier to forgo his normal cycle of planting and harvesting for a year, if that was what Hashem commanded. Therefore, to ensure that the people would keep this commandment, it could only be given at Mount Sinai. And thus the Torah stresses this point.

Similarly, in the time of the prophet Jeremiah, the people slackened their devotion to learning Torah, claiming that they had to devote all their time to their livelihood. Jeremiah showed them the flask of manna that Aaron had preserved for future generations (*Exodus* 16:34), and said, "See the word of Hashem: It is capable of sustaining you just as He sustained your fathers in the wilderness" (see *Tanchuma, Parashas Beshalach* 24).

❈ ❈ ❈

וְהַעֲבַרְתָּ שׁוֹפַר תְּרוּעָה — *You shall sound a teruah blast on the shofar* (25:9).

The *teruah* blast of the shofar was sounded on Yom Kippur at the beginning of the *Yoveil* (the Jubilee year) to proclaim the freedom of slaves and the return of lands to their rightful inheritors. This blast can be interpreted in two different ways.

On the one hand, it reminds us of Hashem's affection for us, since the word תְּרוּעָה, *teruah*, is related to the word רֵעוּת, *rei'us*, (affection). Thus we say in the *Mussaf* of Rosh Hashanah, וּתְרוּעַת מֶלֶךְ בּוֹ, *the affection* [teruah] *of the King is in him* [Israel] (*Bamidbar* 23:21). Secondly, the *teruah* blast of the shofar symbolizes יְבָבָה, the agonized *wailing* that we do on Rosh Hashanah when we think of our sins and the punishment we deserve for them.

Thus the shofar which is blown at the beginning of the *Yoveil* reminds us of the two choices we face. In gratitude for *the affection of the King,* we can crown Hashem with glory by freeing our servants and giving the land back to its inheritors. By doing this, we admit that Hashem is the true owner of the land and and true master of our servants and us as well. If we fail to do so, however, we face the destruction and desolation with which Hashem punishes those who defy Him, and the *wailing* that inevitably follows.

The destruction of the First *Beis HaMikdash* and the desolation of our land are consequences of the failure of earlier generations to observe and respect the Sabbatical and *Yoveil* years (see *Avos* 5:11). Let us hope that by strengthening our resolve to observe these important commandments, we will soon merit to perform them in all of their details, implications and intentions.

❁ ❁ ❁

וְכִי תֹאמְרוּ מַה־נֹּאכַל בַּשָּׁנָה הַשְּׁבִיעִת הֵן לֹא נִזְרָע וְלֹא נֶאֱסֹף אֶת־תְּבוּאָתֵנוּ: וְצִוִּיתִי אֶת־בִּרְכָתִי לָכֶם בַּשָּׁנָה הַשִּׁשִּׁית וְעָשָׂת אֶת־הַתְּבוּאָה לִשְׁלֹשׁ הַשָּׁנִים: — *If you will say: What will we eat in the seventh year? — behold! we will not sow and not gather in our crops! I shall ordain My blessing for you in the sixth year and it will yield a crop sufficient for the three-year period* (25:20-21).

ashi cites the teaching of the Sages that the Babylonian exile lasted for seventy years in punishment for seventy Sabbatical years which the Jews failed to observe when they were on their land. Our verse implies that the produce of the sixth year, the year before the Sabbatical year, was always exceptionally abundant. If this is so, why would anyone ever have reason to plant or harvest during the Sabbatical year? With plenty of food in the storehouses, surely farmers would prefer to have a year's vacation to sit and learn Torah.

In spite of the bountiful crops of the sixth year, however, it still required a high degree of faith to observe the restrictions of the Sabbatical year. It would be very easy to let oneself be led astray into thinking that just as the sixth year was an exceptional one, perhaps the seventh would also be so and enable the farmer to advance from merely making a livelihood to being prosperous. Thus the temptation to plant in the seventh year was very great for those of little faith.

In fact, we can assume that those who planted in the seventh year actually did very well. Thus it required even greater faith to believe that in the long run disobeying Hashem's commandments does not pay off. However attractive the short-term gains may have appeared, temporary profits can disappear more quickly than they came, whereas the reward one receives for observing the commandments, even though it may sometimes seem slow in coming, lasts literally forever.

❦ ❦ ❦

אֶת־כַּסְפְּךָ לֹא־תִתֵּן לוֹ בְּנֶשֶׁךְ וּבְמַרְבִּית לֹא־תִתֵּן אָכְלֶךָ: אֲנִי ה' אֱלֹהֵיכֶם אֲשֶׁר־הוֹצֵאתִי אֶתְכֶם מֵאֶרֶץ מִצְרָיִם — *Do not give him your money at interest, and do not give him your food for increase. I am HASHEM, your God, Who took you out of the land of Egypt* (25:37-38).

Why does the Torah connect the fact that Hashem took us out of Egypt with *ribis*, the prohibition against taking interest? What relation is there between these two topics?

Homiletically, we can say that when Hashem told Abraham that his descendants would suffer exile and enslavement for four hundred years, this became a debt of servitude. However, we did not start to repay the debt, in the literal sense, until the time Jacob went down to Egypt, one hundred and ninety years after the birth of Isaac.

Normally when payment of a debt is postponed, the interest on it accumulates and the total amount owed increases. In our case, however, the Egyptian exile lasted only two hundred ten years, and the period of actual slavery was only one hundred sixteen years, because time was subtracted from the total to compensate for the extremely harsh labor which the Egyptians imposed at the end. Thus we can say that when Hashem took us out of Egypt early, He was doing the opposite of charging us interest, and actually *decreased* the debt.

This, then, is why our verse, which talks about the prohibition against taking interest, reminds us that Hashem took us out of Egypt. Just as Hashem deliberately forgave us the interest we owed

Him and went to the other extreme, so should we be careful never to charge interest.

❦ ❦ ❦

— אֶת־שַׁבְּתֹתַי תִּשְׁמֹרוּ וּמִקְדָּשִׁי תִּירָאוּ אֲנִי ה':
Observe My Sabbaths and revere My Sanctuary — I am HASHEM (26:2).

This verse is an exact repetition of a verse in *Parashas Kedoshim* (19:30). The Torah repeats it because here it refers to something different: The earlier verse refers to the Sabbath and this one to the Sabbatical year.

What is the connection between the Sabbatical year and fearing the Sanctuary? As we noted earlier, the punishment for violating the laws of the Sabbatical year is exile (see *Avos* 5:11). Thus the Torah tells us here that only if we observe the Sabbatical year will we have a Sanctuary to revere. Since we did not, the Sanctuary was destroyed and we were sent into a long and bitter exile.

❦ ❦ ❦

פרשת בחקתי
Parashas Bechukosai

אִם־בְּחֻקֹּתַי תֵּלֵכוּ וְאֶת־מִצְוֹתַי תִּשְׁמְרוּ וַעֲשִׂיתֶם אֹתָם: וְנָתַתִּי גִשְׁמֵיכֶם בְּעִתָּם וְנָתְנָה הָאָרֶץ יְבוּלָהּ וְעֵץ הַשָּׂדֶה יִתֵּן פִּרְיוֹ: — *If you will follow My decrees and observe My ordinances and perform them; then I will provide your rains in their season so that the land will give its produce and the tree of the field will give its fruit* (26:3-4).

In this verse Hashem promises that those who keep His commandments will be rewarded with rains which will make the fields and orchards fruitful. It is noteworthy that He does not promise to cause food to fall directly from the heavens, as He did for forty years in the Wilderness.

This is because Hashem created this world with certain built-in natural laws and processes, and it is His desire that the world proceed in accordance with those processes. Every "miracle" is really an intervention from another world, a deviation from the normal functioning of this one. Such phenomena, while Hashem sometimes deems them necessary, conflict with the purpose of this world, which is to reveal that Hashem controls everything that happens through the laws He created in this world. In this world, Hashem wants to be served according to the laws which He created with it, and not by the laws and processes of some other world. But when people fail to see Hashem's hand in the natural world, it becomes necessary for Him to remind man through miraculous events.

Thus, His promise is to provide for our needs in the terms of *this* world, by causing rain to fall and crops to grow. And it will be to our merit that we do not need a miracle to make us believe that Hashem has paid us.

❧   ❧   ❧

I — וְנָתַתִּי מִשְׁכָּנִי בְּתוֹכְכֶם וְלֹא־תִגְעַל נַפְשִׁי אֶתְכֶם:
will place My Sanctuary among you; and My Spirit will not reject you (26:11).

In most worldly matters, when things do not change we grow tired of them and eventually become disgusted with them. In our relationship with Hashem, however, the opposite is true; when we do what He wants of us, we feel better and better about it, even if it stays the same over a long period of time.

King Solomon said (*Koheles* 1:9), *There is nothing new beneath the sun. Beneath the sun* refers to the normal course of nature. Because there is nothing new, it is very easy to grow tired of the same old unchanging things and to become bitter and unhappy with life. "Above the sun," however, in the world of Torah, there is always change for the better. Someone who devotes himself seriously to acquiring Torah will always be learning and growing; it is so stimulating that it never seems old or boring. (This applies even to those who have only limited time available for Torah study, as long as they make a serious effort to make proper use of whatever time they have.)

Thus, Hashem promises those who go in His ways and keep His laws that His relationship with them will always remain fertile and fresh and never grow old and stale so that He would want to reject them.

❧   ❧   ❧

וְרָדַף אֹתָם קוֹל עָלֶה נִדָּף וְנָסוּ מְנֻסַת־חֶרֶב וְנָפְלוּ וְאֵין
רֹדֵף: — *The sound of a rustling leaf will pursue them, they will flee as one flees the sword, and they will fall, but without a pursuer* (26:36).

The surface meaning of this verse is itself terrifying—Hashem warns the Jews that if they ignore His commandments, they will become so fearful that even the slightest noise will frighten them into running away as if someone with a sword were chasing them.

Allegorically, however, we can say that the verse describes another kind of fear. The "rustling leaves" represent oppressed peoples, those who are flimsy, like leaves, so that even the slightest stirring of the wind makes them fall. The voice of their cries will arouse our sympathies, because we know that we are never far from being persecuted ourselves. Once oppression sets in, we must expect it eventually to reach us. Thus the Talmud states that when there are signs of uneasiness in the world, we must be apprehensive that the signs point to us (*Succah* 29a).

❧ ❧ ❧

וְזָכַרְתִּי אֶת־בְּרִיתִי יַעֲקוֹב וְאַף אֶת־בְּרִיתִי יִצְחָק וְאַף אֶת־בְּרִיתִי אַבְרָהָם אֶזְכֹּר וְהָאָרֶץ אֶזְכֹּר: — *I will remember My covenant with Jacob and also My covenant with Isaac, and also My covenant with Abraham will I remember, and I will remember the land* (26:42).

My covenant with Jacob refers to the covenant of Torah; Hashem will redeem the Jews if they occupy themselves with Torah. *My covenant with Isaac* refers to the covenant of service, that the Jews should perform the commandments and bring the prescribed offerings in the Sanctuary (or, at a time when there is no Sanctuary, recite their required prayers with appropriate concentration). *My covenant with Abraham* refers to the covenant of kind deeds, the quality with which Abraham distinguished himself.

The Sages taught that the phrase, אֶת הַבְּרִית וְאֶת הַחֶסֶד, *the covenant and the kindness,* tells us that Hashem made a covenant with Abraham that his descendants would always have a kind and generous nature (*Yerushalmi Kiddushin* 1:5).

In other words, this verse is a promise by Hashem that however far the Jews stray from the Torah and *mitzvos,* He will remember the covenants which He made with their forefathers and not destroy them completely. Rather, He will always leave them an opportunity to return to Him and to fulfill His covenant in each of the three areas.

What is the signficance of Hashem's promise to remember the land also? *Eretz Yisrael* is the place where the service of Hashem can take place in its purest form, in all three aspects of the covenant. Therefore, whenever Hashem remembers the covenant, He must remember the land as well. Because Hashem remembers that *Eretz Yisrael* is where the Jews were meant to keep these covenants, He will return us to our land so that we can serve Him fully.

❊ ❊ ❊

וְזָכַרְתִּי אֶת־בְּרִיתִי יַעֲקוֹב — *I will remember My covenant with Jacob* (26:42).

In this verse, the word יַעֲקוֹב (Jacob) is written with a *vav. Rashi* points out that this spelling occurs only five times in *Tanach,* corresponding to five times in which the word אֵלִיָּה(וּ) (Elijah) is written without a *vav.* This hints that Jacob took a letter from Elijah's name as a "collateral," so that Elijah would be sure to come and herald the redemption of Jacob's descendants. Why was this Divine promise indicated with a *vav* and not some other letter?

The word *vav* means a connecting hook, as the Torah tells us that the curtains of the *Mishkan* were attached by וָוִים, *hooks,* to the poles that supported them. In terms of the Jewish people, a *vav* symbolizes unity, because the present exile was caused by hatred and dissension, and it cannot be ended until we become united.

It is well known that Elijah will announce the end of the exile, but he will serve another function as well. The last Mishnah in *Eduyos* teaches that Elijah will come to bring peace among Jews. This is why Hashem specifically took a *vav* from Elijah's name, as if to symbolize that he should hurry to reunite the people of Israel and thereby end our exile.

❊ ❊ ❊

ספר במדבר

Sefer Bamidbar

פרשת במדבר
Parashas Bamidbar

שְׂאוּ אֶת־רֹאשׁ כָּל־עֲדַת בְּנֵי־יִשְׂרָאֵל לְמִשְׁפְּחֹתָם לְבֵית אֲבֹתָם בְּמִסְפַּר שֵׁמוֹת כָּל־זָכָר לְגֻלְגְּלֹתָם: — *Count the heads of all the congregation of the Children of Israel by their families, by the houses of their fathers, by the number of names of all males, as a head count* (1:2).

The expression שְׂאוּ אֶת רֹאשׁ literally means *raise the heads*. Thus we see from this verse the fundamental importance that Judaism attaches to each and every individual. The purpose of the census was to "raise" the people by stressing their importance. We see this from the very fact that Hashem commanded Moshe to count the Jews; He would not have caused Moshe all that trouble and effort unless it was important to know exactly how many Jews there were. There would have been no need to count if one person more or less, or even ten or a hundred more or less, were not important.

Similarly, if they had needed to have only a quorum of 600,000 to attain the required degree of holiness, then there would have been no need to record an exact count for each tribe separately. But the totals were not rounded off at all, as we see from the count for the tribe of Gad (45,650). If the Torah had rounded off the figure, it would have been written as a multiple of one hundred. Thus we see that each Jew has value not only as a component of a group, but also as an individual.

This concept also finds expression in other areas of Torah. On the one hand, large masses of people have great importance, as King

Solomon said (*Mishlei* 14:28), *The King is glorified by a multitude of people.* At the same time, however, there is a rule in *halachah* that anything worthy of being counted cannot be nullified, even if it is outnumbered a thousand to one (see *Beitzah* 3b). Thus we see that each individual is valued as a member of a group, but not at the expense of infringing on his personal rights.

❧ ❧ ❧

— וְאֵלֶּה שְׁמוֹת הָאֲנָשִׁים אֲשֶׁר יַעַמְדוּ אִתְּכֶם . . .
And these are the names of the men who will stand with you . . . (1:5).

Why does the Torah specify that these are the *names of the men?* It should have been sufficient to say, *these are the men,* followed by a list of names.

We can say that the Torah wants to draw our attention to the *names* because they reveal the qualifications which made these men suitable to fill the position of *nassi*, or prince. For example, the *nassi* of the tribe of Reuben was named אֱלִיצוּר (Elitzur, *My God is a rock*) בֶּן שְׁדֵיאוּר (the son of Sh'deur, *the Almighty* is a *light*). Most of the other names have similarly significant meanings, suggesting that these men were gifted with exceptional powers to instill knowledge of Hashem's greatness in their people.

❧ ❧ ❧

אִישׁ עַל־דִּגְלוֹ בְאֹתֹת לְבֵית אֲבֹתָם — *Each one by its standard with signs according to their fathers' houses* (2:2).

The flag of each tribe had a design which indicated the nature of the tribe. For example, on the flag of Judah was depicted a lion, the king of the animals, because the royal house of David was descended from him. Similarly, the flag of Issachar showed the sun, moon, and stars, symbolizing their role as heads of the Sanhedrin who made the astronomical calculations on which the calender was based. On Zevulun's flag was a ship, symbolizing their occupation as seafaring businessmen, which enabled them to support the Torah study of the tribe of Issachar.

We know that in exchange for their material support of Issachar, the tribe of Zevulun shared fully in Issachar's merit for studying Torah. If so, with all of this great merit, why were they not worthy to have an easier and less hazardous occupation, which would not require them to venture so far from home?

The Sages say (*Kiddushin 82a*) that sailors tend to be very devout people. Because they do such perilous work, they are continually reminded that their lives are totally in Hashem's hands, and therefore they pray to Him constantly to keep them safe. Of course, even someone who lives in a fortress with all the safeguards in the world is no less dependent on Hashem for his safety, but such a person has fewer reminders of this fact than those who live "dangerous" lives.

As a result, sailors have a much stronger appreciation of the value of Torah, which is one of the reasons why the tribe of Zevulun was so generous in its support of Issachar. Had Zevulun had an easier and safer occupation, they may have come to feel that their wealth was the fruit of their "strength and might of their hands," and been less willing to utilize it to find favor in Hashem's eyes. Thus, Zevulun's difficult livelihood added to the great merit they had in supporting the Torah of Issachar. For this reason, Jacob blessed Zevulun with an occupation that would take him to the sea, in order to increase his recognition of Hashem's constant protection so that his faith would grow and his merit would increase.

❀ ❀ ❀

וַיָּמֶת נָדָב וַאֲבִיהוּא לִפְנֵי ה' בְּהַקְרִבָם אֵשׁ זָרָה לִפְנֵי ה'
בְּמִדְבַּר סִינַי — *And Nadav and Avihu died before HASHEM when they offered an alien fire before HASHEM in the wilderness of Sinai* (3:4).

The Torah tells us that Nadav and Avihu, the sons of Aaron, died *before Hashem*, which means that only Hashem knew why they died. If so, the mere fact that they had brought the "alien fire" was not sufficient reason to cause their death.

The reason is that the two young *Kohanim* had spoken against Moshe and Aaron: "When will these two old men die so that we can take over leadership of the generation?" (*Sanhedrin 52a*). This shows that they felt they could relate more effectively than their elders to the needs and the thinking of the younger generation.

In punishment, Hashem brought about their deaths in a manner and for a reason that everyone could see and understand, the offering of the alien fire, which represented a new and unauthorized form of service. There was poetic justice in this, in that their subversive outlook was truly an אֵשׁ זָרָה, *alien fire*, in contrast to the אֵשׁ דָּת, *fire of religion* (*Devarim* 33:2), with which Moshe kindled the soul of the people until his very last day.

❦ ❦ ❦

וּבָנִים לֹא־הָיוּ לָהֶם — *And they did not have children* (3:4).

The Sages reasoned from these words that if Nadav and Avihu had had children they would not have died (*Yevamos* 64a). How can we understand this? If they had committed a sin worthy of the death penalty, why would their family status have made a difference in their punishment?

It is obvious that when someone is punished with death, his family also suffers. Even though Nadav and Avihu were worthy of the death penalty, perhaps Hashem would have considered it unjust that their children be left orphans and might have spared Nadav and Avihu on that account.

An implication of this is that one should try to form as many connections as possible in his life: children, students, friends, associates and so on. There might come a time when he could be spared from a punishment that had been decreed against him because others would suffer unfairly if the decree were carried out.

This is the meaning of the verse (*Iyov* 33:23), אִם־יֵשׁ עָלָיו מַלְאָךְ מֵלִיץ אֶחָד מִנִּי־אָלֶף לְהַגִּיד לְאָדָם יָשְׁרוֹ, *even if one angel out of a thousand were to testify to one's good deeds,* then he will be saved (*Iyov* 33:23). The more numerous the people who are dependent upon an individual, the more likely it is that the scales of justice will be tipped in his favor by the harm they would suffer if he were to die.

❦ ❦ ❦

פרשת נשא
Parashas Naso

נָשֹׂא אֶת־רֹאשׁ בְּנֵי גֵרְשׁוֹן גַּם־הֵם — *Count the heads of the sons of Gershon, them too* (4:22).

At the end of the previous *parashah* we find a similar command, נָשֹׂא אֶת־רֹאשׁ בְּנֵי קְהָת מִתּוֹךְ בְּנֵי לֵוִי, *Count the heads of the sons of Kehath among the sons of Levi* (4:2). The same expression is used in both verses, נָשֹׂא אֶת־רֹאשׁ, literally *raise up the head,* but this term is not used in connection with the family of Merari. This implies that only the families of Kehath and Gershon enjoyed an elevated status, but not that of Merari.

The hierarchy of the families is indicated by the tasks assigned to them. The family of Kehath had higher status than the other Levites, since they were charged with carrying the most sacred furnishings and implements of the Tent of Meeting. Next came Gershon, who carried the drapings with which the Tabernacle was covered and the curtains that formed the walls of the Courtyard. Finally, Merari carried the walls and pillars of the Tabernacle.

Since each family had responsibilities involving differing degrees of holiness, we may assume that Merari was not allowed to perform the functions of Gershon, and Gershon was not allowed to perform the functions of Kehath, because each was not elevated to the status of the next one. We may assume that the reverse was also true, that a Kehath who did the work of a Gershon was punished for doing a job other than the one he was given. In the same way, an officer in the army who does the work of a private may be punished for demeaning the status of his rank.

Similarly, in the Holy Temple, the Levites were divided into two groups: the gatekeepers, who were of lower status, and those who mounted the platform and sang during the Temple service. A singer who functioned as a gatekeeper was liable to the death penalty, because he had not been assigned to that station.

We learn from this that one should be happy with his station in life. It is wrong to presume to a higher level than the one for which one is qualified. Similarly, one should not degrade himself by seeking a position lower than that for which he is fit. Although one should always aspire to improve himself, this should not be at the cost of usurping a position to which he is not entitled. Thus we find that Rabban Shimon ben Gamliel told Rabbi Nosson that even though Rabbi Nosson was worthy to be the head of the Sanhedrin, he should not aspire to be prince of the nation (*Horayos* 13b).

❧ ❧ ❧

וְהִתְוַדּוּ אֶת־חַטָּאתָם אֲשֶׁר עָשׂוּ וְהֵשִׁיב אֶת־אֲשָׁמוֹ —
They shall confess their sin which they committed and he shall restore his wrong (5:7).

Rashi explains that this section refers to someone who was suspected of theft and takes a false oath to clear himself and then decides to repent and make restitution. We may ask, however, why is there a sudden switch from the plural form to the singular: *They* shall confess *their* sin which *they* committed and *he* shall restore *his* wrong?

The following ruling of the Talmud explains this switch: When someone takes a false oath, his accuser is also considered at fault for bringing about a situation in which someone was tempted to swear falsely (*Shavuos* 39b). Thus, *they,* both the accuser and the accused, should confess to their roles in causing a situation which led to a false oath, and then *he,* the thief, is responsible for righting *his* wrong by paying for what *he* stole.

❧ ❧ ❧

אִישׁ אוֹ־אִשָּׁה כִּי יַפְלִא לִנְדֹּר נֶדֶר נָזִיר לְהַזִּיר לַה':
A man or a woman who will separate himself to make a vow, to become a nazir to HASHEM (6:2).

Th*e Targum Onkelos* gives the Aramaic translation: אֲרֵי יְפָרֵשׁ, which can be understood to mean *when he shall state explicitly.* In other words, someone who wishes to make his vow of *nazirus* binding must phrase the vow explicitly enough to preclude any loopholes. He must obligate himself unequivocally to become a *nazir.*

If, however, there is a loophole, one should take advantage of it to have a court nullify his vow and free him of his obligation as a *nazir.* The Torah prefers that people not add restrictions upon themselves that the Torah does not require.

❦ ❦ ❦

יְבָרֶכְךָ ה' וְיִשְׁמְרֶךָ: — *May* HASHEM *bless you and protect you* (6:24).

Ra*shi* comments that the *blessing* in this verse is a monetary one: May you be blessed with prosperity.

Then, because you have been blessed with property, you will need a special blessing to be *protected,* because property very often brings harm to those who have it. *Rashi* mentions the danger of theft, but we may add to this the very real dangers that wealth poses to the spiritual well-being of those who possess it, such as temptations to indulge in forbidden pleasures and the like. Someone whose property is blessed needs an extra blessing for protection from all of these dangers.

❦ ❦ ❦

וְלִבְנֵי קְהָת לֹא נָתָן . . . בַּכָּתֵף יִשָּׂאוּ: — *And to the children of Kehath he did not give [wagons] . . . on the shoulder shall they carry* (7:9).

Th*e phrase* בַּכָּתֵף יִשָּׂאוּ, *on the shoulder shall they carry,* is grammatically ambiguous. It could equally be translated *they shall be carried by the shoulder.*

To understand what this might mean, let us recall something which we learned in *Parashas Terumah,* that the Ark, with its golden castings and the golden cover and Cherubim, weighed on the order of eight tons, apart from the stone Tablets which it contained. Obviously if four Levites were able to carry it, they must have had a substantial measure of Divine assistance.

We may assume that Hashem made it obvious to anyone who saw them carrying the Ark that a miracle was taking place. They would have borne the Ark lightly and moved more quickly than usual. In a very real sense, therefore, the sons of Kehath who carried the Ark were themselves actually being carried by the "burden" on their shoulders.

❧ ❧ ❧

פרשת בהעלתך
Parashas Beha'alosecha

— אֶל־מוּל פְּנֵי הַמְּנוֹרָה יָאִירוּ שִׁבְעַת הַנֵּרוֹת:
Towards the front of the Menorah shall the seven flames cast light (8:2).

Rashi comments that the wicks of the six outer lamps, three on the eastern side and three on the western side, were pointed towards the central lamp. The wick of the central lamp, in turn, was pointed to the west, towards the Holy Ark. What was the significance of this arrangement?

The Menorah represents חָכְמָה, *wisdom,* and the seven lamps of the Menorah symbolize the seven branches of wisdom. The fact that the six outer lights were directed toward the central one, which was in turn directed toward the point where Hashem's Presence rested in the Tabernacle, teaches that all the different forms of wisdom in the world have to be directed towards the service of Hashem. All areas of study — science, mathematics, history, law — have no independent value except to enable us to understand the Torah and know how better to perform *mitzvos.*

Mathematics, for example, should not be studied for its own sake, but only to provide us with useful tools with which to serve Hashem. In order to observe the Torah, one must know how to measure certain quantities exactly, or how to make the computations required to establish the Jewish calendar. One could easily supply similar examples from a variety of other areas of knowledge.

The beginning of the following verse can be understood in the same light: וַיַּעַשׂ כֵּן אַהֲרֹן, *And Aaron did so.* On an elementary level, this means that Aaron arranged the lamps of the Menorah in the fashion that Hashem commanded. However, these words can also mean that Aaron epitomized this ideal. He approached all of the different forms of knowledge and wisdom not as having any intrinsic interest in themselves, but rather as tools to further his service of Hashem.

Similarly, this interpretation explains why the description of the Menorah is repeated once again. By emphasizing that it was made entirely from one piece of beaten gold, the Torah stresses that, like the Menorah, wisdom should not consist of separate, unrelated branches. Rather, one's knowledge should be a cohesive unit, directed entirely toward the service of Hashem.

❦ ❦ ❦

קַח אֶת־הַלְוִיִּם מִתּוֹךְ בְּנֵי יִשְׂרָאֵל וְטִהַרְתָּ אֹתָם: —
Take the Levites from among the Children of Israel and purify them (8:6).

This verse introduces Hashem's instructions to Moshe to prepare the tribe of Levi for their service in the Tabernacle. It is noteworthy that these procedures were not an *atonement* for wrongdoing, but a *purification*. To understand the distinction, let us remember why the Levites were chosen for their special role.

After the sin of the Golden Calf, only the Levites responded to Moshe's call, *Whoever is for HASHEM, join me!* They passed through the camp and killed all those who had worshiped the idol, including blood relatives. Nonetheless, until Moshe's appeal, they had watched passively while the people strayed after the Golden Calf. Therefore they required purification, but not atonement, since their sin was one of inaction.

Another reason they required purification is the need to suspect that some of the killing may have been tainted by slightly impure motives. Had they killed only family members, it would have been clear to everyone that their desire was solely to avenge the affront to Hashem's honor, since no other motive would overcome their family loyalty. However, because they killed other people as well, they would have had to examine their motives very carefully to rule out the possibility that their zealousness may have been tinged with other motives, such as personal vengeance, anger, or blood lust. Thus even though their actions were in themselves meritorious, since they fulfilled Hashem's will, they were still not free of inner suspicion, and therefore required purification.

❦ ❦ ❦

עַל־מַצּוֹת וּמְרֹרִים יֹאכְלֻהוּ: – *On matzos and marror shall they eat it* (9:11).

Hashem commanded that those who were unable to bring the Pesach Offering on the day before Passover should make up for it by bringing a replacement offering one month later, on the fourteenth of Iyar. This substitute was called *Pesach Sheni*, the Second Pesach Offering. Thus, someone who was too far away to come to Jerusalem or who was unable to eat the Pesach Offering because he was ritually contaminated had a second opportunity to fulfill this *mitzvah*.

Our verse informs us that the *Pesach Sheni* had to be eaten with *matzos* and *marror*. This is difficult to understand: *Chametz* (leavened bread) was allowed to be eaten on that day, even by those who were bringing the *Pesach Sheni,* and surely the person bringing the offering had already eaten *matzah* and *marror* on the first Passover. Why was he required to eat them now a second time?

The word *Pesach* (Passover) means to skip over, because Hashem mercifully skipped over Jewish houses when He killed the firstborn Egyptians on the night of the first Passover. At that time, the Accuser in the Heavenly Court asked Hashem why the Jews were more worthy of being spared than the Egyptians, since both groups had committed idolatry.

Hashem answered that the Jews were still not *chametz*. (Literally this word means *sour,* but it is commonly used to refer to leavened bread or other grain products which have risen until the dough starts to sour.) However much they might have sinned, the spark of the Jewish soul still burned within them. Even though they had descended to the forty-ninth level of impurity, they still had not fallen to the fiftieth level (beyond which the Jewish people can never be redeemed), and therefore there was still hope for them.

Like the regular Pesach Offering, the *Pesach Sheni* commemorates that night when Hashem passed over the houses of the Jews and struck only the Egyptian firstborn. Therefore, it too must be eaten with *matzah,* in order to remind us that we were saved on that night only because we had not become *chametz,* and still retained the essence of the pure Jewish soul.

Similarly, the *Pesach Sheni* has to be eaten with *marror* because Hashem wanted it to remind us of the bitterness of the Egyptian servitude. This reminder will serve to keep us on Hashem's path so that we will never be sent back to a modern-day Egypt, or be tempted to turn back ourselves—and therefore we are worthy to be spared from renewed suffering.

❊ ❊ ❊

וַיֹּאמֶר אַל־נָא תַּעֲזֹב אֹתָנוּ כִּי עַל־כֵּן יָדַעְתָּ חֲנֹתֵנוּ בַּמִּדְבָּר — *And he said: "Please do not leave us inasmuch as you know our encampment in the desert"* (10:31).

As the Jews prepared to depart from their encampment at Mount Sinai, where they had remained for nearly a year following their acceptance of the Torah, Moshe invited his father-in-law Yisro to accompany them and join the congregation. Yisro answered that he would not go with them because he wanted to return to his land and his birthplace. It was at that point that Moshe, in an attempt to persuade him to stay, spoke the above words.

The expression כִּי עַל־כֵּן literally means *for because of this* (see our commentary on this expression in *Parashas Vayeira*). Moshe was telling Yisro that the purpose of his being shown the glory of the Jewish encampment, with all of the wonders and miracles that had been done for Israel, was to give him an impetus to convert to Judaism. It would disappoint Hashem if he failed to embrace the Torah, whose beauty he had seen not only theoretically but also in practice.

The Talmud (*Berachos* 17b) relates several stories of communities that were exposed to the beauty of Torah and were called foolish because they did not produce any converts. Similarly, Moshe argued to Yisro that he should become a Jew because Hashem had shown him the glories of Torah only to inspire him to convert. If he failed to respond, Hashem might be disappointed.

❧ ❧ ❧

וְאָצַלְתִּי מִן־הָרוּחַ אֲשֶׁר עָלֶיךָ וְשַׂמְתִּי עֲלֵיהֶם וְנָשְׂאוּ אִתְּךָ בְּמַשָּׂא הָעָם — *And I will take from the spirit which is on you and place it on them, and they shall bear with you the burden of the people* (11:17).

After hearing the grievances of the people concerning the manna, Moshe told Hashem that the burden of leading the people was too heavy for him to bear alone. Hashem answered by ordering Moshe to choose seventy of the elders of the congregation who would share in the leadership. In our verse, Hashem promised to give them the greatness of spirit which they will need to help lead the people.

In explaining the word וְאָצַלְתִּי, *Rashi* cites the Aramaic translation of *Onkelos, and I will make them great from the spirit which is on you,* meaning that Moshe's spirit will make the others great. How would this help Moshe? If his spirit was not strong enough for him to bear the people, how would sharing his spirit with others create additional strength?

Rashi provides an eloquent image to answer this question. Moshe, he says, was like a candle. No matter how many candles are lit from it, its own light is not diminished. In other words, Hashem intended to use Moshe's greatness of spirit to kindle the spirits of the elders; he would remain unchanged, but the others would grow from their exposure to him. Together they would be able to bear the burdens of the people.

This concept suggests an important principle in education: A teacher cannot give abilities to a student as such; rather, his objective must be to arouse the potential which is latent in the student and to channel it toward desirable goals.

❧ ❧ ❧

פרשת שלח
Parashas Shelach

שְׁלַח־לְךָ אֲנָשִׁים — *Send men for yourself* (13:2).

At the beginning of *Parashas Lech Lecha* (*Bereishis* 12:1), *Rashi* comments that the word לְךָ means *for your benefit.* When Hashem told Abraham to go to another land, it was for his benefit, because his life would improve in the new place.

Perhaps we can apply this interpretation to the same word in our verse. Yet, how was the mission of the spies to Moshe's benefit since, after all, the result was that the people had to dwell in the desert for an extra forty years?

At the end of *Parashas Shemos* (6:1), *Rashi* says that Hashem had already decreed that Moshe could not enter the land, in punishment for his complaint, "Why did You do bad to this people?" Thus, as soon as the people were ready to enter the land, Moshe would have to die. Had it not been for the bad report of the spies, Moshe would have died then, at the age of eighty-one. It was obviously to his benefit to remain alive for thirty-nine more years.

It might be objected that Moshe would have preferred not to send the spies, thereby protecting the Jews from their rebellion, so that they could have entered the land immediately, even if this cost him years of his life. In the long run, however, this would only have made matters worse for the people. At that time, the Jews had not yet fully absorbed the lesson that Hashem demanded strict and uncompromising obedience to His commandments. Their will to rebel was still strong and, if they had entered *Eretz Yisrael* then, they would have rebelled there in some way. Since the land does not easily forgive those who sin in it, their punishment would have been far greater than it was in the Wilderness.

Because the nation was not sufficiently sophisticated, and because one year of preparation was inadequate to make them ready for a life of Torah and *mitzvos* in *Eretz Yisrael,* they needed the additional thirty-nine years in the hands of a teacher of Moshe's caliber to acquire a thorough grounding, a training which would last them for ever.

❈   ❈   ❈

וְאֵלֶּה שְׁמוֹתָם לְמַטֵּה רְאוּבֵן שַׁמּוּעַ בֶּן־זַכּוּר: — *And these are their names: for the tribe of Reuben, Shamua ben Zakur* (13:4).

At the beginning of *Parashas Bamidbar,* we said that the names of the *nesi'im* revealed personal qualities that made those men suitable for their positions. Here also, in the names of the men whom Moshe chose to be spies, we should be able to find hints of their special capabilities.

Thus the name Shamua suggests that he was a good listener and could be expected to listen to Hashem's commandments. His father's name, Zakur, indicates memory, that he would remember Hashem no matter what happened to him.

If so, why did he sin? King Solomon said, *A fool believes everything (Mishlei* 14:15). Unfortunately, Shamua listened too well to his evil inclination and not well enough to Hashem. Likewise, the spies evoked the wrong memories in the people, as we see from their complaints in *Parashas Beha'alosecha (Bamidbar* 11:5), *We remember the fish which we ate in Egypt for free, and the squash and the melon and the leeks and the onions and the garlic.*

Moshe tried to screen the spies by selecting men with desirable qualities, as revealed by their names. Unfortunately, the men he chose diverted their good qualities to bad purposes.

❈   ❈   ❈

וַיִּקְרָא מֹשֶׁה לְהוֹשֵׁעַ בִּן־נוּן יְהוֹשֻׁעַ: — *And Moshe called Hoshea bin Nun Yehoshua* (13:16).

R ashi explains that Moshe wanted Joshua's name to start with Hashem's Two-Letter Name, so that it would protect him from being sucked into the wicked counsel of the spies.

After the battle with Amalek in *Parashas Beshalach,* Hashem told Moshe, *Write this as a memorial in a book and place it in Joshua's ears, for I will surely eradicate the memory of Amalek from under the heavens* (*Shemos* 17:14). Then Hashem said, **כִּי יָד עַל כֵּס יָ־הּ**, *for it is a monument on the throne of God, the war of HASHEM with Amalek in every generation* (ibid. v. 16). The word **כֵּס**, *throne,* is an abbreviated form of **כִּסֵּא**; and the verse uses the Two-Letter instead of the Four-Letter Name. The Sages interpreted this as an oath—Hashem swore that His throne and His Name would not be complete until the memory of Amalek is erased from under the heavens.

This promise, to destroy the memory of Amalek, was especially relevant to Joshua, since he was the one who would bring the Jews into *Eretz Yisrael* and preside over the distribution of the land to them. Thus he was in the best position to ensure that Hashem's oath would be remembered and to transmit the *mitzvah* of destroying Amalek.

This is why Moshe changed Joshua's name to include an allusion to Hashem's Two-Letter Name, **יָ־הּ**. If Hashem would bring this name to mind every time He thought of Joshua, He would spare Joshua from the punishment of the other spies so that he, Joshua, could bring the Jews to *Eretz Yisrael.* Only in the Holy Land could they complete the total eradication of Amalek, which Hashem had sworn was a necessary precondition to making His Name complete in the world. In effect, therefore, Moshe was saying to Hashem, "If You want Your Name not to be two letters, save Joshua so that he can bring the people to *Eretz Yisrael* and destroy Amalek."

❈ ❈ ❈

וַיֵּלְכוּ וַיָּבֹאוּ אֶל־מֹשֶׁה וְאֶל־אַהֲרֹן — *And they went and came to Moshe and to Aaron . . .* (13:26).

T his verse comes when the spies were returning from Canaan to report to Moshe and the people. If so, why does it include the word וַיֵּלְכוּ, *and they went*? It would have been sufficient to say וַיָּבֹאוּ, *and they came.*

Through this seemingly unnecessary word, the Torah may wish to imply that from the time the spies first went on their mission, they planned to return with an unfavorable report. As *Rashi* explains, they left with the same evil intention with which they returned. Accordingly, they looked at the negative side of everything they saw and sought out ways to buttress the gloomy description that they had already decided on.

❀ ❀ ❀

אֲנִי ה' אֱלֹהֵיכֶם אֲשֶׁר הוֹצֵאתִי אֶתְכֶם מֵאֶרֶץ מִצְרַיִם — *I am HASHEM, your God, Who brought you out of the land of Egypt* (15:41).

W hy does the Torah choose the *parashah* of *tzitzis* to remind us that Hashem took us out of Egypt? What is the connection between the Exodus and *tzitzis*?

A few verses earlier, the Torah says that looking at *tzitzis* will protect us from straying after our hearts and our eyes. This is a warning not to be like the spies, who were led astray by the desires of their hearts. Instead, says Hashem, we should learn from His behavior in taking us out of Egypt. If He had not remembered His commitment to the Fathers, our unworthiness at the time would have given Him many excuses to follow the urgings of His heart, as it were, to leave us there. It was only by suppressing the natural inclination of His heart that He was able to free us and give us His Torah.

❀ ❀ ❀

פרשת קרח
Parashas Korach

. . . וַיִּקַּח קֹרַח — *And Korach took . . .* (16:1).

The Torah says that Korach took something, but does not tell us what he took. Many commentators over the centuries have dealt with this question, but we will suggest a new approach.

The truth is that Korach took everything for himself. Hashem entrusted him with great wealth to use for His service, and Korach made the mistake of thinking that he had earned it himself. He treated it as if it belonged to him and he could do with it as he pleased. Thus, Korach's very wealth, in other words, his trait of always taking, was his downfall.

King Solomon had just such a situation in mind when he wrote in *Koheles* (5:12), *Wealth is held for its owners* [i.e., for those who feel that it is theirs] *to harm them.*

On the other hand, a wealthy person — who acknowledges that his money really belongs to Hashem and regards himself as nothing more than the administrator of a trust fund — will find his wealth to be a true blessing. If he diligently and faithfully oversees the fund which has been entrusted to him, in accordance with all the wishes and instructions of its true Owner, then he can be assured of a handsome reward in this world and in the next.

❧ ❧ ❧

לָכֵן אַתָּה וְכָל־עֲדָתְךָ הַנֹּעָדִים עַל־ה' וְאַהֲרֹן מַה־הוּא כִּי תַלִּינוּ עָלָיו׃ — *Therefore, you and all of your congregation are assembling against HASHEM. But Aaron! — what is he that you should complain against him?* (16:11).

Moshe told Korach and his co-conspirators that their accusation — that Aaron aspired to be *Kohen Gadol* and asked Hashem for that position — was wrong. Aaron was only מַה, *nothing at all,* because that is how he thought of himself. On his own, he would never think himself worthy of being the *Kohen Gadol.*

Moshe made the same point earlier, when the Jews complained about the lack of food after the matzah they had brought from Egypt ran out and before the manna started to fall. There, in *Parashas Beshalach,* he said, *What are we? Your complaints are not against us but rather against HASHEM* (*Shemos* 16:7). Moshe and Aaron did not believe themselves to be of any worth because everything they did was directly ordered by Hashem. Indeed, the Sages teach that the humility of Moshe and Aaron, who described themselves as nothing, was even greater than that of Abraham, who spoke of himself as dust and ash (*Chullin* 89a).

❦ ❦ ❦

הָאִישׁ אֶחָד יֶחֱטָא וְעַל כָּל־הָעֵדָה תִּקְצֹף׃ — *If one person sins, will You be angry with the whole congregation?* (16:22).

Let us examine closely Hashem's charge against the congregation and Moshe and Aaron's plea in their defense. Korach and a handful of men had protested against what they saw as Aaron's usurpation of power and had succeeded in arousing a large congregation to join them. Hashem told Moshe and Aaron to distance themselves from this assembly so that He could destroy them.

To this Moshe responded, "You, Hashem, want to punish these people for coming out in support of Korach and his band. You are the God of the spirit of all flesh Who knows what is in each person's heart. Therefore You know that really they came to support Korach's rebellion. But we ordinary people do not know their true intentions. To us, it may seem as if they have come to witness Korach's downfall, not to support him. Therefore, unless it becomes clear to us that they agree with Korach, it is not right for You to be angry with them for the sin of one man."

Hashem accepted this claim and spared the congregation at that time. The next day, however, when the people blamed Moshe for killing Korach and his assembly, this argument was no longer credible, and Moshe could say nothing to vindicate them. All he could do was order Aaron to bring incense, which the Angel of Death had taught him to use as an antidote to the spread of pestilence.

❧ ❧ ❧

וַיְדַבֵּר ה' אֶל־אַהֲרֹן וַאֲנִי הִנֵּה נָתַתִּי לְךָ אֶת־מִשְׁמֶרֶת תְּרוּמֹתָי . . . לְךָ נְתַתִּים לְמָשְׁחָה — *And* HASHEM *spoke to Aaron: "Behold, I am giving you the guardianship of My offerings . . . I have given them to you for greatness"* (18:8).

In this passage, Hashem grants Aaron and his descendants perpetual rights to the priestly offerings, which He calls a token of the greatness of Aaron and his children. What is the significance of this "greatness"?

The answer is evident from the earlier part of the verse, where Hashem speaks of *My* offerings. These priestly gifts are, in reality, presents which are offered to the King of the Universe. One who receives a gift on behalf of the king must behave with regal dignity. Therefore, when the *Kohanim* receive *terumah* from the people, they must have the proper frame of mind. It is not fitting for a *Kohen* to receive the King's presents as a beggar who is grateful for any scraps he can get. On the contrary, a *Kohen* must see himself as an emissary of the exalted King, Who bestows honor on the people who bring presents for their Master. Thus, far from being a supplicant, the recipient is in truth a great person.

❧ ❧ ❧

בְּרִית מֶלַח עוֹלָם — *An eternal covenant of salt*
(18:19).

I n what way can Hashem's gift of priestly offerings to Aaron and his descendants be described as "a covenant of salt"? *Rashi* says that just as salt never rots, and even acts as a preservative for many other things, so this covenant will stay fresh and preserve Aaron's dynasty forever.

This has a very powerful implication: Even if some *Kohanim* go astray and pollute their special holiness, Hashem promises that in every generation there will always be some who remain true to the covenant. Thus, just as salt preserves food and does not allow it to spoil, so the covenant will preserve Aaron's priestly family and ensure that its holiness is preserved in every generation.

❀ ❀ ❀

פרשת חקת
Parashas Chukas

זֹאת חֻקַּת הַתּוֹרָה — *This is the decree of the Torah* (19:2).

Rashi explains that the word חֹק means *decree,* a law which the Torah requires us to accept without question because human minds are not capable of understanding it. We may ask, then, why does the Torah go out of its way to point out that this particular law is *the* decree of the Torah, suggesting that it is the Torah's only, or most important, decree? Many of the commandments fall into the category of decrees, which are beyond our comprehension. Indeed, the Torah is filled with references to חֻקִּים וּמִשְׁפָּטִים, *decrees and* [rational] *laws.* Such laws as *shatnez* and *kashrus* are above rational human analysis. If so, why is the law of *parah adumah* (the red cow) singled out to be called *the* decree of the Torah?

The answer is that the *parah adumah* is a metaphor for the Torah itself. Water mixed with the ashes of a totally red cow has the power to cleanse someone from the form of *tumah* (ritual impurity) caused by contact with a dead person. This is a supra-rational decree, and we will never be able to understand how or why it works.

So also, the Torah has the power to cleanse its followers from many types of impurity, and, if one pursues it diligently and with proper intentions, it will transform him into a pure and sincere person. Just as we do not, and cannot, understand the workings of *parah adumah,* we do not understand how Torah study and observance has this purifying effect on individuals.

The *parah adumah* purifies a person who is spiritually unclean in a miraculous and almost mystical fashion. We see no apparent nexus between the sprinkling of the ashes upon the person and the spiritual transformation that ensues. In the same manner, the study of Torah effects an equally astounding transformation in a person without any external clue as to what is happening or why. Yet we have *prima facie* evidence of this metamorphosis in the thousands of *baalei teshuvah* who have radically modified their character traits as a result of Torah study.

The sprinkling of the ashes catapults a person from being defiled—barred from the Holy Temple—to being welcomed into the House of Hashem. Similarly, Torah study enables a "coarse" spiritual personality to shed his "rough exterior" and come close to Hashem.

Logically, there is no reason why mastering the myriad technicalities of the laws of sacrifices and other offerings, for example, should affect the ways in which we relate to one another. Yet it is well known to those in the Torah world that the more learning one has, the more likely he is to be humble and straightforward in his dealings with his fellows. All we can say is that, like *parah adumah,* Hashem has decreed for the Torah a mysterious power to purify those who apply themselves to it in the proper fashion. Thus, the "decree" of the red cow is illustrative of the "decree" of Torah study—both bring about miraculous transformations.

❧ ❧ ❧

From — מֵעֲפַר שְׂרֵפַת הַחַטָּאת וְנָתַן עָלָיו מַיִם חַיִּים
the ash of the burnt purification-offering and he shall add to it fresh [lit. living] water (19:17).

The purifying water was a mixture of the ashes of the red cow and "living water," fresh spring water which had never been placed in a vessel. There is an interesting symbolism in this combination.

Everyone has an animal instinct which draws him after the base pleasures of the world. Hashem instilled these instincts in us and commanded us to work to overcome them, or to channel them into permitted activities which further our service of Hashem. Someone who follows his base instincts without making any effort to control them is wicked, and the Sages considered him like a dead person, even in his lifetime.

However, if one devotes himself to Torah, it transforms him into a *tzaddik,* a righteous person, and even after he dies he is considered to be among the living. How does the Torah do this?

For one thing, the Torah is called *aish das,* the fire of the law (*Devarim* 33:2). This means that it has the power to "purge" a person's evil inclination. Once this has been accomplished, the Torah gives him *mayim chaim,* living water, which strengthens his good inclination and enables his pure instincts to attain dominance. This living water of Torah nourishes and refreshes the person so that he will be truly and meaningfully alive—even after death. Together these forces make up the process of סוּר מֵרָע וַעֲשֵׂה־טוֹב, *Turn away from evil and do good* (*Tehillim* 34:15). This process is similar to the refining of precious metals. First the impurities are burnt off, then the hot, pure remains are plunged into water to be strengthened.

A further question presents itself. Why is the Torah's capacity to purify compared to the purification from the contamination of a human corpse, rather than from any of the many other sources of contamination, none of which require the ashes of a red cow?

The two elements that contribute to the purification process of the red cow are water and fire (ashes). As noted above, the Torah is likened to water and fire.

Similarly, since our Sages say that evil people are called dead—*meisim*—even during their lifetime, whereas righteous people are referred to as living—*chayim*—even after their deaths, a Jew who does not live up to his calling as a *tzelem Elokim,* someone created in the image of God, is, in reality, spiritually comatose, a "walking zombie." Through these two allegorical elements of water and fire, that same person can be resuscitated into everlasting life!

❊   ❊   ❊

וַיָּבֹאוּ בְנֵי־יִשְׂרָאֵל כָּל־הָעֵדָה מִדְבַּר־צִן בַּחֹדֶשׁ הָרִאשׁוֹן וַיֵּשֶׁב הָעָם בְּקָדֵשׁ — *And the Children of Israel, the entire congregation, came to the Wilderness of Zin, in the first month, and they dwelt in Kadesh* (20:1).

ashi comments on the words כָּל־הָעֵדָה, *the entire congrega-tion,* that now the congregation was complete, since all of the generation which had sinned in the incident of the spies had already died. Thus the new generation returned to the place from which the spies had been sent on their tragic mission (cf. *Bamidbar* 13:26), in preparation for their long-awaited entry into the land.

Perhaps this explains why the Torah chooses this point to insert the laws of *parah adumah,* which seems on the surface an unconnected interruption in the narrative of the Jews' travels through the Wilderness. However, as *Rashi* tells us (19:22), one of the reasons Israel was given the law of the red cow was to atone for the sin of the Golden Calf. Now that no one remained of the old generation, the nation was purified of that very sin for which the *parah adumah* provides atonement, and they were finally ready to enter *Eretz Yisrael.*

❀ ❀ ❀

קַח אֶת־הַמַּטֶּה וְהַקְהֵל אֶת־הָעֵדָה אַתָּה וְאַהֲרֹן אָחִיךָ וְדִבַּרְתֶּם אֶל־הַסֶּלַע לְעֵינֵיהֶם וְנָתַן מֵימָיו — *Take the stick and assemble the congregation, you and your brother Aaron, and speak to the rock in front of their eyes and it will give its waters* (20:8).

f Moshe was supposed to speak to the rock and not hit it, why was he commanded to take the stick?

There is an American saying, "Speak softly and carry a big stick." Even though Moshe was only supposed to talk, words carry more weight when they are backed up with a stick in the hand. Thus, by holding the stick, Moshe was meant to convey a symbolic teaching to the nation. As parents and teachers, we must always be prepared on two levels: to teach and to have the means to mete out punishment if it becomes necessary.

❦ ❦ ❦

וַיַּעַשׂ מֹשֶׁה נְחַשׁ נְחֹשֶׁת וַיְשִׂמֵהוּ עַל־הַנֵּס וְהָיָה אִם־נָשַׁךְ הַנָּחָשׁ אֶת־אִישׁ וְהִבִּיט אֶל־נְחַשׁ הַנְּחֹשֶׁת וָחָי: — *And Moshe made a copper snake and placed it on a pillar. If the snake bit a man and he looked at the copper snake, he would live (21:9).*

Rashi comments that Hashem had not told Moshe to make the snake from copper. Moshe did so on his own initiative, based on the following reasoning: "Hashem spoke of נְחָשׁ [*nachash*], *snake* or *magic,* so I will make it from נְחֹשֶׁת [*nechoshes*], *copper,* since one word alludes to the other." Surely Moshe had something in mind other than a mere similarity in spelling; exactly what connection did he see between these words, and how did he plan to make use of it?

The fiery snakes had been sent by Hashem to punish the Jews for speaking *lashon hara* (gossip or slander) about Hashem, by complaining that He had lead the people out into the desert to die. If we look closely, we find a common thread between the sin, the punishment, and Moshe's cure. It seems "magical" that a snake can kill just by spitting out venom. Similarly, when people speak *lashon hara,* they are "magically" fooling themselves into thinking that it is proper for them to spread a particular piece of gossip, when really they are transgressing one of the Torah's most serious prohibitions.

Moshe saw this similarity between the snake's magic and the magic of *lashon hara,* and tried to fight it with a third form of "magic," copper's ability to fool people into thinking it is gold, a far more precious substance. In *Rashi's* explanation, this is how Moshe used a play on words to eradicate the pestilence.

❦ ❦ ❦

פרשת בלק
Parashas Balak

וַיַּרְא בָּלָק בֶּן־צִפּוֹר אֵת כָּל־אֲשֶׁר־עָשָׂה יִשְׂרָאֵל לָאֱמֹרִי
וַיָּגָר מוֹאָב מִפְּנֵי הָעָם מְאֹד — *And Balak, the son
of Tzippor, saw everything that the Israelites
did to the Emorites. And Moab was very
frightened of that nation* (22:2-3).

The Torah does not say merely that he saw *what* the Jews did
to the Emorites, it says that he saw *everything* that they did.
He saw something that made him think that the Israelites
were a cruel people, a people to be frightened of. What was that?

At first glance, it is hard to understand what Balak was afraid of.
The Jews did not attack the Emorites, or even threaten to attack
them. They asked only for permission to pass through their land,
and promised that they would stay on the main road and not trample
the fields. There was nothing belligerent about their attitude.

How did the Emorites respond to this request? They might simply
have said, "No, we don't want you to come through our land." Or,
to be safe, they could have stationed an army at the border to make
sure that the Jews didn't encroach on their territory. Instead, they
launched an all-out attack on the Jews, who were then forced to
retaliate in self-defense.

Balak knew all this, and it should have been obvious to him that
as long as he did not bother the Jews, they would leave him alone.
As we will soon see, Balak was apprehensive that they would eat up
only the surrounding kingdoms but not his own. True, there might
have been a few border skirmishes here and there, but essentially he
was safe. So why was he worried?

The Moabites [led by their king Balak] said to the elders of Midian,
"Now the assembly will lick up all of our surroundings as an ox licks
up the grass of the field" (Bamidbar 22:4). *Rashi* says that when an
ox eats grass, whatever is left will never again prosper. Normally a
grazing animal leaves over enough stubble to grow back and
replenish itself. But an ox eats everything, all the way down to the
roots, so that it will never grow again. What was there about the
Jews' behavior that convinced Balak that they were so destructive?

To answer this, let us look at Moshe's account of his battles with
Sichon and Og in *Devarim* (2:31). After defeating the enemy
armies, the victorious Israelites, acting on Hashem's command,
killed everyone. Even the cities were destroyed, and only the
livestock and other booty remained. *Rashi* (v. 34) comments that
when the Jews came to the land of Og, they were so satiated with the
plunder they had taken from Sichon that they destroyed everything
except the silver and gold.

This was the cruelty that frightened Balak, that the Israelites
destroyed whatever they did not want for themselves, without
leaving anything over for others who might be able to use it.

Why, however, did they destroy usable property? Normally such
behavior would be forbidden because of *bal tashchis*, the prohibition
against waste. In this case, however, they carried out Hashem's
explicit instructions, for whatever reasons He gave them. This was
the way He wanted it and the people did not question Him.

Balak, however, could not understand how rational people could
destroy valuable property, even if their God had commanded it.
Therefore he concluded that the Israelites were sadists who wanted
to destroy everything in their path, including his people. This is the
everything that Balak saw that made him so frightened of the Jews.

❧ ❧ ❧

כִּי הִכִּיתָנִי זֶה שָׁלֹשׁ רְגָלִים: — *For you have*
struck me now three times (22:28).

Bilam's donkey uses a peculiar word, רְגָלִים, *regalim,* which
normally means *feet*. It is related to the word רָגִיל, *ragil,*
which means *habitual* or *regular*. Thus, we can understand
that the donkey was complaining that his master had become so

habituated to striking him that the master did not comprehend that the animal's strange behavior was a message from Heaven. As the angel told Bilam a few verses later, had he not listened to the third message, there would not have been a fourth one and the angel would have killed him.

Moreover, the donkey's expression, *shalosh regalim* (three times), is the same one that the Torah uses to refer to the three annual pilgrimage festivals (*Shemos* 23:14). Perhaps there also, this word has the same connotation. If so, we can say that the Torah used the word *regalim* in connection with the pilgrimage festivals to indicate that going up to the *Beis HaMikdash* was intended to be a habitual, regular occurrence.

❀ ❀ ❀

אֶת־שִׁבְעַת הַמִּזְבְּחֹת עָרַכְתִּי — *I have set up the seven altars* (23:4).

Bilam instructs Balak to build seven altars for him and then he tells Hashem that he has set up *the* seven altars. *Rashi* explains that Bilam refers to the altars with a definite article to indicate that they correspond to the seven altars which the Patriarchs built. *Rashi* even lists them for us: Abraham built four, Isaac one and Jacob built two. In other words, Bilam asked Hashem to grant his requests because he had matched the combined efforts of all of the Patriarchs.

Or perhaps he thought that the number seven had a special power: Since the Jews had seven altars to their credit, his seven altars would cancel out theirs and his case would prevail over theirs. This is why he used the word שִׁבְעַת, *shivas*, which indicates a group of seven (septet) rather than the normal word שֶׁבַע, *sheva*, which is simply the number seven. As a "magician" of sorts, Bilam believed that the *set* of seven altars would produce the desired effect.

❀ ❀ ❀

מָה אֶקֹּב לֹא קַבֹּה אֵל — *What shall I curse which* **HASHEM** *has not cursed?* (23:8).

One way of understanding Bilam's rhetorical question is as follows: Why should I curse them? If I curse them, it will be only my curse but not Hashem's. No matter what I say, Hashem will turn it into a blessing. Therefore, I will essentially be blessing, not cursing, them. So why should I say anything?

❧ ❧ ❧

וַיַּרְא פִּינְחָס בֶּן־אֶלְעָזָר בֶּן־אַהֲרֹן הַכֹּהֵן וַיָּקָם מִתּוֹךְ הָעֵדָה וַיִּקַּח רֹמַח בְּיָדוֹ: — *And Pinchas, the son of Elazar, the son of Aaron the Kohen saw, and he rose up from among the congregation and he took a spear in his hand* (25:7).

The word בְּיָדוֹ, *in his hand,* seems superfluous; certainly Pinchas took the spear in his hand. However, we can understand it to mean not his *hand* but rather his *possession* (we often find in the Talmud the word *hand* used to refer to one's property). What is the significance of this term here?

Since Pinchas had grown up in the priestly family of Aaron, one would not expect him to be proficient in the use of weapons. However, when he took the spear, he took it as a *possession,* something he was as adept at using as a trained warrior. The truth is that because of his pure desire to avenge Hashem's honor, he was granted this professional-level skill. Those who saw him, however, could not imagine that this was so. They were sure he was a practiced warrior and therefore accused him of cold-blooded murder.

❧ ❧ ❧

פרשת פינחס
Parashas Pinchas

פִּינְחָס בֶּן־אֶלְעָזָר בֶּן־אַהֲרֹן הַכֹּהֵן — *Pinchas, the son of Elazar the son of Aaron the Kohen* (25:11).

ccording to the *trop* (cantillation marking), the title *Kohen* in this verse refers not to Pinchas but to Aaron, his grandfather. However, when Pinchas' name and lineage are given a few verses earlier (25:7), פִּנְחָס בֶּן־אֶלְעָזָר בֶּן־אַהֲרֹן הַכֹּהֵן, *Pinchas the son of Elazar, the son of Aaron, the Kohen*, the *trop* indicates that the title *Kohen* refers to Pinchas himself. What significance is there in this distinction?

The earlier verse comes in the account of the nation's sinfulness in straying after idols when they were seduced by the daughters of Midian. Pinchas rose up in righteous anger and slew a nobleman of the tribe of Simon in the midst of an immoral act with a Midianite princess. This act assuaged Hashem's anger and stopped a plague which had already killed twenty-four thousand Jews. This was an act of sincere zealotry worthy of a *Kohen* and therefore the cantillation marks stress that he was acting like a *Kohen*.

In our verse, Hashem praises Pinchas to the people through Moshe because the people were deriding him, "Did you see this man, whose maternal forebear (Yisro) fattened animals for sacrifice to idols, suddenly turn blood thirsty and kill a member of the Jewish nobility?" In response to these charges, Hashem emphasizes that Pinchas was like his *Kohanite* grandfather Aaron, who was renowned for his love of peace (cf. *Avos* 1:12). Just as Aaron would have killed only out of a purely selfless zealotry to defend Hashem's honor and stop the plague, so Pinchas also acted only out of totally pure motives.

❊ ❊ ❊

וַיַּקְרֵב מֹשֶׁה אֶת־מִשְׁפָּטָן לִפְנֵי ה': — *And Moshe brought their case before HASHEM* (27:5).

This verse appears in the account of the plea of the daughters of Tzelafchad, a man who had died without sons, that their father's inheritance pass to them rather than disappear.

According to the Masoretic tradition, the final *nun* of the word מִשְׁפָּטָן, *their case,* is written enlarged. Had this letter been written normally, it might have been possible to misread the word as מִשְׁפָּטוֹ, *his case*, with a *vav*. Read in this way, it would have indicated that the daughters were selflessly representing the interests of their deceased father. This seems to be what they believed they were doing, as we see from their argument, *why should our father's name be removed from among his family?* (v. 4).

Written with the *nun* enlarged, however, it seems to indicate that Moshe considered their claim to be more selfish. Perhaps he thought that whenever someone's own personal gain is involved, it is impossible for him to be completely objective, and therefore he suspected that they were acting more in their own interests than in their father's. Likewise, one who performs an unselfish deed yet stands to gain from it should not claim that the deed was done "for the sake of heaven," since people may then suspect him of lying. This is why he stressed the *nun,* which emphasized that it was *their* case and not their father's.

Hashem, however, looked into their hearts and saw that they were indeed sincere. This is why He answered Moshe, כֵּן בְּנוֹת צְלָפְחָד דֹּבְרֹת נָתֹן תִּתֵּן לָהֶם, *the daughters of Tzelafchad speak correctly, you shall surely give to them* (27:7). The word לָהֶם, *to them*, is in the masculine form, which appears to be grammatically incorrect. According to what we have said, however, the land was to be given to them only for their father's sake, as they had claimed all along. To stress that it was for *him,* Hashem deliberately used the masculine pronoun.

❊ ❊ ❊

וַיֹּאמֶר ה' אֶל־מֹשֶׁה קַח־לְךָ אֶת־יְהוֹשֻׁעַ . . . וְנָתַתָּה
מֵהוֹדְךָ עָלָיו — *And HASHEM said to Moshe:*
Take Joshua to yourself . . . and give of your
glory to him (27:18, 20).

W hat exactly was Moshe's *glory* that Hashem told him to
give to Joshua? Perhaps it refers to the glory of the
miracles Moshe performed. The Sages (*Taanis* 20a)
taught that Joshua was not the first to cause the sun to stand still in
the heavens for a whole day (see *Yehoshua* 10:12-13); Moshe had
also performed that same miracle.

Thus, it was the ability to perform such miracles that Moshe was to
confer upon Joshua.

❦ ❦ ❦

צַו אֶת־בְּנֵי יִשְׂרָאֵל וְאָמַרְתָּ אֲלֵהֶם אֶת־קָרְבָּנִי לַחְמִי
לְאִשַּׁי רֵיחַ נִיחֹחִי תִּשְׁמְרוּ לְהַקְרִיב לִי בְּמוֹעֲדוֹ:
— *Command the Children of Israel and tell*
them: My offering, My food for My fires, My
satisfying aroma, you are to be scrupulous to
offer Me in its appointed time (28:2).

T his verse introduces the enumeration of the public offerings,
including the daily continual offerings, and the *mussaf*
offerings of the Sabbath, Rosh Chodesh, and the festivals.
This is the primary listing of offerings in the Torah and an
appropriate portion from it is read on each festival in place of the
offerings.

We may ask why the Torah presents this important catalogue of
offerings immediately following the account of Joshua's appointment as Moshe's successor.

The Torah wanted to stress to Joshua the importance of the
offerings in establishing and maintaining Jewish settlement in *Eretz*
Yisrael. In *Parashas Lech Lecha,* we said that Hashem promised
Abraham that, whatever else happened, He would allow the Jews
to remain in the land as long as they continued to bring the public
offerings. Thus, it was vital that Joshua be informed of the order of

the public offerings as soon as he was designated to lead the Jews in conquering, distributing, and settling the land.

❈   ❈   ❈

וּבַחֹדֶשׁ הַשְּׁבִיעִי בְּאֶחָד לַחֹדֶשׁ מִקְרָא־קֹדֶשׁ יִהְיֶה לָכֶם . . . יוֹם תְּרוּעָה יִהְיֶה לָכֶם: וַעֲשִׂיתֶם עֹלָה לְרֵיחַ נִיחֹחַ לַה' — *And in the seventh month, on the first of the month, there shall be a holy convocation for you . . . a day of shofar blowing. And you shall make an elevation-offering for a satisfying aroma to HASHEM* (29:1-2).

It is interesting to note that in discussing the offerings of Rosh Hashanah, the Torah uses the term וַעֲשִׂיתֶם, *you shall make,* while concerning all the other festivals it says וְהִקְרַבְתֶּם, *you shall offer.* What can we learn from this discrepancy?

The Sages taught (*Yerushalmi, Rosh Hashanah* 4:5) that on Rosh Hashanah, each person should feel that he makes *himself* into an offering before Hashem. The purpose of blowing the shofar, which has the sound of a person crying in spiritual agony over his sins and imperfections, is to raise us up to the level of offering ourselves totally and sincerely to Hashem. Thus, after telling us that Rosh Hashanah is to be a day of shofar blowing *for us,* the Torah uses the expression *making,* to indicate that the shofar will make us reach that level.

❈   ❈   ❈

וּבַחֲמִשָּׁה עָשָׂר יוֹם לַחֹדֶשׁ הַשְּׁבִיעִי מִקְרָא־קֹדֶשׁ יִהְיֶה לָכֶם . . . וְחַגֹּתֶם חַג לַה' שִׁבְעַת יָמִים: — *And on the fifteen day of the seventh month, there shall be a holy convocation for you; . . . and you shall celebrate a festival to HASHEM for seven days* (29:12).

In listing the offerings for the festival of Succos, the Torah does not mention the name Succos at all, but refers to it simply as the festival on the fifteenth day of the seventh month.

We may say that the reason for this strange omission is because this section prescribes the seventy bulls that comprised the *mussafim* (additional offerings) of Succos. (Thirteen bulls were offered on the first day, twelve on the second, and so on for the seven days, making a total of seventy.) The Sages taught that these seventy bulls atoned for the seventy nations of the world (*Succah* 55b). It is possible to say, then, that these offerings are not entirely related to Succos, which is a Jewish festival commemorating the tents in which the Jews dwelt during their sojourn in the Wilderness after the Exodus from Egypt. And thus the Torah omitted the name of the festival.

This point gives further meaning to *Rashi's* explanation that the eighth day, Shemini Atzeres, is reserved for the "private" feast which Hashem makes in honor of His special relationship with Israel. For, as indicated by the single bull of its *mussaf* offering, Shemini Atzeres is strictly a festival for the Jews, and, unlike Succos, is not shared with the nations.

❧ ❧ ❧

פרשת מטות
Parashas Matos

וַיְדַבֵּר מֹשֶׁה אֶל־רָאשֵׁי הַמַּטּוֹת לִבְנֵי יִשְׂרָאֵל לֵאמֹר זֶה הַדָּבָר אֲשֶׁר צִוָּה ה': — *And Moshe spoke to the heads of the tribes of the Children of Israel, saying: This is the matter which HASHEM commanded* (30:2).

*R*ashi comments that as a gesture of respect, Moshe taught these laws to the *nesi'im* (princes) before he passed them on to the rest of the people. We may ask: Why were the laws of *nedarim* (vows) singled out to be taught first to the *nesi'im*? Also, why were these laws discussed at this point in the Torah, in middle of the account of the preparations to enter the land?

Eretz Yisrael was given to the Jews as *morashah,* a heritage. As long as we remain true to His Torah and *mitzvos*, Hashem promises that we will continue to dwell on the land and have it to pass on to our children. Now, the Sages taught that the punishment for reneging on a vow is the death of one's small children, may Heaven protect us (*Shabbos* 32b). Therefore in order for Israel to assume eternal occupation of the land, it was necessary for the people to learn the laws of vows, in order to avoid this punishment and ensure that there would be future generations to occupy the Land.

As we will see in *Parashas Masei* (*Bamidbar* 34:29), the *nesi'im* were given responsibility for allocating and distributing parcels of land, each to members of his tribe. We may assume that they were also responsible to ensure that the land remained in its proper hands. In order to do this, they would need to have a thorough knowledge of the laws of vows, to help assure that their followers would have offspring to whom to pass on their land. For this reason the *nesi'im* were singled out to be taught these laws in particular, so that, by knowing how to annul vows whenever possible, they would be able to protect people from violating them.

❦ ❦ ❦

וְאִם־הָפֵר יָפֵר אֹתָם אַחֲרֵי שָׁמְעוֹ וְנָשָׂא אֶת־עֲוֺנָהּ: — *And if he will annul them [the vows] after he hears, then he shall bear her sin* (30:16).

Rashi explains that, *after he hears,* describes a situation in which the husband consented to his wife's vow when he first heard of it, and then later annulled it. Such an annulment is not valid, since once the husband has confirmed the vow, he may no longer annul it, even on the same day that he heard it. Therefore, if his wife violated the vow in the mistaken belief that it was no longer in effect, her husband is held guilty. In this situation, the husband suffers the punishment for violating a vow, which, as we saw above, is the loss of his children.

However, the words אַחֲרֵי שָׁמְעוֹ, *after he hears,* seem to limit the applicability of this rule. He bears her sin *only* if he has heard of her vow. If, however, the husband never heard that his wife had made a vow, then even if she violated it, perhaps he will not be punished in this way. After all, he did not do anything wrong and therefore does not deserve to be punished for a sin that is solely his wife's, even if she committed it intentionally. For why should *his* children suffer for *her* sin?

❦ ❦ ❦

נְקֹם נִקְמַת בְּנֵי יִשְׂרָאֵל מֵאֵת הַמִּדְיָנִים — *Take the vengeance of the Children of Israel from the Midianites* (31:2).

In this verse, Hashem refers to the *vengeance of the Children of Israel.* In the next verse, however, when Moshe passes Hashem's instructions on to the Jews, he speaks of HASHEM's *vengeance against Midian.* Indeed, since Moshe uses a different expression, the Torah does not say that Moshe was quoting Hashem's words; it says only that *Moshe spoke to the people, saying,* which implies that his words were his own rephrasing of the Divine command. Why did Moshe paraphrase Hashem's words and what right did he have to do so?

Rashi says that whenever someone stands up against Israel, it is as if he stood against Hashem. Thus Moshe was merely restating Hashem's words in a way that would be more compelling to the people. If Moshe had ordered the Jews to extract vengeance for transgressions against them, they might have been willing to forgive any wrongs done them and forgo taking vengeance. However, they had no right to forgive offenses against Hashem. Therefore, once Moshe said that HASHEM's honor was involved, the people had no choice but to follow his orders.

❦ ❦ ❦

וַיִּקַּח מֹשֶׁה וְאֶלְעָזָר הַכֹּהֵן אֶת־הַזָּהָב מֵאֵת שָׂרֵי הָאֲלָפִים וְהַמֵּאוֹת וַיָּבִאוּ אֹתוֹ אֶל־אֹהֶל מוֹעֵד זִכָּרוֹן לִבְנֵי־יִשְׂרָאֵל לִפְנֵי ה': — *And Moshe and Elazar the Kohen took the gold from the commanders of thousands and hundreds, and they brought it to the Tent of Meeting as a memorial for the Children of Israel before* HASHEM (31:54).

The expression זִכָּרוֹן לִבְנֵי־יִשְׂרָאֵל, *a memorial for the Children of Israel,* suggests that this gold was preserved forever afterwards as a reminder to the Jews of the war against Midian. It seems strange to us that the Sages did not mention this memorial anywhere in their descriptions of the contents of the *Mishkan* or the *Beis HaMikdash.*

❦ ❦ ❦

הָאָרֶץ אֲשֶׁר הִכָּה ה' לִפְנֵי עֲדַת יִשְׂרָאֵל אֶרֶץ מִקְנֶה הִיא וְלַעֲבָדֶיךָ מִקְנֶה: — *The land which HASHEM smote before the congregation of Israel is a land [suitable] for cattle and your servants possess cattle* (32:4).

If we examine the claim of the tribes of Gad and Reuben carefully, we will see that it had considerable justification. They assumed that Hashem would surely give each tribe the portion that was most appropriate for it, and therefore thought they could reasonably expect that the land conquered from Sichon would eventually come to them, as the suitable territory for their abundant herds.

Furthermore, there was a basis for their being excused from participation in the battles to conquer *Eretz Yisrael*. It is related in *Yehoshua* (ch. 18) and *Shoftim* (ch. 1) that only after the land had been apportioned to the tribes did each tribe set out to capture the land which had been allotted to it. Since each tribe would have to fight for its own portion anyway, there was no reason to single out Gad and Reuben to fight the battles of the other tribes.

Moshe, however, saw the matter from a different perspective. Even though their arguments may have been valid, he was concerned that the other tribes would think that their real motive was a lack of confidence in the new nation's ability to prevail against the nations they would confront on the other side of the river. If this happened, panic would spread and it would be impossible to induce anyone to enter the land. Then Hashem would grow angry at the people for their lack of trust in Him, just as He had grown angry with them after the incident of the spies almost four decades, years earlier. A close analysis of Moshe's reproof of Gad and Reuben in verses 6 through 15 will show that this was his real concern.

❅ ❅ ❅

פרשת מסעי
Parashas Masei

— **אֵלֶּה מַסְעֵי בְנֵי־יִשְׂרָאֵל אֲשֶׁר יָצְאוּ מֵאֶרֶץ מִצְרָיִם**
*These are the journeys of the Children of
Israel who went out from Egypt* (33:1).

I t is noteworthy that the Torah does not speak of these journeys
as the route to *Eretz Yisrael;* rather, it associates them with the
road *away from* Egypt. This suggests that the Torah views the
Exodus from Egypt as more than just a process of physical or
geographical relocating. Leaving Egypt was a spiritual process,
which involved weaning the people from the Egyptian manner of
thought and instilling them with a commitment to Torah, so that
they would never desire to return to Egypt. (See our commentary at
the beginning of *Parashas Beshalach.*)

We may say further that all of the journeys through the
Wilderness described here represented stages in the spiritual
journey from Egypt to *Eretz Yisrael.* In a sense, this spiritual journey
did not reach its true goal until the building of the *Beis HaMikdash,*
as is suggested by the fifteen steps involved in the departure from
Egypt, as enumerated in the *Dayeinu* passage in the Pesach
Haggadah. This also explains why the Prophet (*Melachim I* 6:1)
connects the two events by saying that the *Beis HaMikdash* was
completed 480 years after the Exodus from Egypt. This suggests
that the spiritual process of eradicating Egyptian thought took a full
480 years.

❧ ❧ ❧

וַיִּכְתֹּב מֹשֶׁה אֶת־מוֹצָאֵיהֶם לְמַסְעֵיהֶם עַל־פִּי ה' וְאֵלֶּה
מַסְעֵיהֶם לְמוֹצָאֵיהֶם: — *And Moshe wrote their*
goings out according to their journeys by the
word of HASHEM, and these are their journeys
according to their goings out (33:2).

At the beginning of this verse, the Torah mentions their *goings* before their *journeys,* and at the end it reverses the order. What is the significance of this change?

This is not difficult to understand, according to what we said earlier in this *parashah.* At the beginning, the journeys were required to complete the Jews' spiritual journey away from Egypt. The process of weaning the Jews from the influence of Egypt — *their goings out* — would have required all of these stops, even if the entire journey had taken less than forty years. At the end, the Torah speaks of the historical, rather than the spiritual, aspect of their travels: These are their journeys — that took a total of forty years — to eradicate their sins, in order to achieve the necessary degree of *going out.*

❧ ❧ ❧

וְאַהֲרֹן בֶּן־שָׁלֹשׁ וְעֶשְׂרִים וּמְאַת שָׁנָה בְּמֹתוֹ בְּהֹר
הָהָר: ס וַיִּשְׁמַע הַכְּנַעֲנִי מֶלֶךְ עֲרָד — *And Aaron*
was one hundred twenty-three years old when
he died at Hor HaHar. And the Canaanite, the
King of Arad, heard . . . (33:39-40).

In our printed versions of the *Chumash,* a letter *samech* separates these two verses, indicating a "closed *parashah,*" which appears as a space left open in the middle of a line in the written *Sefer Torah.* Such a break usually indicates the beginning of a new topic and therefore its presence in the middle of the enumeration of the Jews' resting places through the wilderness is strange.

We can explain this with reference to a passage in *Parashas Eikev* (*Devarim* 10:6). *Rashi* there says that after Aaron's death, the Jews feared doing battle with the King of Arad and retreated towards Egypt as far as Moseirah, a distance which had taken them eight journeys to traverse. At Moseirah, the tribe of Levi rose up and forced the rest of the people to continue on their journey. In that battle there were casualties on both sides. Finally the Jews decided to resume their progress towards *Eretz Yisrael* and continued on their way.

These events described by *Rashi* occurred at the point where the closed *parashah* interrupts the account of the journeys through the Wilderness. In light of the above, it seems obvious that the closed *parashah* is an allusion to this whole series of unstated events, which interrupted the journey toward *Eretz Yisrael*.

❈ ❈ ❈

וְהָיוּ לָכֶם הֶעָרִים לְמִקְלָט — *And these cities shall be for you for a refuge* (35:12).

To whom did the Torah refer with the words *for you*? At first glance it would seem to refer to *beis din*, the religious courts which were responsible for enforcing the Torah. Yet we can ask, the *beis din* was not composed of killers; why did they need cities of refuge?

However, as the *Mishnah* in *Avos* warns (5:11), bloodshed leads to the exile of the Jews from their land. The cities of refuge were to protect accidental killers from the vengeance of their victims' relatives. If the *beis din* did not take adequate steps to protect such killers from the hands of their avengers, the innocent blood spilled would be on the heads of the *beis din*. They would then be held accountable in Heaven for the resulting exile.

Furthermore, if the *beis din* was not diligent in protecting innocent lives, people would see that the leaders of the nation did not place a high value on human life. This could result in a general cheapening of life, which in turn would encourage people to be less careful about preventing accidents. (See our commentary to *Parashas Mishpatim* 21:13.)

❈ ❈ ❈

וַיְצַו מֹשֶׁה אֶת־בְּנֵי יִשְׂרָאֵל עַל־פִּי ה' לֵאמֹר כֵּן מַטֵּה בְנֵי־יוֹסֵף דֹּבְרִים: — *And Moshe commanded the Children of Israel according to the word of HASHEM, saying: The tribe of the sons of Joseph are speaking correctly* (36:5).

In *Parashas Pinchas* (*Bamidbar* 27:1-11), the daughters of Tzelafchad, a man who died without sons, requested and were granted the right to inherit their father's property in place of the brothers they did not have.

In our *parashah,* the elders of Tzelafchad's tribe, Manasseh, came to Moshe and the elders of the nation to express their concern that ownership of their relative's land might pass to another tribe if Tzelafchad's daughters were to marry men from other tribes. Their unstated request was that the daughters be required to marry within their own tribe to prevent this from happening.

In response, Moshe reassured them that their fears were ungrounded. "You are speaking correctly," he told them. "Not only is the law as you say, that such heirs may not marry out of their tribe, but you may also be assured that Tzelafchad's daughters do not want to even though they are permitted to do so (*Bava Basra* 120a). Their whole concern from the outset was to protect their father's standing in his family, as they themselves said, '*why should our father's name be removed from among his family?*'" (ibid. v. 4).

This is the meaning of the clause, *the tribe of the sons of Joseph are speaking correctly*: They are right that the daughters of Tzelafchad will marry their cousins from Manasseh, because they want to preserve their father's name *in his family.*

❧ ❧ ❧

ספר דברים

Sefer Devarim

פרשת דברים
Parashas Devarim

אֵלֶּה הַדְּבָרִים אֲשֶׁר דִּבֶּר מֹשֶׁה . . . בֵּין־פָּארָן
וּבֵין־תֹּפֶל וְלָבָן — *These are the words which*
Moshe spoke . . . between Paran and Tofel and
Lavan . . . (1:1).

Rashi comments that these were words of rebuke, and the
places which Moshe mentioned refer to occasions when the
Jews angered Hashem. "Paran" refers to the spies who were
sent from the Wilderness of Paran (*Bamidbar* 13:3), and "Tofel and
Lavan" refers to the Jews' complaints about the manna (ibid. 21:5).

Two questions present themselves. For one thing, the word
between suggests that there was a connection *between* these two
incidents. Yet the mission of the spies occurred near the beginning of
the forty-year trek through the Wilderness, while the complaint
about the manna was near the end. What connection is there
between these two events that occurred thirty-eight years apart?

Secondly, the name "Tofel and Lavan" is strange. The Hebrew
word תֹּפֶל means *attach* and לָבָן means *white,* implying that the
people attached one word to another to formulate their complaint
about the manna, which was *white.* Why, in alluding to the manna,
does the Torah focus on its white color?

In both incidents the nation did wrong by complaining about gifts
that Hashem gave them. In the case of the spies, it was the land of
Israel, which they were about to inherit, and later it was the manna,
which they called לֶחֶם הַקְּלֹקֵל, *the light bread* (ibid., see *Rashi*).

Really, the nation had the same basic complaint in both cases:
They were tired of living under Hashem's constant observation. We
see this from the Sages' teaching (*Yoma* 75a) that the manna was

white שֶׁמַּלְבִּין עֲוֹנוֹתֵיהֶם שֶׁל יִשְׂרָאֵל, *because it cleansed* (lit., *whitened*) Israel's sins.

How did the manna do this? Each day they were able to gather only one measure of manna per family member, and that amount was edible only on that day. Anything extra they tried to gather would disappear by the time they arrived home; and any manna remaining uneaten on the day it was gathered would grow wormy overnight. So they had to have faith that there would be a new gift the following day. The result was that they had to examine their actions every day, because they knew that if they were not worthy, there would be no manna the next day.

In the incident of the spies, they had the same worry about the land of Israel, that their every deed would be scrutinized. As Moshe was later to tell the Jews about the land, עֵינֵי ה' אֱלֹהֶיךָ בָּהּ מֵרֵשִׁית הַשָּׁנָה וְעַד אַחֲרִית שָׁנָה, *the eyes of HASHEM are on it from the beginning of the year until the end of the year* (*Devarim* 11:12). They knew that once they were in the land, Hashem would watch them very closely and judge their every action; this was very likely one important reason why the report of the spies made them want to go back to Egypt.

Thus we see the relationship between the incident of the spies and the complaints about the manna: The people complained that Hashem was watching them too closely.

❧   ❧   ❧

וְדִי זָהָב: — *And Di Zahav* (1:1).

Di Zahav literally means "enough gold," and *Rashi* explains this as a reference to the Golden Calf. "Since Hashem gave you so much gold," Moshe chastises the people, "you became spoiled and made the Golden Calf." However, this seems more like a defense than a rebuke, so we have to determine how the Sages understood Moshe's words as a rebuke.

Another thing is puzzling about *Rashi's* interpretation. In *Parashas Lech Lecha,* he says that Hashem's promise to Abraham, וַאֲבָרֶכְךָ, *and I will bless you* (*Bereishis* 12:2), was a blessing for wealth. However, here he suggests that wealth leads only to evil. How could Hashem bless Abraham with evil?

There are two different attitudes towards wealth, one good and one bad. Someone who is arrogant about his money because he feels he made it through his own efforts is very likely to ignore the extra responsibilities Hashem gave him to use his wealth wisely.

On the other hand, someone who thinks that, in the words of King David, מִמְּךָ הַכֹּל וּמִיָּדְךָ נָתַנּוּ לָךְ, *Everything is Yours and from Your hand we have given to You* (*Divrei HaYamim I* 29:14), recognizes that all wealth belongs to Hashem and that he is only a banker in Hashem's employ. Whatever Hashem has given him is *everything* he needs—he has what he requires for himself and whatever is necessary to distribute to the poor and for other *mitzvos*. For such a person, money is a blessing and he does not feel that he has more than he needs.

My father, זצ״ל, noted that when Esau said (*Bereishis* 33:9), "יֶשׁ־לִי רָב, *I have plenty*," he meant that he had more than he could use, because it was all his and he did not feel responsible to anyone else for it. Jacob, however, said (ibid. v. 11), "יֶשׁ־לִי־כֹל, *I have everything*," because he understood that he had everything he was supposed to have and that it was his responsibility to figure out what the One Who entrusted it to him wanted him to do with it.

This, then, was Moshe's rebuke to the Jews: "You thought you had 'enough' money, that your money was a plaything to amuse yourselves with. That is why you strayed after your desires and built the Golden Calf."

On the other side, Hashem knew that Abraham would make proper use of any wealth he was given, to help those in need and to glorify Hashem's Name in the world. Moreover, he will receive ample remuneration for his role as a trustee of that money. For someone with that attitude, wealth is truly a blessing.

❀ ❀ ❀

וּשְׁפַטְתֶּם צֶדֶק — *And you shall judge right-eously* (1:16).

The question presents itself: Why does Moshe choose this moment, on the eve of the Jews' entry into the land of Israel, to admonish judges to be fair in their judgments? We can say simply that he wanted to make the point that a high standard of justice was a prerequisite to their settling in the land. This is why we say, in the *Shemoneh Esrei* prayer, the blessing הָשִׁיבָה שׁוֹפְטֵינוּ, *Restore our judges*, before the blessing וְלִירוּשָׁלַיִם עִירְךָ, *And to Jerusalem, Your city, may You return in compassion*, to indicate that we will not be worthy of possessing our land until true Torah justice has been restored.

There is another reference to this at the end of this week's *Haftarah*: צִיּוֹן בְּמִשְׁפָּט תִּפָּדֶה וְשָׁבֶיהָ בִּצְדָקָה, *Zion will be redeemed with justice and those who return to her with righteousness* (*Yeshayahu* 1:27).

❦ ❦ ❦

וַתֵּרָגְנוּ בְאָהֳלֵיכֶם — *And you complained in your tents* (1:27).

This verse describes the reaction of the Jews to the report of the spies on their return from their mission to explore the land. The Sages (*Taanis* 29a) tell us that the spies returned from their mission on the eighth of Av, so that the nation cried on the night of Tishah B'Av. Therefore, that night was established as a time of בְּכִיָּה לְדוֹרוֹת, a time of catastrophe and *crying through the generations*.

Perhaps, then, *in your tents* is an allusion to Jewish wives and mothers, who maintain the home and nurture future generations. It is upon this allusion that the Sages base their teaching that the tears shed unnecessarily that first Tishah B'Av would bring untold suffering throughout the generations. Since the fundamentals of Judaism are passed on from *mother* to child, this tragic tradition would be perpetuated in future generations through the mothers, who are the mainstay of the *tents,* the Jewish home.

❦ ❦ ❦

וַיְהִי כַאֲשֶׁר־תַּמּוּ כָּל־אַנְשֵׁי הַמִּלְחָמָה לָמוּת מִקֶּרֶב הָעָם: וַיְדַבֵּר ה' אֵלַי לֵאמֹר: — *And it was when all of the men of war ceased to die from among the people. And HASHEM spoke to me, saying* (2:16-17).

ashi points out that in his narrative of the Jews' wanderings through the Wilderness, Moshe does not use the word וַיְדַבֵּר, which denotes fond "face-to-face" speech, to describe Hashem's conversations with him from the time of the incident with the spies until this verse. Instead, וַיֹּאמֶר is always used. This was because as long as any of the rebellious generation was still alive, Hashem was angry with the Jews and therefore did not favor Moshe, their leader, with the closeness which he had enjoyed earlier.

There is something very puzzling about this *Rashi*. In other places, *Rashi* tells us that וַיֹּאמֶר indicates a soft, gentle kind of speech (*Shemos* 19:3), while וַיְדַבֵּר is used more harshly, to convey a strict command (ibid. 6:2). Yet here *Rashi* seems to be reversing himself.

Really, however, there is no contradiction. It is true that וַיֹּאמֶר connotes softness, but it is the softness of two people who are not on intimate terms and have to "walk on eggs" to avoid confronting each other directly, to avoid coming "face-to-face." וַיְדַבֵּר, on the other hand, describes the direct speech of two people who are so close to each other that they are not afraid of saying exactly what they think.

Thus, it was only when Hashem wanted to draw Moshe close to Him that He spoke in the commanding fashion expressed by וַיְדַבֵּר, knowing that in Moshe's worshipful love for Him, Moshe would take it as a gesture of love to receive Hashem's commands. Our Sages hinted at this in their dictum (*Kiddushin* 31a) גָּדוֹל הַמְּצֻוֶּה וְעוֹשֶׂה מִמִּי שֶׁאֵינוֹ מְצֻוֶּה וְעוֹשֶׂה, *Greater is the one who is commanded and does than the one who is not commanded and does.*

❦   ❦   ❦

וְאֶת־יְהוֹשׁוּעַ צִוֵּיתִי — *And I commanded Joshua* (3:21).

Joshua's name is usually spelled with only one *vav*, יְהוֹשֻׁעַ, but here the Torah inserts an extra *vav*, יְהוֹשׁוּעַ.

Normally, Joshua's name signifies יְשׁוּעָה, *salvation*, Spelled as it is here, however, we can relate it to the word שׁוּעַ, *prayer.* Joshua had exceptional powers of prayer, as evidenced by the incident of Achan ben Carmi.

Achan had secretly stolen silver, gold, and clothing from the spoils of Jericho. As a result, Hashem grew angry and the Jews lost a battle against the people of Ai, a battle which they should have won easily, and their courage melted. Therefore, Joshua tore his garments and prostrated himself in prayer before the Holy Ark, begging Hashem not to destroy His people. Hashem answered that Israel had sinned and that Joshua should cast lots to find out who was responsible. The lot fell on Achan, who confessed his thievery and was executed. With his death, his sin was atoned and Hashem again allowed the Jews to be victorious in battle (cf. *Yehoshua* 7).

In our verse, Moshe tells Joshua not to be afraid of doing battle with the enemy because Hashem will fight them, just as He had already delivered the two kings Sichon and Og into their hands. Moshe must already have known of this power of Joshua's prayers, and by placing an extra *vav* in Joshua's name, he hinted that Joshua should pray before doing battle. In the merit of conquering the land and distributing it to the Jews, his prayers would certainly be answered.

Our Sages said (*Arachin* 32b) that Joshua should have used his great power of prayer to destroy the inclination for idol worship. Because he missed this opportunity, his name appears in one verse (*Nechemiah* 8:17) as יֵשׁוּעַ, with the *vav* of prayer but without the *hei* which represents Hashem's name. This spelling stresses his power of prayer but indicates that he did not use this power to the extent he should have.

❧ ❧ ❧

פרשת ואתחנן
Parashas Vaeschanan

וָאֶתְחַנַּן אֶל־ה' בָּעֵת הַהִוא לֵאמֹר: — *And I pleaded
to HASHEM at that time, saying* (3:23).

The word וָאֶתְחַנַּן, *I pleaded,* is derived from the Hebrew word
חֵן, which means *favor.* Moshe relates that before he presented his plea, he tried to get Hashem into a mood to show
him favor, not to answer him according to the strict letter of the law.

How did he do this? The Sages (*Berachos* 32a) derive from this
passage that one should always first say Hashem's praises and then
ask for his personal needs. Therefore Moshe said in the next verse,
*HASHEM, You have started to show Your servant Your greatness
and Your strong hand. Who is so powerful in the heavens and on
the earth who can do like Your mighty works* (3:24)?

Only after this introduction did Moshe make his request in the
following verse: *Please allow me to go and to see the good land on
the other side of the Jordan, this good mountain and the forest of
Lebanon* (3:25).

When a good lawyer wants to present a client's claim in court, he
first asks which judges are available. Next he investigates the
backgrounds of the judges and tries, as much as he can, to bring his
case before the judge who will be the most sympathetic to his client.

In the Heavenly Court, of course, Hashem is the only Judge. Still,
He reveals different aspects of Himself at different times —
sometimes His mercy is dominant, other times His strict justice, and
so on — and it is obviously in our interest to bring our judgments to
Him at a time when He is most favorably disposed toward us. In
order to do this, we should follow the lead that Moshe set in these

verses, by reciting Hashem's praises before we make our requests.

❦ ❦ ❦

וַיִּתְעַבֵּר ה' בִּי לְמַעַנְכֶם — **And HASHEM grew angry with me because of you** (3:26).

R ashi says that when Moshe said, *"because of you,"* he meant that you, the Jewish people, caused my punishment by bickering about the lack of water. On the surface, it seems that Moshe was accusing the people of causing him to do wrong, but this is unlikely. Surely Moshe knew that, however much the people may have provoked him, he was responsible for his own actions. If so, why did he blame them?

Really, Moshe's charge against the people was different. He admitted that he alone was responsible for his mistake, but he felt, that on his own merits, Hashem would have forgiven him. However, because the people had sinned by complaining about the lack of water and thus showed that they had too little trust in Hashem, they had to be shown the stringency of His judgment — that even as righteous a person as Moshe is punished for a comparatively small sin.

This point is made more clearly in *Parashas Chukas* (*Bamidbar* 20:13), where the Torah says that Hashem was sanctified by the incident of the water. *Rashi* comments on this, "When Hashem judges those who are holy to Him, He becomes more fearful and holy in the eyes of His creatures."

This, then, was Moshe's real complaint to the people: "Because you needed to be taught a lesson, Hashem made an example of me and punished me by not allowing me to enter the Land."

❦ ❦ ❦

לֹא תֹסִפוּ עַל־הַדָּבָר אֲשֶׁר אָנֹכִי מְצַוֶּה אֶתְכֶם וְלֹא תִגְרְעוּ מִמֶּנּוּ — **Do not add to the word which I command you and do not subtract from it** (4:2).

T he order of these commands requires explanation. One would think that, *do not subtract,* should come first because that is more obvious. Then, *do not add,* would come to warn us not to try to become more pious than the Creator by adding things to the Torah.

The truth is, however, that Moshe says, *do not subtract,* only in order to explain what he meant by, *do not add.* Whenever you try to add something to the Torah, you are really subtracting from it because, in effect, you are saying that it is not complete as is, and therefore needs something more. By taking the liberty of adding, you detract from the greatness of the Torah.

❀ ❀ ❀

כִּי אָנֹכִי מֵת בָּאָרֶץ הַזֹּאת אֵינֶנִּי עֹבֵר אֶת־הַיַּרְדֵּן וְאַתֶּם עֹבְרִים . . . הִשָּׁמְרוּ לָכֶם פֶּן־תִּשְׁכְּחוּ . . . וַעֲשִׂיתֶם לָכֶם פֶּסֶל — *For I die in this land, I am not crossing the Jordan, but you are crossing . . . Beware lest you forget . . . and make yourselves a graven image . . .* (4:22-23).

Moshe relates these two points to each other: Because I am not crossing the Jordan River with you, you have to beware not to forget Hashem's commandment against idolatry. What connection is there between his death and the prohibition against idolatry?

We find the answer to this question in the words of our Sages in Tractate *Arachin* (32b). They point out that Joshua was criticized for not praying to Hashem to destroy the inclination for idolatry. The Talmud then asks why Moshe did not pray for the same thing. The answer is given that the merit of the land of Israel would have been required in order for such prayers to be successful. Because the punishment for idolatry is the exile of the Jewish people from their land, such a prayer can be effective only when they are in the land — then *Eretz Yisrael* itself intercedes to prevent the loss of her children (cf. *Avos* 5:11).

This explains the warning that Moshe gave the people: "If I could enter the land with you, then I would be able to pray to expunge your desire to worship idols and you would not have to worry. Since I am to die here, however, I cannot protect you and therefore you must yourselves be wary."

❀ ❀ ❀

לֹא תִרְצָח וְלֹא תִנְאָף וְלֹא תִגְנֹב וְלֹא־תַעֲנֶה בְרֵעֲךָ עֵד שָׁוְא: וְלֹא תַחְמֹד — *Do not kill, and do not commit adultery, and do not steal, and do not bear false witness against your fellow. And do not covet.* (5:17-18).

These prohibitions seem to be in logical, descending order: The most serious sin comes first, followed by the others. Presented in this way, they warn us that all of them are forbidden, not just the more serious ones. Why, though, are they joined together with the prefix ו, *and*?

We may say that the Torah wants to stress to us that we are never to think that some commandments are more important than others. Had the Torah not said these *ands*, we might have felt that some were less stringent than others. The *ands* teach us that we must be equally zealous in avoiding all of these sins. If someone *covets* (in violation of the last transgression on the list), he may well come to kill to obtain the object of his desire.

Conversely, someone who rejects murder primarily because Hashem so commands will be equally careful not to transgress any of the other sins as well. Thus, by connecting these prohibitions with *ands*, the Torah teaches us that they are equal expressions of Hashem's will and therefore *all* of equal importance. If someone refrains from killing for this reason, he will likewise not covet.

❧ ❧ ❧

שְׁמַע יִשְׂרָאֵל ה' אֱלֹהֵינוּ ה' אֶחָד: — *Hear, O Israel: HASHEM is our God, HASHEM, the One and Only* (6:4).

Why does the Torah require us to make a public proclamation—*Hear, O Israel*? Why would it not be enough for each Jew simply to make a personal affirmation of his belief in Hashem's unity—*Hashem is our God, Hashem, the One and Only*?

The answer is that everyone sees Hashem in a different way, depending on his wisdom, his nature and his experiences in life. Some are more afraid of Hashem's ability to punish, others are enthused by His mercy, others focus on His glory. If we were to make only a personal declaration, it could be thought that each individual is speaking only about his personal perception of Hashem. By proclaiming publicly that all His ways and manifestations are One, we affirm that even though everyone has a different understanding of Him, all of those differing perceptions of His ways show us His unified glory. "Hear, O Israel, Hashem, Who each person sees in a different way, is One." It is all His glory.

❦ ❦ ❦

וְעָשִׂיתָ הַיָּשָׁר וְהַטּוֹב בְּעֵינֵי ה' לְמַעַן יִיטַב לָךְ וּבָאתָ וְיָרַשְׁתָּ אֶת־הָאָרֶץ — *Do what is right and good in* HASHEM'*s eyes [i.e., go beyond the letter of the law (Rashi)] so that He will do good to you and you shall come and inherit the land* (6:18).

The Sages learned from the beginning of this verse that a Jew should feel obligated to go beyond the strict requirements of the Torah. Thus, our verse brings together the two concepts of doing beyond the letter of the law and possession of the land. The Sages referred to this connection in the following teaching: לֹא נֶחְרְבָה יְרוּשָׁלַיִם אֶלָּא עַל שֶׁלֹּא דָּנוּ בָהּ לִפְנִים מְשׁוּרַת הַדִּין, *Jerusalem was destroyed only because they did not judge there beyond the letter of the law* (Bava Metzia 30b). The people lost their land because they insisted on doing only what was absolutely required, and no more.

❦ ❦ ❦

פרשת עקב
Parashas Eikev

וְהָיָה עֵקֶב תִּשְׁמְעוּן אֵת הַמִּשְׁפָּטִים הָאֵלֶּה . . . וְשָׁמַר ה' אֱלֹהֶיךָ לְךָ אֶת־הַבְּרִית — *And it shall be because you will listen to these laws . . . and Hashem, your God, will keep for you the covenant* (7:12).

The use of the word עֵקֶב, *because,* is strange in this expression. It would seem that בִּשְׁבִיל, *for the sake of,* or תַּחַת, *because of,* would have been more fitting. Many commentators have given explanations for this unusual word, but we will suggest still one more.

The word עֵקֶב really means *heel*; in other words, the extremity of something. Every law has not only the requirements which make up the essence of the law but also an indefinite end point that is called לִפְנִים מִשּׁוּרַת הַדִּין, *more than the boundary of the law.* An observant Jew is expected to observe more than the strict requirements of the law; upholding the law is the minimum obligation, but he should try to do more, to whatever degree he can.

This is the significance of the word עֵקֶב. Everyone should try to go to the *extremity* of his abilities, doing not only what is strictly required of him but more than that, to do whatever he possibly can to fulfill the will of the Creator. If he does this, the Torah promises him that Hashem will keep His covenant on the heels of the minutiae of this *mitzvah.*

❈ ❈ ❈

וְשָׁמַר ה' אֱלֹהֶיךָ לְךָ אֶת־הַבְּרִית — *And* HASHEM, *your God, will keep for you the covenant* (7:12).

Usually when the Torah talks about keeping the covenant, it uses the word קַיֵּם, *uphold*. What is the signficance of the word וְשָׁמַר, which suggests "watching" something or holding it in storage?

The answer is that normally Jews do not need this promise. When they keep the Torah and *mitzvos*, Hashem protects them from harm because of their own merits. It is only at a time when, Heaven forbid, we do not merit Hashem's exceptional protection, that He, so to speak, relies on the covenant, which He had *kept* in storage, and safeguards His people only because of it.

❧ ❧ ❧

וְאָמַרְתָּ בִּלְבָבֶךָ כֹּחִי וְעֹצֶם יָדִי עָשָׂה לִי אֶת־הַחַיִל הַזֶּה: וְזָכַרְתָּ אֶת־ה' אֱלֹהֶיךָ כִּי הוּא הַנֹּתֵן לְךָ כֹּחַ לַעֲשׂוֹת חָיִל — *And you will say in your heart, "My strength and the power of my hand has made me this wealth." You shall remember* HASHEM, *your God, for it is He Who gives you strength to make wealth* (8:17,18).

How fortunate is the person who is given the strength to provide for his own needs, without having to ask Hashem to intervene overtly in his affairs. This is what Hashem wants of us, and those who achieve this goal are indeed blessed.

Such a person, however, is in danger of forgetting that, in spite of surface appearances, really all of his strength and all of his wealth come from Hashem. This is why the Torah has to remind him that what he has is the greatest present Hashem can give anyone—the ability to do for himself.

❧ ❧ ❧

וַיִּתֵּן ה' אֵלַי אֶת־שְׁנֵי לוּחֹת הָאֲבָנִים — *And Hashem gave me the two Tablets of stone* (9:10).

Normally we find the word לוּחֹת written with a *vav* to designate the plural. *Rashi* explains why it is left out here. In our verse, it is spelled deficiently so that it can be vowelized לוּחַת, in the singular, as well as לוּחֹת, in the plural, to indicate that the two Tablets were equal, as if they were one.

We may further say that the word שְׁנֵי, *two*, also indicates that the two were equal. It is not needed to indicate how many Tablets there were because this is already obvious from the plural form, *Tablets*, and the Sages taught that a plural noun by itself, without a modifying number, means two, the minimum possible. Thus the word שְׁנֵי in this context indicates that the two Tablets are equal. [Similarly, the Sages (*Yoma* 62b) interpreted the word שְׁנֵי to mean that the two he-goats offered on Yom Kippur should resemble one another as closely as possible.] In any case, we see that each of the Tablets was just as important as the other.

The *Talmud Yerushalmi* (*Shekalim* 6:1) mentions an opinion that all Ten Commandments were written on each of the two Tablets. Why was this so? Perhaps we can learn from it that one cannot fulfill the first five commandments, which concern man's relationship with Hashem, unless one also fulfills the second five, which concern relations among human beings. Thus, one Tablet gives primacy to the first five commandments and lists the others as an explanation for them, while on the second Tablet the reverse is true. In any case, we see that there is an unshakable connection between the two: One cannot truly fulfill either set of five commandments unless he fulfills all ten of them. To fulfill only five is tantamount to fulfilling none at all.

❧ ❧ ❧

הָאֵל הַגָּדֹל הַגִּבֹּר וְהַנּוֹרָא . . . עֹשֶׂה מִשְׁפַּט יָתוֹם
וְאַלְמָנָה — *the great, mighty and awesome God
. . . He performs justice for orphan and widow*
(10:17-18).

Rabbi Yochanan (*Megillah* 31a) cites these verses in support of his dictum: *Wherever you find the greatness of the Holy One, Blessed is He, there you find His humility.* Thus, after telling us of Hashem's infinite greatness, the Torah tells us that He is concerned with the plight of the helpless.

We may ask: What does Rabbi Yochanan add to our understanding of the Torah with his comment? Simply from reading the verses we would know that both Hashem's greatness and His humility are evident in them.

We may say that Rabbi Yochanan wants to teach a most fundamental message: Hashem's greatness rests *precisely* in His humility. We can see that our Sages recognized this meaning of greatness in the *Mishnah: Who is mighty? He who subdues his personal inclination (Avos* 4:1).

The Talmud (*Yoma* 69b) relates that Daniel, contemplating the oppression of our people in exile, asked, "The nations enslave His children; where are His mighty deeds?" Because of this, Daniel omitted the declaration of Hashem's might from his prayer (see *Daniel* 9:4). Later the Men of the Great Assembly answered Daniel's question: "To the contrary, it is proof of Hashem's might that He can subdue His personal inclination and display patience toward the wicked." Thus, when the Men of the Great Assembly formalized the *Shemoneh Esrei* prayer, they inserted the complete phrase, הָאֵל
הַגָּדוֹל הַגִּבּוֹר וְהַנּוֹרָא.

❦ ❦ ❦

פרשת ראה
Parashas Re'eh

רְאֵה אָנֹכִי נֹתֵן לִפְנֵיכֶם הַיּוֹם בְּרָכָה וּקְלָלָה: — *See! I am placing before you today a blessing and a curse* (11:26).

We may ask, why does Moshe say רְאֵה, *see*, in the singular form? He was, after all, talking to the whole assembly, as we see from the use of the plural word לִפְנֵיכֶם, *before you,* rather than the singular form לְפָנֶיךָ. Furthermore, why does he use the word "see" at all when he could have said more simply, "I am placing a blessing and a curse before you"?

In answer, we can say that each person has his own idea of what is a blessing (or its opposite, Heaven forbid). Some would say that mild sickness is really a blessing, since it warns us to examine our life-style and make healthy changes before there are worse conse-quences; while others say that health is always a blessing. Some feel the greatest blessing is children, others say it is wealth, and so on.

When Moshe said רְאֵה, *see*, in the singular, he meant that each individual will be given whatever he personally considers a blessing. However, sometimes the things that people think are blessings turn out not to be good for them, such as wealth, which may expose its owner to temptations best avoided, or may make him a target for dangerous criminals. Conversely, things that seem bad can turn out to be great blessings, such as situations we hear of in which people miss travel connections and thereby avoid fatal accidents.

This is why Moshe used the word רְאֵה, *see*. Not only will you be given blessings, but you will actually *see* how they are blessings and why they are good for you, even though others may not agree. In

KOL DODI ON THE TORAH

this vein, someone once defined a שָׁנָה טוֹבָה וּמְתוּקָה, *a good and sweet year*, as a year so sweet that even a child understands that it is good.

❦ ❦ ❦

אַבֵּד תְּאַבְּדוּן אֶת־כָּל־הַמְּקֹמוֹת אֲשֶׁר עָבְדוּ־שָׁם הַגּוֹיִם — *You shall surely destroy all of the places where the gentiles worshiped [idols]* (12:2).

The repetitive expression אַבֵּד תְּאַבְּדוּן connotes persistent, recurrent destruction. Why is this point stressed — once a site of idolatry was destroyed, surely it would remain destroyed? However, Moshe knew that in time the Jews would revert to idol worship. He therefore told them that every time they built a new idol or a new altar and later repented, they would have to go back and destroy their idols again.

Joshua was not aware of this danger, since in his time the people were still fresh and enthusiastic in their new land, and he did not suspect that they would return to idolatry once they had destroyed the idols of the previous inhabitants. This is why he did not pray, as Ezra later did, that the urge to worship idols be eradicated from people's minds. (See our commentary to *Devarim* 3:21.)

❦ ❦ ❦

שְׁמֹר וְשָׁמַעְתָּ אֵת כָּל־הַדְּבָרִים הָאֵלֶּה אֲשֶׁר אָנֹכִי מְצַוֶּךָּ לְמַעַן יִיטַב לְךָ . . . כִּי תַעֲשֶׂה הַטּוֹב וְהַיָּשָׁר בְּעֵינֵי ה' אֱלֹהֶיךָ: — *Keep and hear all these words which I command you, so that it will be good for you . . . when you will do what is good and just in the eyes of HASHEM, your God* (12:28).

It would seem that the first two words of this verse should be reversed: First *hear* the commandments and then you will be able to *keep* them. Why does Moshe change the order?

Really, however, Moshe was saying the following: "If you *keep* the letter of the law, then you will merit to *hear* what Hashem really wants of you, which is to do לִפְנִים מִשּׁוּרַת הַדִּין, more than the requirement of the law." This is the meaning of the end of the verse,

כִּי תַעֲשֶׂה הַטּוֹב וְהַיָּשָׁר, *when you will do what is good and just*, even when the law does not strictly require it. It is from this verse that the Sages (*Bava Metzia* 30b) derive the requirement to go beyond the minimum demands of the law.

❧ ❧ ❧

עַשֵּׂר תְּעַשֵּׂר אֵת כָּל־תְּבוּאַת זַרְעֶךָ — *Tithe, you shall tithe all the produce of your sowing* (14:22).

The Sages (*Taanis* 9a) interpreted this verse homiletically, עַשֵּׂר בִּשְׁבִיל שֶׁתִּתְעַשֵּׂר, *tithe so that you will become wealthy* (from the similar spelling of the two words עַשֵּׂר, *tithe,* and עָשֵׁר, *wealth*).

This saying could also be transposed: עַשֵּׁר בִּשְׁבִיל שֶׁתִּתְעַשֵּׂר, *become wealthy in order to tithe*. Wealth is given to people only so that they can distribute to the needy the portion that is rightfully theirs.

❧ ❧ ❧

וְשָׂמַחְתָּ בְּחַגֶּךָ . . . וְהָיִיתָ אַךְ שָׂמֵחַ: — *And you shall rejoice in your festivals . . . And you shall be only joyous* (16:14-15).

Why is this dictum, which refers to the festival of Succos, repeated twice? The second time is a promise that someone who rejoices during Succos will merit to be joyful all year long.

We can see this in an interesting *gematria*: By rejoicing for the 7 days of Succos, he adds 7 (days) to 348, the numerical value of the word שָׂמֵחַ (joyous) to make up 355, the numerical value of the word שָׁנָה (year).

Why does Succos have this power to spread its joyousness throughout the year? On Succos, Hashem makes us leave our homes and the protection they provide in order to make us realize that everything in this world is transitory and that ultimately, He protects *us,* not our material goods and fortresses.

Furthermore, we are especially enjoined during these days to use the money which we consider to be "ours" to provide for the needs of the poor (cf. *Avos* 5:12). In spite of this, we feel greater joy on Succos than at any other time.

In reward for accepting these privations joyfully, the Torah promises that we will rejoice the whole year in our homes with all of our normal supports.

We see this in the *Mishnah* in *Avos* (4:11), כָּל הַמְקַיֵּם אֶת הַתּוֹרָה מֵעֹנִי סוֹפוֹ לְקַיְּמָהּ מֵעשֶׁר, *Whoever fulfills the Torah despite poverty, will ultimately fulfill it in wealth.* If we do not let poverty deter us from serving Hashem, He will allow us to serve Him in comfort and good fortune. And — we may add — in both situations we will be בְּשִׂמְחָה, *joyful.*

❧ ❧ ❧

פרשת שופטים
Parashas Shoftim

וְלֹא־תִקַּח שֹׁחַד כִּי הַשֹּׁחַד יְעַוֵּר עֵינֵי חֲכָמִים וִיסַלֵּף
דִּבְרֵי צַדִּיקִם׃ — *Do not take a bribe, for bribery blinds the eyes of the wise and corrupts righteous words* (16:19).

It is interesting to note that even though a judge has accepted a bribe, the Torah does not call *him* corrupt. It says merely that the bribe corrupts his words. This is because the bribe he takes makes him into a lawyer for one side. From then on, all of his thoughts are directed to the benefit of his "employer," and he becomes convinced of the justness of the briber's case; even though if he were impartial he would realize that he is thinking illogically. Thus the Talmud (*Kesubos* 105b) states, "מַאי שׁוֹחַד? שֶׁהוּא חַד, Why is bribery called שׁוֹחַד? Because it makes the giver and recipient חַד, as one."

He may think that he is righteous and attempt to judge honestly, but his words are no longer "straight" and logical. He is deceiving himself for such is the power of bribery, that it buys his partiality.

❧ ❧ ❧

יַד הָעֵדִים תִּהְיֶה־בּוֹ בָרִאשֹׁנָה לַהֲמִיתוֹ — *The hand of the witnesses shall be on him first to kill him* (17:7).

There are two reasons why witnesses whose testimony convicts someone of a capital offense are required to perform the execution themselves. For one thing, such a rule obviously forces the witnesses to take their testimony very seriously. Since they will literally have blood on their hands, they will think very carefully before they accuse someone. Without this rule, someone might well testify about a crime that he had not actually seen being committed, relying on logic or probability to convince himself and others that his story was correct. However, if he had to carry out the execution himself, he would hesitate to do this. If someone else were to do the actual killing, it might not have the same effect.

The second reason is more abstract: The Sages said that seeing something is a much surer way of knowing it with certainty than hearing it. [אֵינָה דוֹמָה שְׁמִיעָה לִרְאִיָּה, *hearing is not equivalent to seeing,* is a phrase oft repeated by the Sages (e.g., *Mechilta Yisro* 19:9.)] Anyone other than an eyewitness knows what happened only through hearsay, but the witnesses have actually seen the crime take place and can be more certain who was responsible. Therefore they should be the ones to take action.

❧ ❧ ❧

כִּי יִפָּלֵא מִמְּךָ דָבָר לַמִּשְׁפָּט . . . וְקַמְתָּ וְעָלִיתָ אֶל־הַמָּקוֹם אֲשֶׁר יִבְחַר ה' אֱלֹהֶיךָ בּוֹ: וּבָאתָ . . . וְאֶל־הַשֹּׁפֵט אֲשֶׁר יִהְיֶה בַּיָּמִים הָהֵם וְדָרַשְׁתָּ וְהִגִּידוּ לְךָ אֶת דְּבַר הַמִּשְׁפָּט: — *When a matter of judgment shall be hidden from you . . . you shall stand and go up to the place which HASHEM, your God, will choose. And you shall come to the . . . judge who will be in those days and ask and they will tell you the matter of the judgment (17:8-9).*

Rashi comments on the words, *who will be in those days,* that even if he is not the equal of the judges who lived in the generations before him, you still have to obey him because you have only the judge who is in your time. We can ask why the Torah had to add this phrase — had it said simply, *and come to the judge and he will tell you . . .* we would know that the Torah meant that we have to obey *the judge,* whatever his abilities, even if he is not the equal of earlier judges.

However, the Torah means to teach us that if the judges rule on the basis of their own logic but someone disagrees with them based on the teaching he received from the leaders of previous generations — who were greater than the current judges — he must still obey the ruling of those in authority in *his* own time.

❀ ❀ ❀

שָׁלוֹשׁ עָרִים תַּבְדִּיל לָךְ — *Separate for yourself three cities* (19:2).

In speaking about the cities of refuge, the Torah uses the concept of *separating*, not just choosing or naming. This suggests that there was something distinctive about these cities: a special respect for life that could be felt in the cities of the Levites. Exile was the punishment of someone who killed through carelessness, in a manner that indicated a light-hearted attitude toward the value of human life. One who reveres life to the proper degree would not have been so careless. Consequently, he was exiled to live among exalted people, the Levites.

Thus, someone who had accidentally taken a life could use the time of his exile to learn more clearly the value of life and be more careful to avoid fatal accidents in the future.

❀ ❀ ❀

וַעֲשִׂיתֶם לוֹ כַּאֲשֶׁר זָמַם לַעֲשׂוֹת לְאָחִיו וּבִעַרְתָּ הָרָע מִקִּרְבֶּךָ — *And you shall do to him as he had planned to do to his brother, and you shall remove the evil from your midst* (19:19).

When witnesses who testified about a murder are later proven false by testimony which places them elsewhere at the time the alleged murder occurred, the false witnesses are executed in place of the person they accused. (This rule is subject to many intricate provisions, as discussed in Tractate *Makkos*.) However, if the accused had already been executed, then the false witnesses are free from this special, reciprocal, punishment. This is derived from the words in our verse, *as he had 'planned' to do to his brother*, but not if he had actually done it.

By close analysis, we can understand the Torah's justification for this rule. Hashem, Who is just in all His ways, would not have allowed the accused to be executed unless he actually deserved that punishment. Therefore the false witnesses, even though they did wrong, did not cause an unjust death and so do not deserve execution.

On the other hand, if their conspiracy is uncovered before the accused is executed, so that his life is spared, we know that Hashem saved him because he did not deserve death. Thus it turns out that these false witnesses tried to have an innocent man killed, and for this they are themselves executed.

❧ ❧ ❧

פרשת כי תצא
Parashas Ki Seitzei

כִּי־תֵצֵא לַמִּלְחָמָה עַל־אֹיְבֶיךָ וּנְתָנוֹ ה' אֱלֹהֶיךָ בְּיָדֶךָ
וְשָׁבִיתָ שִׁבְיוֹ: — *When you go out to war against
your enemies, and* HASHEM *your God will give
him into your hand, and you will capture a
prisoner* (21:10).

The phrasing of this verse seems to imply a guarantee:
Hashem *will* deliver your enemies into your hands. How
can the Torah offer such a blanket promise that every war
will be victorious? Has the Jewish people never been defeated?

Rashi says that this verse refers to a מִלְחֶמֶת הָרְשׁוּת, *an elective war,*
since it was forbidden to take captives in mandatory wars (wars
dictated by Torah law, such as Joshua's battles to oust the seven
Caananite nations). Now, the Sages (*Berachos* 3b) taught that
before a ruler was permitted to wage an elective war, he was
required to consult the *Urim VeTumim*, the stones on the
breastplate of the High Priest, which would light up in patterns
revealing Hashem's will in the matter.

Obviously, they would undertake only those wars which were
sanctioned by the *Urim VeTumim* and which it said they would win.
Thus the Torah could promise that the Jews would emerge
victoriously from any elective war which was fought.

❀ ❀ ❀

אֵינֶנּוּ שֹׁמֵעַ בְּקֹלֵנוּ — *He does not listen to our voice* (21:20).

uch is the complaint to the judges by the parents of the "stubborn and rebellious son." The word קֹלֵנוּ appears in the singular, *our voice*, rather than *our voices*. This suggests that the two parents speak with a single voice, agreeing that what their child did was wrong.

A few verses earlier, however, we find written, אֵינֶנּוּ שֹׁמֵעַ בְּקוֹל אָבִיו וּבְקוֹל אִמּוֹ, *He does not listen to the voice of his father and the voice of his mother* (v.18). Here two separate voices are mentioned, implying that there was discord between the parents.

The lesson is that a child is more likely to be ruled by his own desires when the parents disagree about how to deal with him; and that lack of unity between the parents caused the problem in the first place. Even though they later realized that he was doing wrong and joined together to correct the damage, by then it was already too late and he would not listen to them about anything.

❧ ❧ ❧

כִּי יִקָּרֵא קַן־צִפּוֹר לְפָנֶיךָ — *If you come upon a bird's nest* (22:6).

he word יִקָּרֵא, *to come upon*, is normally spelled with a *hei*. When it is written with an *aleph*, as it is here, it usually means *to call* or *announce*. This suggests that there was an "announcement" that you should come upon this nest. What is the significance of this announcement?

One purpose of this *mitzvah* is to teach compassion, that we should respect the feelings of the mother bird by not making her witness the taking of her eggs. Someone who already has this quality does not need the lesson of the *mitzvah*. Therefore, if Hashem arranged for a particular person to find a nest with eggs, it is because that person needs the lesson it teaches.

The next verse promises reward for doing this *mitzvah*: לְמַעַן יִיטַב לָךְ וְהַאֲרַכְתָּ יָמִים — *so that it will be good for you and your days will be lengthened*. The first part of this blessing, *so that it will be good for you,* refers to the fruits which he will enjoy in this world, and the second part, *and your days will be lengthened,* refers to the principal which remains intact for him in the World to Come. Now, the Sages taught (*Kiddushin* 46a) that the only *mitzvos* which are rewarded in this world are those which concern relations between human beings. If so, why should this *mitzvah* be rewarded in this world?

The answer is that the *mitzvah* teaches compassion. It is inevitable that one who develops compassion for a bird will learn to be kind to human beings, as well. Therefore it is appropriate that when one learns that lesson, one should have reward in this world, as well as in the next.

❦ ❦ ❦

עַל־דְּבַר אֲשֶׁר לֹא־קִדְּמוּ אֶתְכֶם בַּלֶּחֶם וּבַמַּיִם —
Because they did not greet you with bread and water (23:5).

In these words, the Torah explains that male converts of Ammonite and Moabite origin were never to be allowed to marry into the Jewish people [i.e., they could only marry converts, but not full-born Jews], because they did not show compassion to their Jewish "cousins" in their time of need. We must understand how this historical event justifies such a sweeping disqualification, and how these converts differ from Egyptian converts and converts from the descendants of Esau, who are permitted to marry into the Jewish nation after three generations.

Our father Abraham was exceptionally distinguished in the quality of compassion, and his descendants inherited this quality from him, to one degree or another. The Torah realized that callous behavior, like that of the Ammonites and Moabites, would inevitably pollute the Abrahamitic genetic pool with undesirable traits.

This does not apply to Esau's descendants, however, since he was Abraham's grandson and had the same genetic inheritance as Jacob. Therefore, even though the Edomite descendants of Esau displayed the same behavior as the Ammonites and Moabites, it did not indicate a trait inherent in their genetic makeup.

As for the Egyptians, in spite of the fact that they afflicted the Jews with slavery, earlier they had given them refuge in time of need.

From this we see that they must have had some measure of compassion in their make-up, albeit a weak one. Thus, in these two cases, after three generations of exposure to Torah and *mitzvos*, they were allowed to marry into the mainstream.

❧ ❧ ❧

וּלְאָחִיךָ לֹא תַשִּׁיךְ לְמַעַן יְבָרֶכְךָ ה' אֱלֹהֶיךָ — *Do not take interest from your brother so that HASHEM, your God, will bless you* (23:21).

The Torah gives a reason not to take interest: *so that* Hashem will bless us. Why should this be a reason?

Someone who takes interest is, so to speak, blessing himself and saying that he can take care of his own needs. Therefore Hashem does not want to help such a person. However, someone who lends without taking interest, because Hashem commands that we do so, does not rely on his own means; instead, he risks his own funds without earning any return, showing that he depends entirely on Hashem's help. This is the person whom Hashem will bless.

❧ ❧ ❧

פרשת כי תבוא
Parashas Ki Savo

וְהָיָה כִּי־תָבוֹא אֶל־הָאָרֶץ אֲשֶׁר ה' אֱלֹהֶיךָ נֹתֵן לְךָ
נַחֲלָה וִירִשְׁתָּהּ וְיָשַׁבְתָּ בָּהּ: וְלָקַחְתָּ מֵרֵאשִׁית כָּל־פְּרִי
הָאֲדָמָה — *And it shall be when you come
to the land which HASHEM, your God, is
giving you as an inheritance and you shall
occupy it and dwell in it. And you shall take
from the first of all produce of the land . . .*
(26:1-2).

From our verse we learn that the Jews did not have to fulfill
the *mitzvah* of *bikkurim*, the offering of the first fruits, until
after they had come to the land, occupied it, dwelled on it,
and divided it among the tribes, a series of activities that took
fourteen years.

Why did this particular *mitzvah* not take effect immediately when
the Jews entered their land? To answer this question, we must
understand that the offering of the first fruits had a specific purpose:
to give thanks to Hashem for keeping His promise to Moshe, וְהֵבֵאתִי
אֶתְכֶם אֶל־הָאָרֶץ, *and I will bring you to the land* (*Shemos* 6:8). In
other words, it was a thanksgiving offering for the land.

Now, until the land was fully divided and occupied, the people
could not say that the promise had been completely fulfilled.
Therefore, until then it was not appropriate to give thanks. Had the
Jews started to bring *bikkurim* earlier, it might have implied a feeling

on their part that Hashem did not intend to finish giving them the land, or, Heaven forbid, was not capable of it, and therefore they were giving thanks for what they already had, but they did not expect any more. That is why this *mitzvah* did not apply until the land was completely distributed and every family was settled in its portion.

❈ ❈ ❈

וּבָאתָ אֶל־הַכֹּהֵן . . . וְאָמַרְתָּ אֵלָיו הִגַּדְתִּי הַיּוֹם לַה' אֱלֹהֶיךָ כִּי־בָאתִי אֶל־הָאָרֶץ — *And you shall come to the Kohen . . . and you shall say to him: Today I have related to HASHEM, your God, that I have come to the land . . .* (26:3).

One who brings *bikkurim* is commanded to present them to a *Kohen* and recite a short speech of thanksgiving containing a capsule history of the Egyptian exile. It is this speech which we say on *Seder* night as part of the Haggadah.

The word הִגַּדְתִּי, *I have related,* can be homiletically interpreted to recall two similar Hebrew words. One is גִּידִים, *sinews,* suggesting things which are hard as sinews. The other is אַגָּדָה, *aggadah,* the teachings of the Sages which draw a person's heart and inspire faith and commitment to Torah. Both of these can be understood as references to sections in the recitation which follows.

The "sinews" refer to the beginning of the recitation, which tells the harsh story of Jacob's descent to Egypt because of hunger, וַיֵּרֶד מִצְרַיְמָה, *and he went down to Egypt* (v. 5). The *aggadah* is the uplifting story of the redemption of the Jews from Egypt, וַיּוֹצִאֵנוּ ה' מִמִּצְרַיִם בְּיָד חֲזָקָה וּבִזְרֹעַ נְטוּיָה, *and HASHEM took us out from Egypt with a strong hand and an outstretched arm* (v. 8).

The Passover *Seder* prescribes this same progression in answering the Four Questions: מַתְחִיל בִּגְנוּת וּמְסַיֵּם בְּשֶׁבַח, *One should begin with disgrace and end with praise,* meaning that the narrative of the Haggadah begins with the degrading story of our idol-worshiping ancestor Terach and our slavery in Egypt. Only then does it go on to the miracles of the Exodus.

❈ ❈ ❈

וְעָנִיתָ וְאָמַרְתָּ — *And you shall respond and say* (26:5).

fter the *Kohen* takes the *bikkurim* from the hand of its owner, the owner is told to "respond and say" the short speech mentioned earlier. It is not at all obvious, however, what he is to respond to. The Torah has not told us that the *Kohen* is supposed to say anything, nor do we know of anyone else who has spoken to him. Therefore, to whom or to what is he responding?

In answer, we may say simply that he is responding to the blessing which Hashem gave him in bringing him to the Land and giving him its fruits to eat. This is what prompted him to separate the first fruits from his harvest and to bring them to the Holy Temple, there to follow the procedure for offering them, with the recitation of thanksgiving which he is about to say. In other words, a Jew must learn to appreciate the significance of events. God "speaks" to us through history and nature, and when He does, we are called upon to respond properly. Even though we work hard to produce our bread, we still thank Hashem before we eat it.

※ ※ ※

תַּחַת אֲשֶׁר לֹא־עָבַדְתָּ אֶת־ה' אֱלֹהֶיךָ בְּשִׂמְחָה וּבְטוּב לֵבָב מֵרֹב כֹּל: — *Because you did not serve HASHEM with joy and with a good heart out of an abundance of everything* (28:47).

wo words in this verse, רֹב, *abundance*, and כֹּל, *everything*, create opposing impressions. When Esau said, "יֶשׁ־לִי רָב, *I have plenty*," he was boasting that he had more than anyone needed. Yet רָב is not *all*. Jacob, on the other hand, said, "יֶשׁ־לִי־כֹל, *I have everything*," meaning that he had everything he needed and was happy with it. However much or little it was, he did not need more.

Someone who prides himself on possessions that he regards as his alone, and does not feel that he is responsible to anyone else for them, will never be satisfied, because he will always want more than he has. But someone who views his property as an opportunity from Hashem to do more *mitzvos* will always be satisfied, because he recognizes that he has literally everything he needs.

This was Moshe's warning to the Jews: "If you are not happy when you serve Hashem, it is because you think that your property is yours to use as you please. With such an attitude, you will never be satisfied with what you have, but will always want more. You had כֹּל, *everything* you needed, but you weren't satisfied with that. Instead you said רֹב כֹּל, an *abundance of everything* — not just *everything!*"

❧ ❧ ❧

וְלֹא־נָתַן ה' לָכֶם לֵב לָדַעַת וְעֵינַיִם לִרְאוֹת וְאָזְנַיִם לִשְׁמֹעַ עַד הַיּוֹם הַזֶּה: — *And HASHEM did not give you a heart to know and eyes to see and ears to hear until today* (29:3).

Moshe is consoling the Jews: "Until now, Hashem did not give you the ability to see and understand His great kindnesses to you. It is not your fault that you did not appreciate them because in the past you were not capable of it. Now, however, that He has given you these powers, you will be held responsible for your actions." And now that they were capable of doing so, Moshe was able to charge them with the responsibilities he speaks of in *Parashas Nitzavim*.

❧ ❧ ❧

פרשת נצבים
Parashas Nitzavim

אַתֶּם נִצָּבִים הַיּוֹם כֻּלְּכֶם לִפְנֵי ה' אֱלֹהֵיכֶם רָאשֵׁיכֶם שִׁבְטֵיכֶם זִקְנֵיכֶם וְשֹׁטְרֵיכֶם כֹּל אִישׁ יִשְׂרָאֵל: — *You are standing today, all of you before HASHEM, your God, the chiefs of your tribes, your elders, and your officers, every man of Israel (29:9).*

The word נִצָּבִים, *standing*, suggests a rigid, unchanging erect-ness, like מַצֵּבָה, *a stone monument*. Yet every Jew has a re-sponsibility to progress, to move ever high. Surely Moshe did not mean to suggest that the Jews were frozen like stone, never to change or grow. In what sense, therefore, did he describe them as erect?

When Moshe told the Jews that they were standing erect and unchanging, he was referring to their position as כֻּלְּכֶם לִפְנֵי ה', *all of you, before HASHEM.* He meant that every Jew stands equal in Hashem's eyes, every one of them together in His front row, with the same duty to serve Him according to his own ability. Even though some are leaders with tens of thousands of followers, and others are only infants, each one is equal in his obligation to do as much as he can to serve Hashem.

We take it for granted that children are expected to grow and change, but they are not the only ones. *Every Jew is required to strive for higher levels in his service of Hashem, every day of his life. In every situation that he finds himself, he must exert himself to the* utmost. Still, however much anyone grows, his position relative to Hashem remains ever fixed and unchanging in the front row of the Jewish people, among those with the highest commitments to Hashem.

❧ ❧ ❧

וְלֹא אִתְּכֶם לְבַדְּכֶם אָנֹכִי כֹּרֵת אֶת־הַבְּרִית הַזֹּאת וְאֶת־הָאָלָה הַזֹּאת: כִּי אֶת־אֲשֶׁר יֶשְׁנוֹ פֹּה עִמָּנוּ עֹמֵד הַיּוֹם לִפְנֵי ה' אֱלֹהֵינוּ וְאֵת אֲשֶׁר אֵינֶנּוּ פֹּה עִמָּנוּ הַיּוֹם:
— *And not with you alone do I make this covenant and this oath. But with those who are standing with us here today before* HASHEM, *your God, and with those who are not with us today* (29:13-14).

Rashi explains that, *those who are not with us today,* refers to future generations. Thus the covenant which Moshe forged between Hashem and the people is obligatory on Jews of all times, not only on those who were present. This raises two questions: First, how could the children present at that time, who were not yet capable of obligating themselves *halachically* to anything, have entered into the covenant? Furthermore, how could someone of that time bind unborn generations, spanning thousands of years, to such a demanding and all-encompassing commitment?

The answer to the first question is that the *neshamah* (soul) of a child is mature from birth and is fully capable of entering into such a bond; it was those souls which Moshe brought into the covenant. Similarly, while the future generations were not present, the genetic base that would later produce them was present in the persons of that generation of Jews. That was sufficient to create a national commitment that was binding on future generations as well.

❧ ❧ ❧

וַיִּתְּשֵׁם ה' מֵעַל אַדְמָתָם בְּאַף וּבְחֵמָה וּבְקֶצֶף גָּדוֹל
וַיַּשְׁלִכֵם אֶל־אֶרֶץ אַחֶרֶת כַּיּוֹם הַזֶּה: — *And*
HASHEM removed them from their land in
anger and rage and fury, and He threw them
out to a different land like this day (29:27).

According to the Masoretic tradition, the letter *lamed* of the word וַיַּשְׁלִכֵם, *and He threw them out,* is written enlarged. We may interpret this homiletically. The name of the letter *lamed* denotes the concept of teaching. Hashem will exile the Jews from their land in order to *teach* them the consequences of straying from the Torah. Hashem's primary purpose is instruction rather than punishment. If the nation could learn from its fate that the result of sin is banishment and persecution, it would be zealous in its observance of the Torah and its commandments.

Another way of looking at this enlarged *lamed* is to read the word as if that letter were not there at all. This would leave us with the word וַיַּשְׁכֵּם, *and He arose early,* a reference to the teaching of the Sages (*Gittin* 88a) that the Jews were expelled from their land two years before the time of no return. Had Hashem waited two more years, Israel's accumulated sins would have been so numerous that the destruction would have been much greater, Heaven forbid. Had that happened, Israel might not have been able to survive. To avert that, God brought the exile two years earlier.

According to this interpretation, however, it might have been more appropriate if the *lamed* had been written smaller than normal, as usually occurs when a word is interpreted without the indicated letter. We can say, however, that the Torah wanted to stress another meaning of the letter *lamed*, as a prepositional prefix meaning "to" or "for." In the context of our verse, it could have the meaning "for our benefit," indicating that the expulsion from our land was really to our benefit. We may go further and say that no matter how much we have suffered during our exile, eventually we will understand that it was for our benefit.

❀   ❀   ❀

וְשָׁב ה' אֱלֹהֶיךָ אֶת־שְׁבוּתְךָ — And HASHEM, your God, will return with your captivity . . . (30:3).

ashi on this verse cites the teaching of our Sages that the Shechinah (Divine Presence) joins the Jewish people in their exile, and will Itself be redeemed only together with them. In this week's *Haftarah*, we find a similar idea: בְּכָל־צָרָתָם לֹא צָר (לוֹ קרי) — *In all of their hardship it is hard for Him* (*Yeshayahu* 63:9).

There is an obvious question to be asked on both of these verses: If Hashem is in exile with us and shares our suffering, why has He extended the exile for so long when it is surely in His power to end it whenever He wants?

To answer this question, let us examine a discrepancy in the Masoretic tradition between the written and the pronounced texts of the verse from the *Haftarah*. The written version, לֹא צָר, *it is not hard,* seems to say that Hashem is not bothered by our difficulties; this would explain why He leaves us in exile for so long.

This verse is read, however, לוֹ צָר, *it is hard for Him*. Even though Hashem shares our pain, He nonetheless does not end the exile because He knows it is for our good. Like a father who punishes his son to force him to improve his character but nonetheless cries as he does so, or like a surgeon who can save a patient's life only by performing a painful operation, Hashem shares our suffering, but perseveres in continuing the exile for our sake.

❧ ❧ ❧

וּבָחַרְתָּ בַּחַיִּים — Choose life! (30:19).

hy does the Torah see fit to enjoin us to do something which is so patently obvious? Surely these words were not written only for suicidal people, Heaven forbid. What is the Torah trying to tell us?

Very often we see people doing things which are clearly detrimental to their health and well-being. Even though they don't die immediately from their actions, over the course of time they wind up taking years from the lives they could have lived had they behaved more wisely. And why do they do this? Because the temporary pleasure they have at the time is more important to them than the life of some future time that it costs them.

If we were to be honest with ourselves, we would admit that most of us fall into this category in one way or another. Therefore, it is to all of us that the Torah addresses the commandment *Choose life,* telling us to be strong and forgo ephemeral pleasures which will shorten our lives in the long run.

❃ ❃ ❃

פרשת וילך
Parshas Vayeilech

בֶּן־מֵאָה וְעֶשְׂרִים שָׁנָה אָנֹכִי הַיּוֹם לֹא־אוּכַל עוֹד
לָצֵאת וְלָבוֹא וַה' אָמַר אֵלַי לֹא תַעֲבֹר אֶת־הַיַּרְדֵּן הַזֶּה:
— *I am one hundred and twenty years old
today, I can no longer go out and come in, and
HASHEM said to me: "You will not cross this
River Jordan"* (31:2).

The questions on this verse abound. Why did Moshe find it important to stress his age? As interpreted by the Sages (*see Rashi*), he was telling them that he would die on that day — how did he know this? As the reason for his imminent death he explained, *I can no longer go out and come in,* meaning that he could no longer be their leader — but why did this necessitate his death? What is the relationship between the fact that Hashem told him that he would not cross the Jordan and his death?

This verse teaches that several strands came together to dictate that Moshe was to die on that day. As the climax of man's moral downfall from the creation of Adam to Hashem's decision to bring about the Flood, the Torah states, בְּשַׁגַּם הוּא בָשָׂר וְהָיוּ יָמָיו מֵאָה וְעֶשְׂרִים שָׁנָה, *since he is but flesh, his years will be one hundred and twenty* (*Bereishis* 6:3). This verse indicates that man could no longer live for centuries, as did the first ten generations recorded in the Torah. Because of Adam's sin, death had to be decreed upon his descendants, and a hundred and twenty years would become an ideal lifespan with the passage of time. The Sages (*Chullin* 139b) derive from this verse an allusion to Moshe's lifespan, because the numerical value of מֹשֶׁה, *Moshe,* is equal to that of בְּשַׁגַּם, *since he is but [flesh],* indicating that he would die at the age of a hundred and twenty, because all flesh must die.

The Sages further teach that Moshe's leadership came to an end that day, because it was decreed that Joshua was to assume the mantle. This was what Moshe meant when he said, *I can no longer go out and come in.* Conceivably, Moshe could have lived longer if Israel's entry to *Eretz Yisrael* had been delayed, because it was there that Joshua was to be their leader, and Moshe had been forbidden to cross the Jordan. But that would have meant extending Israel's sojourn in the Wilderness — and this Moshe did not want. Therefore, his life had to end on that day.

Thus, this one verse ties together several different issues: Moshe had reached the age of one hundred and twenty, the end of his allotted years; he was not allowed to cross the Jordan; and, therefore, he did not want to stand in the nation's way when they were ready to embark on a new phase in their history.

❧ ❧ ❧

חֲזַק וֶאֱמָץ כִּי אַתָּה תָּבוֹא אֶת־הָעָם הַזֶּה אֶל־הָאָרֶץ . . . וְאַתָּה תַּנְחִילֶנָּה אוֹתָם: — *Be strong and courageous because you will come with this people to the land . . . and you will cause them to inherit it* (31:7).

Moshe called to Joshua and exhorted him to take courage in front of the whole people. Yet there is a contradiction in Moshe's words: *You will come with this people to the land* suggests that Joshua will enter on equal terms with everyone else; while *you will cause them to inherit it* clearly indicates that he will have authority over the people.

We may say, however, that both of these elements were part of the encouragement that Moshe wanted to give to Joshua. He meant to say, "It is very difficult to strike the proper balance between the humility and the assertiveness that are required of any Jewish public figure, particularly in the land, where Hashem scrutinizes every last deed and thought. On the one hand, you must be humble despite your exalted position, but on the other hand, you must be authoritative in order to control this proud and stiff-necked people. This is the challenge that I pass on to you. Therefore, חֲזַק וֶאֱמָץ, *you need to be strong and courageous.*

❦ ❦ ❦

הַקְהֵל אֶת־הָעָם הָאֲנָשִׁים וְהַנָּשִׁים וְהַטַּף — *Assemble this people, the men, the women and the children (31:12).*

This is the commandment of *Hakheil*, that all the people were to gather in the *Beis HaMikdash* during the *Succos* immediately following the Sabbatical year, to listen to the king read the Book of *Devarim*. *Rashi* explains that the children came to these assemblies, even though they could not understand the proceedings, so that their parents would be rewarded for bringing them.

My father, ל"ז, said that the *mitzvah* of educating children should be performed with the same motivation as any other *mitzvah*, not because we believe we understand its purpose, but לִשְׁמָהּ, for the simple reward of fulfilling Hashem's will. If we were to educate children based on our grasp of who should be educated and why, we might well make the mistake of concentrating our efforts only on those children we think are likely to do well. This would be a mistake, however, because very often our judgments are wrong and children do much better than we expect them to.

Instead, we must approach the *mitzvah* of educating children as גְּזֵרַת הַכָּתוּב, something the Torah decrees us to do. This approach, by the way, was expressed by the Sage R' Elazar ben Azariah. The Talmud relates that when R' Yehoshua ben Chananiah heard that R' Elazar had said this, he said, "Our generation is truly blessed with such a leader."

Why did R' Yehoshua consider this statement worthy of such effusive praise? His mentor, Rabban Yochanan be Zakai, said of him (*Avos* 2:11), אַשְׁרֵי יוֹלַדְתּוֹ, *Fortunate is the one who bore him.* The Talmud explains that R' Yehoshua's mother used to take him as an infant into the *beis midrash* (study hall) so that his tender ears would become attuned to the sound of Torah. Therefore, he was especially well-equipped to recognize the value of study just for the sake of the *mitzvah,* and to appreciate R' Elazar's wise approach to it.

☙ ☙ ☙

וְאָנֹכִי הַסְתֵּר אַסְתִּיר פָּנַי בַּיּוֹם הַהוּא . . . וְעַתָּה כִּתְבוּ לָכֶם אֶת־הַשִּׁירָה הַזֹּאת . . . לְמַעַן תִּהְיֶה־לִּי הַשִּׁירָה הַזֹּאת לְעֵד בִּבְנֵי יִשְׂרָאֵל: — *And I will surely hide My countenance on that day . . . And now write for yourselves this song . . . so that this song shall be for Me a witness on the Children of Israel* (31:18-19).

The "song" refers to the Torah, for this is the commandment to write a Torah scroll. The word לִי, *for Me,* indicates that by means of the *song,* we can see Hashem's Presence (*Shechinah*). Thus there is a very important point hidden in these verses. At a time when Hashem, so to speak, "hides His face" and does not make His Presence manifest, then it is most important that we immerse ourselves in the "song," meaning the Torah. For in it we see the *Shechinah* and the truth that there is a God.

☙ ☙ ☙

וַיְצַו אֶת־יְהוֹשֻׁעַ בִּן־נוּן — *And He [i.e., Hashem] commanded Yehoshua bin Nun* (31:23).

In this verse, Hashem urges Joshua to be strong and includes his father's name. Moshe, however, in his own exortation, referred to him only as Joshua, without saying בִּן נוּן (31:7). Why is there this omission? As *Rashi* notes on verse seven, Moshe told Joshua to rule in partnership with the Elders, paying deference to their views. Hashem, however, told Joshua to be a strong leader and to insist on obedience to his views.

In the discussion of the letters of the Hebrew alphabet (*Shabbos* 104a), the Sages teach that the regular נ, which is bent, alludes to the concept of נֶאֱמָן כָּפוּף, *a trusted person who is humble,* because humility is an essential character trait. The final ן is straight, alluding to נֶאֱמָן פָּשׁוּט, a *straight* or *upright trusted person,* meaning that he does not bow to others, but maintains his authority over others. By telling Joshua to be subservient to the Elders, Moshe was telling Joshua to be like the bent נ. Hashem said otherwise. The word בֵּן alludes to בִּינָה, *understanding.* The name נוּן contains both forms of the letter נ. Thus, Hashem was telling Joshua that a leader must be both authoritative *and* deferential. He should consult others, but he must make the final decision on his own. To know when to defer and when to insist — he must exercise the בִּינָה, *understanding,* necessary for the proper balance of the two letters, נ and ן.

❧ ❧ ❧

פרשת האזינו
Parashas Ha'azinu

הַאֲזִינוּ הַשָּׁמַיִם וַאֲדַבֵּרָה וְתִשְׁמַע הָאָרֶץ אִמְרֵי־פִי:
Listen, O Heavens, and I will speak, and may the earth hear the sayings of my mouth (32:1).

Moshe addressed the Heavens with דִּיבּוּר, a very forceful expression of command: "הַאֲזִינוּ . . . וַאֲדַבֵּרָה, Listen carefully to what I am about to speak to you!" But, for the earth he used אֲמִירָה, a much softer tone, "וְתִשְׁמַע הָאָרֶץ אִמְרֵי־פִי, *Let the earth hear the sayings of my mouth.*" Why did Moshe use stern words in speaking to the Heavens and soft words in speaking to the earth?

Because the Heavens are a spiritual entity, they do exactly as they are commanded even if they do not understand why. And since they are being called upon to do something they do not understand and which is not self-evident, they must listen carefully in order to remember well.

The earth, on the other hand, being entirely physical, needs to understand what it is doing. This is why Moshe speaks to it in a different tone. Physical beings are less responsive than the spiritual Heavens and must be put in a receptive frame of mind to understand what they are told to do. It is difficult for them to be responsive unless they are given logical and easily understood instructions. Once they do understand, however, they will remember. Therefore, Moshe addresses the earth in softer and more subtle terms than the ones he used with the Heavens.

❧ ❧ ❧

כִּי שֵׁם ה' אֶקְרָא הָבוּ גֹדֶל לֵאלֹהֵינוּ — *When I call out the Name of HASHEM, ascribe greatness to our God* (32:3).

I n these verses, Moshe calls on the Heavens and the earth to be witnesses to the Jews' acceptance of the Torah. Like all witnesses in the Torah, they will be the first to administer reward and punishment. However, the words, כִּי שֵׁם ה' אֶקְרָא, *when I call out the Name of HASHEM,* limit this role; the witnesses are to punish the Jews only when the honor of Hashem's Name is at stake.

This is what happened in the time of the prophet Elijah. Under the leadership of the wicked King Ahab, the Kingdom of Israel turned away from the Torah and became ensnared in the idolatrous service of the Baal. To punish them for this desecration of Hashem's Name, Elijah called on the Heavens to withhold rain and dew for three years.

The Sages (*Sanhedrin* 113a) described the circumstances of this drought. The prophet Elijah and King Ahab went to be *menachem avel* (pay a condolence call) a man named Chiel who had transgressed Joshua's ban on rebuilding Jericho and whose sons subsequently died in fulfillment of Joshua's curse. On that occasion, Ahab, who was far from God-fearing, scoffed and said, "How is it possible that Moshe's curse is not fulfilled and his disciple Joshua's is?" He meant, "Moshe said that if the nation turns idolatrous, rain will be withheld from it. Nevertheless, we worship idols and we have abundant rainfall!" When Elijah heard this, he viewed Ahab's words as blasphemous — a *chillul Hashem* — and swore that no rain would fall for three years.

❧ ❧ ❧

וַיֵּנִקֵהוּ דְבַשׁ מִסֶּלַע — *And he will suckle honey from a rock . . .* (32:13).

M oshe promises the Jews that the fruits they will grow in the land will be as sweet as honey. Really, however, the dry, stony soil of *Eretz Yisrael* is not naturally capable of producing such rich, succulent fruits. This is possible only because Hashem overrides the normal forces of nature in the land. Even though the land is a "rock," Hashem promises the Jewish people that it will nurture them with "honey." That is why no people other than the Jews have succeeded in making *Eretz Yisrael* fertile. As the Torah says, לִמְטַר הַשָּׁמַיִם תִּשְׁתֶּה־מָּיִם, *from the rain of heaven shall you drink water* (*Devarim* 11:11), meaning that *Eretz Yisrael* lacks the natural capacity to nourish crops, but prosperity will come nonetheless, thanks to Hashem's blessing, the rains of heaven.

❦ ❦ ❦

חִצַּי אֲכַלֶּה־בָּם: — *I will use up My arrows against them* (32:23).

Rashi notes that this threat contains a hidden blessing: "My arrows will be used up but they (the people) will not be totally destroyed." However much Hashem punishes the Jews, they will always survive.

Hashem never inflicts difficulties on His people merely for the sake of punishment — only to teach and to stimulate them to improve themselves. Thus, Hashem complained to the prophet Yirmiyahu (2:30), *"In vain did I strike your children, for they did not learn the lesson."* The punishments He sent were only for the constructive purpose of causing His children to mend their ways. Since they did not do so, the punishments were in vain.

❦ ❦ ❦

וּמֻת בָּהָר . . . כַּאֲשֶׁר־מֵת אַהֲרֹן אָחִיךָ — *And die on the mountain . . . as your brother Aaron died* (32:50).

In this verse, Hashem seems to promise Moshe that he would die in the same way as his brother. *Rashi* comments that Moshe envied the way in which Aaron died and desired the same death for himself. What was it about Aaron's death that Moshe so coveted?

As *Rashi* explains, just before Aaron died, Moshe dressed Aaron's son Elazar in the priestly garments so that Aaron would have the pleasure of seeing his son take over his position as High Priest while he was still alive. Similarly, in *Parashas Pinchas* (*Bamidbar* 27:16), when Hashem told Moshe that he would be permitted to see the land from the other side of the Jordan River before going to his death, *Rashi* says that Moshe asked Hashem to allow his sons to inherit his greatness.

This raises a question: Moshe desired to see his sons assume his role as leader of the people and envied his brother the privilege of seeing Elazar dressed in the garments of his office at the moment that he left the world. And here, Hashem seems to promise Moshe that he would be granted his desire to die in the same way Aaron did — yet, we know that Hashem did not allow Moshe's sons to take over leadership of the people and instead appointed Joshua. It is unthinkable that Hashem made a promise which He did not fulfill: How then did Moshe see his children inherit his greatness?

Moshe's greatness did not lie in his role as king or political leader. Instead, he was מֹשֶׁה רַבֵּנוּ, *Moshe Our Teacher*, the teacher of Torah *par excellence*, who first introduced the holy Torah to the Jewish people. Our Sages taught (*Bava Metzia* 33a) that a father gives his son a place in *this* world but a Torah teacher brings his students into the World to Come and gives them a place there. In the eternal world, a teacher is, in a very real sense, a father to all of his students.

Thus, as he left the world, Moshe was privileged to see his most devoted and beloved disciple, his "first-born son" so to speak, inherit his Torah leadership role, and all his "children," an entire nation of students, inherit his true greatness, the Torah which Hashem gave them through him. All of us are his heirs, and we have him to thank for the place which is waiting for students of Torah in the World to Come, as the Sages said, "All Israel has a share in the World to Come" (*Sanhedrin* 90a).

❈ ❈ ❈

פרשת וזאת הברכה
Parashas Vezos HaBerachah

וְזֹאת הַבְּרָכָה אֲשֶׁר בֵּרַךְ מֹשֶׁה אִישׁ הָאֱלֹהִים אֶת־בְּנֵי
יִשְׂרָאֵל לִפְנֵי מוֹתוֹ: — *And this is the blessing which Moshe, the man of God, bestowed upon the Children of Israel before his death* (33:1).

The word, *and,* at the beginning of this verse prompts us to look for a connection between this verse and the preceding ones. At the end of *Parashas Ha'azinu*, Hashem tells Moshe that the time had come for him to go up to Mount Nebo, from where he could see the land, and die there. What continuity is there between these two seemingly unrelated matters?

Later in our *parashah,* the Torah relates that when Moshe actually went up on the mountain, he surveyed the whole of *Eretz Yisrael,* including the portions of each of the tribes, עַד הַיָּם הָאַחֲרוֹן, *until the farthest sea (Devarim 34:2). Rashi* mentions the homiletical interpretation of the Sages that this phrase may also be read עַד הַיּוֹם הָאַחֲרוֹן, *until the last day,* to say that Hashem showed Moshe everything that was destined to happen to the Jews until the "last day," namely the Resuscitation of the Dead.

It is also possible to interpret this in another way: On the last day of his life, Moshe saw the physical portion of the Land that would be given to each tribe and he was shown each tribe's destiny until its *last day.* Based on his knowledge of the tribe and its destiny, and the physical characteristics of its portion, he gave each one the blessing that was most appropriate for it.

וּלְלֵוִי אָמַר תֻּמֶּיךָ וְאוּרֶיךָ לְאִישׁ חֲסִידֶךָ אֲשֶׁר נִסִּיתוֹ
בְּמַסָּה תְּרִיבֵהוּ עַל־מֵי מְרִיבָה: — *Of Levi he said:*
Your Tumim and Your Urim befit Your devout
one, whom You tested at Massah and whom
You challenged at the waters of Meribah
(33:8).

In blessing Levi, Moshe addresses Hashem and tells Him that the tribe is worthy of the special forms of service with which Hashem entrusted them because they passed the test of responding to Moshe's call to slay everyone who had served the Golden Calf (cf. *Shemos* 32:26-27). The Levites obeyed Moshe and killed all of the idolaters, even their relatives, as Moshe says here, וְאֶת־אֶחָיו לֹא הִכִּיר וְאֶת־בָּנָיו לֹא יָדָע, *he disregarded his brothers and ignored his own children* (*Devarim* 33:9).

Their reward for this service is also spelled out: יוֹרוּ מִשְׁפָּטֶיךָ לְיַעֲקֹב וְתוֹרָתְךָ לְיִשְׂרָאֵל, *Thus it is they [who are worthy to] teach Your law to Jacob and Your Torah to Israel* (ibid. 33:10). This is an assurance that the Levites will always be teachers of Torah. How could Moshe know that just because the tribe had once shown itself worthy they would always remain on such a high level?

To understand this, let us look back to something Moshe said in *Parashas Eikev* (ibid. 10:8): בָּעֵת הַהִוא הִבְדִּיל ה' אֶת־שֵׁבֶט הַלֵּוִי לָשֵׂאת אֶת־אֲרוֹן בְּרִית־ה', *At that time HASHEM separated the tribe of Levi to carry the Ark of HASHEM's covenant*. From this we see that, after the incident of the Golden Calf, the Levites were put in a class by themselves, since the word "separated" implies that from then on they would be in a different category. In reward for punishing the idolaters, Hashem infused the Levites with an unfading devotion to His service, one that would raise them above the rest of the people. Moshe knew that this quality would always make them worthy to teach Hashem's Torah to the Jews, and to always respond to the call, "מִי לַה' אֵלַי" "Whoever is for HASHEM, come join me" (*Shemos* 32:26), as they had done then.

❧ ❧ ❧

— וּלְיוֹסֵף אָמַר מְבֹרֶכֶת ה' אַרְצוֹ מִמֶּגֶד שָׁמַיִם מִטָּל
Of Joseph he said: His land is blessed by
HASHEM *with the heavenly bounty of dew*
(33:13).

J oseph's blessing is longer and more fulsome, in material
terms, than those of the other tribes. Perhaps this was
because Joseph sustained his brothers during their stay in
Egypt, as he said to them (*Bereishis* 50:21), *"I will sustain you and
your children."* As his reward for undertaking the role of provider,
his descendants were blessed with plentiful sustenance so that they
could continue to be the breadbasket of the nation.

❈   ❈   ❈

וַיָּמָת שָׁם מֹשֶׁה עֶבֶד־ה' — *So Moshe, servant of*
HASHEM, *died there* (34:5).

T he Torah relates that Moshe died *there,* implying that in
other places he did not die. And indeed, his soul lives on to
inspire Jews of all times and all places where the Torah he
brought to his people is studied and lived.

❈   ❈   ❖

לְעֵינֵי כָּל־יִשְׂרָאֵל: — *Before the eyes of all of*
Israel (34:12).

E very Jew has a different conception of Hashem, a different
way of seeing and understanding Him, based on his
education and experiences. Yet all of these varying
perspectives trace back to a single source — the Torah that Moshe
passed on to his people, which gives each individual the power to
see and recognize in his own way Hashem's greatness and His
rulership of the world.

❈   ❈   ❈

This volume is part of
THE ARTSCROLL SERIES®
an ongoing project of
translations, commentaries and expositions
on Scripture, Mishnah, Talmud, Halachah,
liturgy, history, the classic Rabbinic writings,
biographies, and thought.

For a brochure of current publications
visit your local Hebrew bookseller
or contact the publisher:

Mesorah Publications, ltd

4401 Second Avenue
Brooklyn, New York 11232
(718) 921-9000